Go Ahead or Go Home

TRETHEWEY

Go Ahead or
Go Home

The Trethewey Story

DAPHNE SLEIGH

Vicarro Publishing Abbotsford, B.C.
1994
Mail order: Box 29, Deroche, B.C. V0M 1G0

Printed by Hemlock Printers
7050 Buller Avenue
Burnaby, B.C.

Canadian Cataloguing in Publication Data
Sleigh, Daphne.
Go Ahead or Go Home

Includes bibliographical references and index.
ISBN 0-9698678-0-8
1. Trethewey family. 2. Fraser Valley (B.C.)–Biography
3. Frontier and pioneer life–British Columbia–Fraser Valley.
4. Lumbermen–British Columbia–Fraser Valley–Biography.
I. Title.
FC3845.F7Z48 1994   971.1′03′0922   C94-910815-4
F1089.F7S63 1994

Acknowledgements

No work of research can be undertaken without the assistance and co-operation of a great many people. Foremost among these is Alan Trethewey, whose dream it has been for many years to see the history of the Trethewey family recorded and who has commissioned the writing of this book. His interviews with older family members (none of whom, unfortunately, has lived to see it published) have provided invaluable insights into the lives and characters of an earlier generation, and his own personal memoirs and family records have afforded a wealth of detail concerning more recent times. Equally, in this respect, I owe a debt to his cousin, the late Clarke Trethewey, whom I never met but without whose colourful family memoirs this book would be lacking much of the early background. Alan's brothers, Richard, Bill, and J.O., and his sister, Phyllis, have also given of their time to further the project.

Other family members too have contributed in various ways. Doug Bowell, the late Helen Cambray, Roger Cambray, Nicola Cunningham, Joy Fairbarns, Richard Fairbarns, Brenda Jackson, the late Mildred Kitching, Donna Logan, Verne Logan, Elaine Mitten, Donna Pound, Frank Taylor, John Taylor and Shirley Taylor have willingly answered queries, provided stories or lent photos. Several Trethewey family friends have also identified with the project. Margaret Weir has been a fund of information about life in Abbotsford in earlier days; Dave Falconer and Bill Holden have offered many useful suggestions while the manuscript was in progress, and Marie Elliott has unearthed some fascinating archival items relating to the Tretheweys in the course of her own research. Heather Coupland has freely shared her own research into Muskoka history; Sally Whiffing has done likewise with her research into Cornish family history. Cornish historian Dorothy Sweet and Derbyshire historians Lynn Willies and Peter Naylor, have also been more than generous in their response. My brother, John Swan, has kindly procured some of the English Vital Statistics records for me. And, not least, my husband, Francis Sleigh, has taken much time and trouble in drawing up the maps.

Many archival repositories have been consulted in the course of the project, and I should like to acknowledge the assistance I have unfailingly received from the officials of the institutions listed below:

Provincial Archives of British Columbia
Provincial Archives of Ontario
Chilliwack Archives
Kamloops Museum & Archives
Kilby General Store Museum
Matsqui-Sumas-Abbotsford Museum
Mission Community Archives
United Church Archives, Toronto
United Church Archives, Vancouver
Bracebridge Public Library
Cloverdale Public Library, Genealogical Section
Metropolitan Toronto Reference Library
New Westminster Public Library
Sutro Library, Library of Calfornia
Vancouver Public Library
Land Registry Office, Barrie
Land Registry Office, Bracebridge
Land Registry Office, New Westminster
Oblate House, Vancouver

Contents

Foreword

Thomas Carlyle called history "the essence of numerous biographies." It was one of his more succinct sentences, but one to remember. British Columbia history, like any other, is bound by Carlyle's rule, and the changes wrought her in the past century and a half are told in the biographies of a few people who are seized with the divine discontent of mankind.

The Trethewey family were such a bunch. The family tree's roots are in Cornwall, near the tin mines established by the Phoenicians. Like all families, their fortunes rose and fell there. In the 15th century Tretheweys held royal titles and sat in England's Parliament. By the middle of the 18th century they were shoemakers in a part of Cornwall which one chronicle describes as "a direful strag of rocks, . . . affording shelter for little else besides sheep, rabbits, hares, goats and horses." They made their way to British Columbia by way of log cabin pioneering in Ontario, at a time when many considered this province to be nothing more than a direful straggle of rocks.

There have now been five generations of Tretheweys in B.C. and they appear to have involved themselves in everything except the arts, politics and protest parades. Nobody is good at everything. The Tretheweys seem to have been invariably attracted to the primary production industries, ranching, farming, logging and finally, the industry which attracts dreamers and incorrigible optimists, mining.

Readers will pick their favourites. Among mine are Sam, who loved dancing but couldn't do it, and Will, who found the Cobalt mines in Ontario and for the hell of it staged what was probably the world's first aerial bombardment, pre-dating even those of a Mexican Revolution, as a spectacle for his guests at a party. Many Trethewey wives emerge as women with whims of iron, and frequently husband and wife relationships were so sporadic that the reader may wonder that reproduction could occur and keep the family line moving.

One way or another, almost all of them were fitted to life in our strag of rocks. It's a book that's fun to read.

Paul St. Pierre.

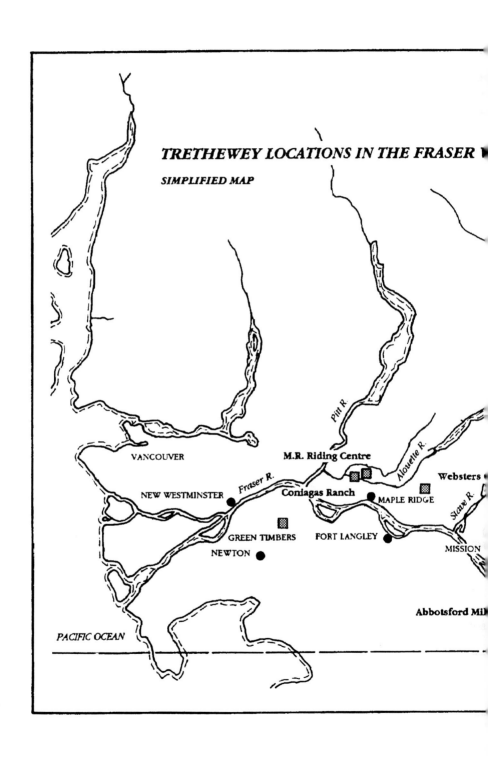

TRETHEWEY LOCATIONS IN THE FRASER V

SIMPLIFIED MAP

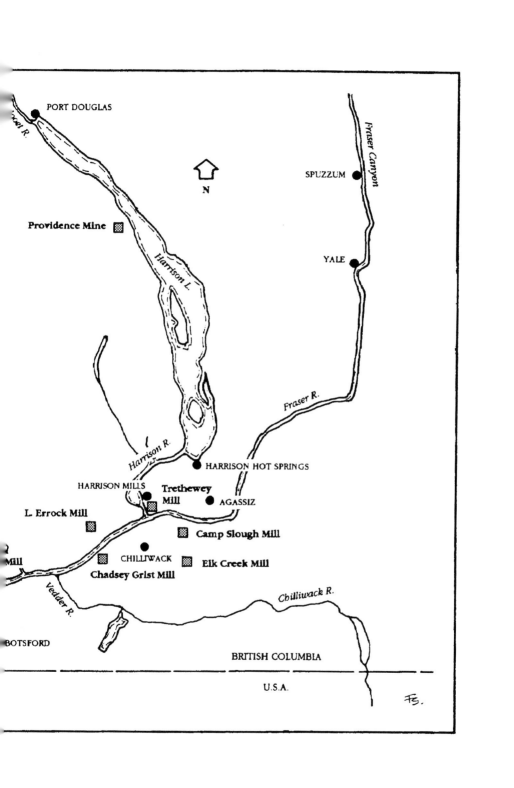

DESCENDANTS OF SAMUEL TRETHEWEY, *Cornish engineer, b.1794*

(simplified chart)

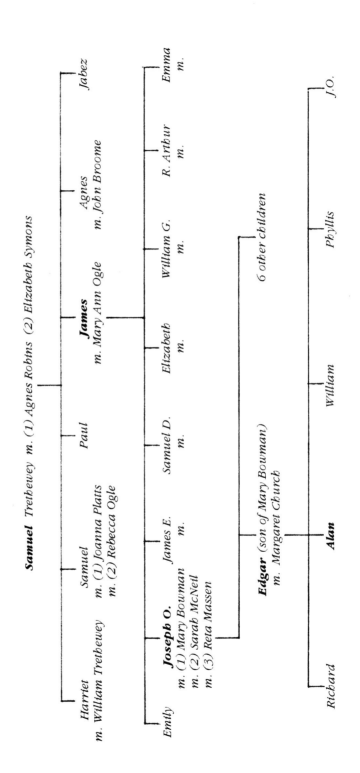

Samuel *Trethewey m. (1) Agnes Robins (2) Elizabeth Symons*

Harriet
m. William Trethewey

Samuel
m. (1) Joanna Platts
m. (2) Rebecca Ogle

Paul

James
m. Mary Ann Ogle

Agnes
m. John Broome

Jabez

Emily

Joseph O.
m. (1) Mary Bowman
m. (2) Sarah McNeil
m. (3) Reta Massen

James E.
m.

Samuel D.
m.

Elizabeth
m.

William G.
m.

R. Arthur
m.

Emma
m.

Edgar *(son of Mary Bowman)*
m. Margaret Church

6 other children

Richard

Alan

William

Phyllis

J.O.

1

The Adventure of a Lifetime

At first it was nothing more than a thin, undulating line of silver on the far distant horizon. It looked to James like a low bank of cloud on the edge of the vast landscape. Suddenly realisation dawned. He turned to Joe. "It's the Rockies! It's the Rockies at last!" He could hardly contain his elation. The greatest adventure of the whole journey was about to begin.

There really was no need for this trip to be an adventure at all—in order to reach British Columbia it was certainly not necessary to cross the Rocky Mountains on horseback. This was doing it the hard way. Any normal pioneer entering British Columbia from Ontario in the early 1880s could have done so in relative comfort, travelling by train across the United States to San Francisco and then by steamship up the coast to Victoria harbour.

But to James Trethewey and his son Joe the whole of life was one big adventure, and if adventure did not already exist, then they would make it happen. If no challenge presented itself, then the Tretheweys would create one. For them, the right way to start their new life in western Canada was to enter the province of their choice with a flourish of achievement.

James had lived in British Columbia before. He had come out by the conventional route several years earlier to have a look at this new province, and he had quickly fallen under the spell of its primeval forests and mountains. Soon he knew with certainty that one day

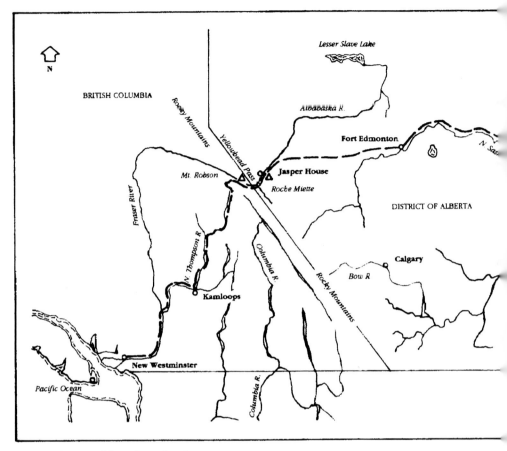

he would make it his home.

Now in 1881 he was returning with his eldest son, twenty-three-year-old Joe, and this time it was to stay. The rest of the family would follow later. In the meantime here was a glorious opportunity. Soon the journey would merely be a routine matter of boarding a train for the West, for at last the Canadian Pacific Railway was starting the construction of its transcontinental railway. But before this happened, he and Joe would cast themselves in the role of the early explorers and fur traders. They would take the trail and slog their way through 2,000 miles of unfamiliar country on horseback or on foot. And the ultimate challenge would be that rampart of mountain peaks that they saw before them now.[1]

It was an amazing undertaking for them to have thought of at all. It was true that they would be taking the train as far as Win-

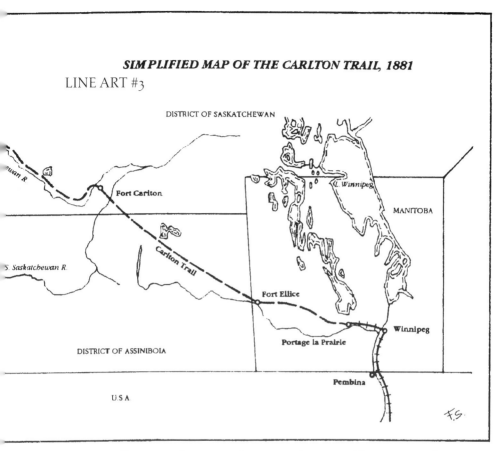

SIMPLIFIED MAP OF THE CARLTON TRAIL, 1881

LINE ART #3

nipeg, travelling via the United States. They would even use the CPR's solitary 70 miles of track that pushed westward though the prairie grassland from Winnipeg to Portage la Prairie. But after that, nothing lay between them and the mountains but open prairie and a few Hudson's Bay trading posts.

The way across the prairies was still the old fur trade route along the historic Carlton trail, but it had fallen into disuse beyond Edmonton, and the eastern side of the Rockies was relatively unknown country. Very few people had any reason to travel that way or cross the Rockies now that the fur trade had died out and the fur brigades no longer came through. The only travellers these mountains had seen for many years were the native traders and hunters, and the railway surveyors. Once they were in the heart of the Rockies James and Joe would have to find their way as best they could.

It was not hard to follow the trail across the prairies. All they had to do was to let their horses follow the rutted tracks which the caravans of the Red River carts had ground into the prairie dust, as they creaked their way across the plains year after year. It was not, however, a trip for anyone who valued creature comforts.

Mosquitoes, in huge clouds that darkened the sky, would suddenly blow in out of nowhere, driving the horses to a state of frenzy. The water supply was a constant problem, as so many of the little lakes were too salty or too alkaline to be drinkable—at times like these, the two travellers were thankful to find a lake which merely reeked nauseatingly of sulphur. Sometimes they passed through miles of country without a twig to fuel their campfire. Sometimes they travelled through burnt-off areas that had no grazing for the horses. Fording the streams was perhaps the worst problem of all. Often the banks were soft and marshy, and the horses bogged down in the mud. Elsewhere James and Joe might find themselves faced with the crumbling slope of a steep rocky embankment, as much as a hundred feet or more down to the river. It was a relief to find a ferry to take them across at the major trading posts.

But all this did not matter. They were seeing the country—and what a country! From the moment they glimpsed the prairie in its early summer beauty, James and Joe were entranced by the landscape that lay before them. Almost untouched by the plough, it was a vast expanse of fresh young green, in places sparkling with the brilliant colours of the local flora—asters, sunflowers, golden rod and daisies—in a tapestry of mauve and red and gold. By day they rode on under the great bowl of the blazing sky. In the cool stillness of evening they camped by the light of the incomparable prairie sunsets that shot violent hues of purple, rose and indigo in giant streamers across the far horizon. Never had they experienced such immensity, such solitude, such silence, broken only by the whinnying of their horses or the faint cry of the distant wolf.

When they finally rode into Fort Edmonton after weeks on the trail, it seemed like a return to civilisation. With its trading-post and its crude hotels, it was by far the largest stopping-place on their route, and it was humming with activity. Even though the CPR had just turned down the Edmonton route in favour of the Calgary route, Edmonton was in the grip of a sudden land boom. Already the land speculators were in town, making their appraisals.

James and Joe's departure from Edmonton marked a transition point in their journey, for now they were about to enter very different territory. Gone were the firm compacted paths of the level prairie. Gradually the little cavalcade wound its way up into low hills and woodland. The forest of fir and spruce seemed dense and gloomy by contrast to the little copses of delicate white aspens which they had seen on the plains. Now they were into the the muskeg too, and picking their way through the maze of deep swamps that lay concealed under the spongy moss—deep enough for an animal to be mired in, or even sucked under completely. But already they had had their first faint glimpse of the far-off Rockies, still a hundred miles away, and they had fresh incentive to carry on through the increasingly rugged country.

It was a three-day ordeal, but finally they emerged from the forest and stood on the high banks of the Athabaska River. They gasped at the view that suddenly lay revealed. Shining in the sunlight and filling the whole western horizon, a grand array of icy pinnacles soared sheer into the sky. The Rockies stared them in the face. No longer just a distant gleam of silver, the mountains now stood so close that they gave the illusion of waiting for them just behind the nearest hill.

All next day and the day after, the two travellers rode on in the face of these stupendous peaks, following the Athabaska River up into the mountains. It was not until the third day that they actually entered the remote and awesome mountain world which they had come so far to see.

From a long way off they had seen the narrow cleft which was the passageway into the mountains. This was the gorge of the Athabaska. Above it reared the high square bluff of the Roche Miette, and ahead lay one of the most dangerous passages of the entire journey.

To get around the Roche Miette they could take either an upper route or a lower route. The lower route down by the water would involve several lengthy and difficult fordings of the Athabaska. On the other hand, the higher route was a very dangerous one, especially with horses. It consisted of a narrow path edging around the face of the cliff—a perpendicular rock wall on one side and a giddy precipice of several hundred feet on the other. With good reason, the place was known as Disaster Point.

The Trethewey men, in any generation, have never been lacking in physical courage. Father and son were in total agreement over their course of action. Without hesitation they opted for the higher route. It was a nerve-racking passage. "Here a single blunder, one false step for either man or beast, and no human power could save him from instant destruction," wrote one early traveller.[2] But the luck of the Tretheweys held, and men and horses came safely down. Many times in the future it would be said that the Tretheweys led charmed lives.

They rejoined the Athabaska, but it was rough terrain, and by the time night fell they had also had to scale two or three other steep bluffs that overhung the river. They camped for the night beside a lake at the foot of three huge peaks, the immensity of their surroundings filling them with the eerie consciousness of being alone among the mountains in a world of solitude and silence.

The next day brought them to another of the chief danger-spots of the route—the crossing-place of the Athabaska. The river here was broad and deep—a hundred yards across and as much as twenty feet in depth. They would have to build a raft and hope they could fight the powerful current, which could quickly sweep them downstream into a series of rapids, some small and some large, but any of them capable of overturning their craft. James and Joe had to scour the bank to find enough drift timber to rope together to form a clumsy raft. They lashed the supplies firmly to it, for the loss of these would spell disaster. Then, driving the horses into the water ahead of them, they launched themselves on the fast current, paddling furiously. Luckily the river was not in full spate by now, and all went well in this critical fording. So far, so good. Now it was on to the next set of difficulties.

Much more fording had to be done the following day, and it was totally exhausting. By now they had passed through the broad valley where the town of Jasper stands today, and left the Athabaska for another river, the Miette. This was a rushing mountain stream that twisted and turned in endless convolutions, so that the trail was first on one side of the river and then on the other. In the space of a few hours they found themselves wading across it no fewer than nine times, fighting to keep their footing in the strong current, and half-frozen by the icy water. In between fordings they struggled through a forest full of fallen timber, which also slowed them down.

At last they were out of it. And now, just a few miles farther on, came the biggest moment of the whole trip when they stood at the summit of the Yellowhead Pass. They had reached the Great Divide! Another few steps and they were standing with one foot on either side of a tiny rivulet—the source of the great Fraser River.

As he looked westward into British Columbia, James felt a turmoil of emotions. Elation, thankfulness, and hope for the future came flooding into his mind in a wave of sudden exhilaration. He was about to enter the province of his choice. He was at the brink of a new life. Above all else, he was filled with a sense of the rightness of what he was doing, and a deep inner conviction that the future would be good.

He thought back to the tremendousness of the journey they had already made. So far the luck of the Tretheweys had been with them, though there was a long way still to go. Tomorrow as they descended from the Divide, they would still be in the heart of the Rockies. Like pygmies among the giants, they would remain in the shadow of the great peaks for another two or three days of hard travel before reaching the western edge of the mountains and the great landmark of Mount Robson, towering above all the rest.

But after leaving the high mountains, the journey would be a more straightforward matter of following the surveyors' trail down to Tete Jaune Cache, and on to Kamloops and civilisation. From here, well-travelled water routes and wagon roads would take them safely down to their final destination—the Lower Fraser.

What a magnificent adventure it all was, thought James as he stood at the Divide; and what a magnificent adventure life was going to be in the years ahead! His mind raced with ideas as he considered the opportunities waiting out there in the new province. Visions of success dazzled his thoughts only too easily. He dreamed on of the bright future that lay ahead. What a province for his sons to make their way in! Land and natural resources all waiting for the first comers. Water, forests, minerals. . . . He could envisage so many good things for these five sons—large farms, property, businesses, mills, perhaps even mines. . . .

And, as it turned out, James was absolutely right.

END NOTES

1. The source of the story in this chapter is the late Clarke Trethewey, grandson of James Trethewey. Clarke was the historian of the Trethewey family, who recorded many of the human interest stories that would otherwise be lost to us. Although the basic content of these stories is correct, he was not always quite accurate over the factual framework. In this case, he has stated that James and Joe went by train as far as Calgary in 1881. This would have been impossible, as the rails only reached Calgary in August 1883, at which time James was in Mission, building his house. The usual route in 1881 was the Carlton trail via Edmonton. However, the fact of James and Joe's journey has separate confirmation by Cornelius Kelleher [see Chapter 4.]

2. Thomas McMicking, *Overland from Canada to British Columbia*. Ed. Joanne Leduc. Vancouver and London, U.B.C. Press, 1981, p.36.

2

A Cornish Family

The go-getting spirit that fired James Trethewey and his five remarkable sons was the same Trethewey characteristic that had been the driving force in his father, Samuel. The saga of the Tretheweys in Canada truly begins with this rugged Cornishman, Samuel the engineer, who had so much of the pioneer spirit in his make-up.

The Tretheweys were Celtic in origin, the descendants of those rebel Britons who were forced back into the isolated region west of the River Tamar (today's Cornwall), where they would be unlikely to interfere with the Saxon regime. The very name 'Trethewey' is of Celtic origin. 'Tre', deriving from the Latin 'terra', means 'land' or 'homestead', while 'thewey' is a corruption of the ancient name of 'David'. Together they formed the Celtic 'Trethewey'—the land of David.

Little is known of Samuel's immediate forbears. His early ancestors in the 15th century had been notable achievers. They were men whom James and his sons would certainly have admired—men of action, men of substance. Henry de Trethewy was Member of Parliament for Bodmin in the 15th century. His son Thomas was Member for the whole County of Cornwall, as well as Coroner for Cornwall. Henry was a King's Seneschal, and Thomas a King's Armiger. During the 16th century the family prospered and had substantial land holdings.[1]

But for the following hundred years or more, the line of descent becomes lost in a blur of bloodlines, and when it re-emerges at the end of the 18th century, the family is living in humbler circumstances. They occupy one of the stone cottages in the bleak hilltop village of St. Dennis, and many of the family are in the shoe-making trade.[2]

They are still living in traditional Trethewey territory in the same few square miles of country where Tretheweys have lived for four hundred years or more. A few little stone villages cling to the lower slopes of the moors, and it is here on the western edge of the St. Austell highlands that the Trethewey villages of St. Stephen, St. Dennis and Roche are to be found. It is a harsh environment—an inland region dominated by the sombre scenery of the high moors, which loom over their villages in a gale-swept expanse of granite and stunted grass. Samuel's own home village of St. Dennis was a spot written off by one early chronicler as "a direful strag of rocks . . . affording shelter for little else besides sheep, rabbits, hares, goats and horses."[3]

These uplands were now the heart of the china clay industry, and the skyline of the moors was dominated by the huge white pyramids of spoil from the china clay pits, giving the appearance of some strange lunar landscape. The industry brought welcome prosperity to the villages around the edge of the moor, and many of the local men were employed in these pits. Samuel's father, Richard, however, was an exception. His branch of the family were shoe-makers, and Richard was content to carry on in this tradition.

But if he had expected his son to follow him in the family trade, he was disappointed. Samuel had other ideas. A keen, bright lad, full of initiative, he was fascinated by machinery, and he loved to watch the mechanical processes of the industries near his home—the separators and drying-machines of the china clay pits, the great whims and pumping-engines of the tin mines. How thrilling it would be to operate one of those powerful machines! The occupation of shoe-making held little appeal by comparison: Samuel decided that he was going to become an engineer.

He must have spent his early married years in the St. Austell area, for this was where James and three of the other children were baptised during the 1820s and 1830s. He may very well have been working in the famous tin mine at Carclaze, described as "one of the wonders of the mining world."[4] A tour of this mine was considered an absolute "must" for any visitor to the area, and to work here would have been excellent experience.

Samuel married into a mining family. His young wife, Agnes, was one of the large and prosperous Robins family who lived at nearby Roche.[5] Both her father and brother had good managerial positions in the local mines, and this was a connection which certainly did not hurt Samuel in his career. All the evidence points to the idea that Agnes's brother found a responsible position for Samuel with the Roche Rock Consolidated Tin and Copper Mining Company, and that he was working there until it ran into problems and was sold in 1839.[6]

It was at this point in his career that Samuel made what must have been a very momentous decision. He would break away from his Cornish roots and the tradition of so many centuries of belonging. He would move away from Cornwall.

He had been offered an opportunity too good to refuse: he had been hand-picked to be one of a small group of Cornish engineers who would relocate to Derbyshire to help introduce new methods into the lead-mining industry there. It would be advancement, it would be a challenge, and it would be an opportunity for innovation—in short, it had all the elements that chiefly appealed to Samuel's mind. It was an offer he could not resist.

If challenges were what Samuel wanted, he certainly found them. The part of Derbyshire he had arrived in was one of the very worst in the whole country for flooding in the mines. As one old document picturesquely puts it, it was "a basin heavily indurated with water", and water poured into the mines at the massive rate of 2,000 to 6,000 gallons a minute when conditions were at their most extreme.[7]

All Samuel's resourcefulness came into play in an effort to find some solution to the problems of flooding. He experimented with extra pumps, extra boilers, special iron doors and valves, though all too often these devices had little effect against the tremendous forces of nature. For the mine-owners it was an appalling dilemma. The mines were not producing enough to compensate for all this investment, yet the companies had no choice but to go below the water-table, for all the surface ore was long gone.

Pumping-machines became Samuel's specialty. And now, Trethewey initiative came to the fore—he invented an engine of his own. His design was published in 1845, appearing under the title of *An improved combined expansive steam and atmospheric engine* and consisting of a 4-page booklet of specifications and drawings. It was apparently checked by a civil engineer, Joseph Quick, whose name appears after Samuel's as a co-author. There is no doubt that his work was well regarded and found to be of practical use, because twelve years later it was still in sufficient demand for a reprint to be issued.[8] This talent for invention was to emerge again and again in successive generations of the Trethewey family.

Samuel's independence of mind did not always endear him to his employers. He was a feisty character, inclined to be high-handed and opinionated, even when his position did not entitle him to act this way. At one point, when he was deemed to be exceeding his authority, he was firmly told not to transact any further business and not to leave the mine without permission. This was too much for a Trethewey to take. Samuel quit soon after.

On a subsequent occasion, when transferring to a new job and attempting to lay down conditions of employment, he was bluntly informed that his demands were "quite unreasonable." "If you intend to abide by the propositions already named, the business may be considered at an end," wrote his future employer. "We will engage the first suitable person that may offer himself, who will consider it a pleasure in the interests of his employers to save every sixpence; these are the men we want about us." Samuel hastily backed down.[9] But even though the patience of the directors may have been sorely tried at times, they kept him on and probably allowed him a certain amount of leeway because of his great capability and resourcefulness.

After ten years in the lead mines at Youlgreave and Foolow, Samuel moved on to a different type of engineering job at Crich, near Matlock Bath. He still operated a pumping-engine, but not in one of the mines. He was working for the Cromford Canal Company, and the object of this pumping-engine was to top up the level of the Cromford Canal by bringing in water from the River Derwent which flows parallel. The Canal Company had just invested in a state-of-the-art new engine of massive proportions, which Samuel was only too delighted to have the control of. (This great old engine is still fired up three or four times a year for tour groups, and the picturesque stone pumphouse, peering out of the greenery beside the towpath, is one of the focal points of today's local history trails.)[10]

Samuel was still living at Crich when, between 1854 and 1855, his whole personal world changed.

He had already experienced one major family loss not long after he arrived in Derbyshire. At the age of forty-one Agnes had given birth to their fifth child, Jabez. She never really recovered her health, and as 1839 and 1840 went by she became progressively weaker, the

The Leawood Pumphouse.   *(Arkwright Society)*

victim of some nameless disease. When she died in 1841, her death certificate recorded only the usual vague Victorian diagnosis— a "decline."

Less than two years after her death, Samuel had married again. Eliza was a single woman of forty-six, whom he had met on one of his business trips to Cornwall. The marriage had brought much unhappiness to Samuel's children, for Eliza had not treated her new family very kindly. Little Agnes, the next to youngest child, was left with bitter memories of the harsh treatment she had received, and passed the story of it down to her children and grandchildren.[11]

Nevertheless, the next thirteen years had been a period of relative stability. No one could have foreseen the sudden family break-up that would follow. Abruptly and unexpectedly, within a period of about eighteen months, the family pattern would be shattered. The whole family would be dispersed, and Samuel would be left completely on his own.

It started in the spring of 1854. The young men in the Trethewey family began talking about Canada. Free land was to be had, they had heard—hundreds of fertile acres just for the clearing! In the New

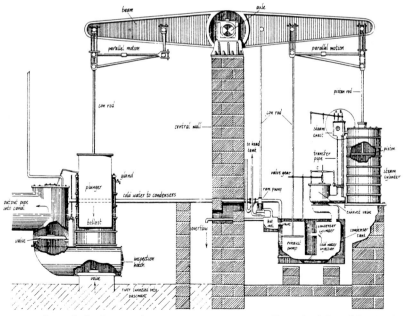

Section through the Leawood Pump   *(Cromford Canal Society)*

World anyone prepared to work could be a landowner and have his own farm, which would be an almost impossible ambition for the ordinary worker in Britain. They decided to try their luck. Two of Samuel's family left that very year—his son Paul and his daughter Harriet, along with her husband William Trethewey (she had married a cousin.)[12]

Then came two deaths in the immediate family. The first of these was Samuel's youngest son, Jabez, who died of typhus fever in September of 1854, after a month's illness. Six months later, Samuel lost his wife as well. Rather suddenly, in March of 1855, Eliza had fallen sick with a "low fever", and within a few days the 58-year-old woman was dead.

Soon after, the rest of Samuel's children left home. In August the younger daughter, Agnes, married John Broome, who became a successful cotton manufacturer. James was in Canada by the end of 1855, and by the following year Samuel junior had crossed the ocean and joined him. The older Samuel was now on his own.

Just at this low point in Samuel's life, incredibly one more crisis was to strike. No one knows exactly how it happened—it may have been an accident at work—but Samuel suffered a serious injury. As a result he lost a leg.[13] This would certainly have meant the end of his working career, since he would have been over sixty at the time, and it might account for the fact that within the next few years he too decided to emigrate to Canada. By the early 1860s, as pioneer records show, he was living on the spacious Ontario homestead with James and Samuel junior—and probably relishing every moment of his new life.

In spite of the trauma he had had to overcome, Samuel was still a forward-looking individual, as he had been all his life. He was tough enough in mind and body to withstand the hard knocks that fate had dealt him—Samuel was a natural survivor. But beyond the mere capacity to endure, he was also the fortunate possessor of an optimistic and enquiring attitude towards life. One has the shrewd suspicion that Samuel may have been tempted just as much as his sons by a very lively curiosity to see for himself what conditions were like on the other side of an ocean.

END NOTES

1. a) Trethewey pedigree. A small booklet, bound in crimson leather, containing a family tree and a coat-of-arms. It was compiled by William Griffith Trethewey as a Christmas card for his family in 1911. His cousin Reginald Trethewey researched parish records in England for this pedigree, and other information came from family Bibles and from living relatives. Recent research has turned up one or two small errors in it.
    b) Everard Green, Somerset Herald, F.S.A., of the College of Heralds, provided a much more extensive pedigree in March 1912. This was derived from the *Heralds' Visitation of Cornwall*, 1620, and Gilbert's *Historical Survey of Cornwall*, ed. Colonel Vivian, 1887.

2. The occupation of shoemaker is noted in various birth, marriage and death certificates.

3. William Lake, *Parochial History of the County of Cornwall*, Vol.1, 1867, p.294.

4. J.A. Buckley, *Cornish Mining—at Surface*, Tor Mark Press, Penryn, 1990, p.4.

5. Some of the Robins family emigrated too. Sampson Paul Robins (baptised in Kent in 1833, and possibly a nephew of Agnes) taught at McGill Normal College, Montreal, for fifty years, and was Principal from 1884 to 1907.

6. Roche Rock Mining Correspondence, J/1304, parts d-g, County Record Office, Truro.

7. Peak District Mines Historical Society, *Lead Mining in the Peak District*, ed. Trevor D. Ford & J.H. Rieuwerts, Peak Park Joint Planning Board, Derbyshire, 1983, p.97.

8. Samuel Trethewey of Watergrove Mine near Stony Middleton & Joseph Quick of Sumner Street, Southwark, *An improved combined expansive steam and atmospheric engine*, No. 10,766, (specification with drawing), London, July 12, 1845. Reprinted Eyre & Spottiswoode, 1857. Fol. pp.4, 9d.

9. a) Lynn Willies, articles on lead mining, *Bulletin Peak District Mines Historical Society*, Vol.6, No.3, 1976; Vol.6, No.5, 1977; Vol.8, No.6, 1983.
    b) Lynn Willies, *Notes on Samuel Trethewey from the Wyatt letters at the Derby Borough Library*. Unpublished research notes.

10. a) Brenda Jackson, *A Cornishman in Derbyshire*, Derbyshire Family History Journal, Autumn, 1992, pp.18 & 19.
    b) Cromford Canal Society, *Guide*, c.1976.

11. Helen Cambray to Alastair Simmonds, Feb.24, 1983.

12. Land records, Archives of Ontario, Toronto.

13. Helen Cambray to Nicky Cunningham, Feb.24, 1983 (quoting information given to her by Ruth Secord.)

James Trethewey.
Mission Community Archives

Mary Ann Trethewey.
Mission Community Archives

Mary Ann and her grand-
daughter Mae.
Trethewey family archives

Mary Ann's home and first general store, Mission.

Mission Community Archives

Mary Ann's second general store, Mission.

Mission Community Archives

The two Trethewey hotels in Mission, (left) Albion House and (right) Ontario House (later the Bellevue), c.1890. The site was at the foot of the hill west of Grand Street.

Mission Community Archives

James built the Elk Creek mills at the foot of the Mount Cheam peaks, whose silhouette dominates the Central Fraser Valley. *D. Sleigh*

Elk Creek grist mill (left) and sawmill (right), 1902. Brett family in foreground: (left to right) Richard, Enos, Earl, Roy, Beatrice, Emma.

Chilliwack Archives

The Trethewey mill at
Harrison Mills, seen
from the railway
bridge, c.1902.
*Kilby General Store
Museum*

William Griffith Trethewey, the Cobalt millionaire, in his study.
Trethewey family archives

The Trethewey mine at Cobalt, c.1911.   *Provincial Archives of Ontario*

The Coniagas mine at Cobalt, c.1911.   *Provincial Archives of Ontario*

(Top to bottom) Will with his hand on the discovery post, his son Frank, Joe Sutton, Bill Fairburn. This plaque, created for Will from a photograph, was presented by the family to the Ontario Department of Mines after his death.

Silver moose.

A depiction of Holmsted Place, Will's mansion in England.

Silverware manufactured from the Trethewey mines at Cobalt.

Trethewey family archives

Canada's First Air Meet ✦ Held on the Trethewey Farm in Toronto, Ontario - 1910

The historic air meet at Will's farm outside Toronto, July 1910. (The photo inscription is inaccurate: a previous air meet had been held in Montreal.)

North Coast Photography and Framing

Postcard of Glen Lince, Will's town home in Toronto, 1906. On the back of the card Lottie wrote to her sister: "This is the shack."   *Arthur Plumridge*

Will's English residence, Holmsted Place, c.1916.

Trethewey family archives

Will in hunting gear.   *Trethewey family archives*

Will in his workshop, Holmsted Place.
                                         Trethewey family archives

Will's yacht, the *Vergemere*.

Customised china used
on the *Vergemere*.

Will (left) aboard his yacht.

Will's yacht, the *Semiramis*.

3

A Mill in Muskoka

As often happens with family history, a certain amount of myth surrounds the Tretheweys' early years in Canada. Legend has it that Samuel's sons, James and Samuel, had arranged to pre-empt land in Canada—sight unseen—before they even left the shores of England. According to this account, they were later shocked to discover that what they had bought was nothing but forest, which they had to cut down before they could create a farm. This first homestead was supposedly in Muskoka, Ontario.[1]

The facts are far less dramatic. The family did not go directly to Muskoka—the land in Muskoka was not even surveyed, much less open for settlement, until several years after they emigrated. The brothers had been living in other parts of Ontario for at least six years before they ever filed for land in Muskoka. When they did, it was with their eyes open. The land they decided to settle on was undoubtedly covered in trees, but it was entirely their own choice: they knew very well what they were doing. More than likely they even thought of the trees as a commercial advantage, since they ended up running a sawmill on one of the properties.

The Tretheweys' first home in Canada was actually not in Muskoka but in Simcoe County. It was a rural area west of Lake Simcoe, with only a sprinkling of settlers, and it must have been a sharp contrast to the cosy village life they were used to in England. But the family had each other for company and support. Harriet and

William's homestead was side by side with Paul's in the township of Tosorontio, and when Samuel junior joined them a year or two later, he found a piece of land only a few miles away from them, in Mulmer on the outskirts of Mansfield.[2]

James too came out to Tosorontio, and was living there at the time of his marriage in 1855. In the months before leaving England, he and Samuel had become romantically involved with two sisters. The two girls, Mary Ann and Rebecca, were from a Derbyshire family living only two miles away from the Tretheweys' old home in Crich. Their father, Joseph Ogle, had worked for the same manufacturing company as Samuel junior—the famous Butterley ironworks, which produced, among other things, the great pumping-engines used in the mines—so the two families had probably known each other for several years.

But besides this connection, the two families had another bond. When James's stepmother Eliza was on her deathbed in the spring of 1855, the family had called in a certificated nurse to attend her. The nurse was young for this sad duty—only just turned twenty-one—but she already had the competence and levelheadedness of a much more experienced professional. Her name was Mary Ann Ogle, and before the end of the year she would be the wife of James Trethewey.[3]

Both couples married in the same year. In the circumstances, one wonders how much of the brothers' courtship was pure romance and how much was practical thinking. Did James and Samuel feel that they must have wives to partner them in the pioneer life? Samuel, who had been widowed in the same month as his father, remarried precipitately only four months after his first wife's death, marrying Rebecca Ogle in England in July 1855.

James and Mary Ann did not marry until six months later, when they were already in Canada. A few days before Christmas 1855, the two of them made the ten-mile trip out to Barrie, which was the nearest large centre for the Tosorontio settlers, and took their marriage vows before the local Wesleyan Methodist minister, with the minister's wife and Samuel Trethewey as witnesses.

It was a marriage of two very strong and very unusual personalities. James was an adventurer by nature, a man of sweeping ideas and ambitious vision, ever ready to embrace the latest impulsive notion and translate it into action, always craving the stimulus of new places and new projects. Mary Ann was the perfect complement to James's volatile personality. Just as enterprising as her husband, she displayed a determination and forceful practicality which may have acted as a balance to some of James's wilder schemes, and certainly held the family together at these times. Her strength of will was formidable: no one crossed Mary Ann and got away with it. In any community in which she lived, Mary Ann stood out, just as James did.

We do not know where the family home was in 1856 when the first child, Emily, was born, but from at least 1858 to 1861 they were living on the Niagara peninsula.Niagara Falls was where the next child, Joseph Ogle, was born in 1858, but the family were living a little west of there—near St. Catharines in Louth—by the time James Everett was born in 1860. All this time, James was pursuing his old trade of grist-milling.

James and Mary Ann were probably not homesteading in these years, but were gradually easing into the ways of pioneer life. They lived in a semi-rural style. Though they kept a cow (valued at $25 in the census), it was just to provide milk and butter for their own use. They had no other livestock such as horses and pigs. They were not living in a crude log shanty, but in a house of frame construction. It was not, in fact, the primitive life-style of the remote rural settler.4

But big changes had taken place in their lives by the time Samuel Dunn was born at the end of 1861. Now they were in the heart of true pioneer country. The uninhabited region of Muskoka had been opened for settlement at last, and the Tretheweys were among the very first of the newcomers to enter this pristine wilderness.

It was an awesome thought to James that no one before him and his contemporaries had ever lived in these virgin forests. Even the Ojibway Indians, who had traditionally hunted here, had never established their villages in such inhospitable territory. Essentially, Muskoka was nothing but a landscape of trees and rock. It was a picturesque countryside of wooded hills and craggy promontories, lavishly scattered with hundreds of pretty little lakes and streams, but from the point of view of the settler it was the worst kind of terrain to try to tame and cultivate. The lumber companies which had been allowed in during the 1850s had taken out the largest of the pines for square timber, but they had barely begun to thin the tangled woodland. It was a primeval scene to impress any immigrant from the old countries of Europe.

But the lush green appearance of the forest was deceptive. Many newcomers read it as a sign of very fertile soil. They fully expected it to blossom forth with crops and orchards once they had cleared and put it under the plough, and were dismayed when they realised that the forest floor was only a thin covering over the mass of bedrock beneath. Disastrously, they would sometimes see even this meagre layer of humus erode rapidly away once it was stripped of trees.

But the Tretheweys were first and foremost millers—farming was secondary. What appealed to them about Muskoka was its tremendous potential for water power. The great watercourse of the Muskoka River, which flows through the region, pours down over tumbled rocks to Muskoka Lake in a series of breathtaking falls and rapids and explosions of white water. Originating in the snows of the Algonquin Dome, the Muskoka carries a larger volume of water than any other river in Ontario. Today many of its waterfalls are harnessed to power Ontario's electric generating stations, but the earliest dams on the river were built for the purpose of servicing the sawmills and grist mills of the pioneer settlers.

To James, this kind of country must have seemed like a miller's dream. Enthusiastically—and with his usual compulsion to explore new ground—he urged the rest of the family to join in with him and live the pioneer life in the depths of the Muskoka forest, where no human being had ever created a settlement before. By the end of 1861 he and Mary Ann were among the first two or three families living in what would one day be the town of Bracebridge.[5]

Now they were living the rugged sort of Canadian life that James had always pictured when he first had thoughts of emigrating. A log cabin and 93 acres of his own in the virgin forest of Upper Canada! This was genuine wilderness country. Until that summer there had not even been a road into the district—only water travel—and to cross the falls at Bracebridge you would have had to edge your way cautiously along a primitive pine log bridge. The only amenities consisted of a boarding-house and a tavern for the road-building crew. No store existed until 1862, and even then it only supplied a few basic needs. To buy such staples as flour and pork you still had to walk all the way to Orillia—a distance of about 30 miles.

Though the property was in James's name,[6] the 93 acres was actually home to a large extended family of Tretheweys and their brood of young children, for Samuel and Rebecca had now been persuaded to join him. It is possible that Paul, the bachelor brother, was with them too at Bracebridge: he did become a Muskoka Falls resident a little later in this decade. Certainly their father, Samuel the elder, had come out to Canada by now to join the family and was as active and vigorous as ever, judging from this story passed on by one of the pioneers.

It seems that Samuel, because of his wooden leg, was having some difficulty with the trail that the Tretheweys used as a short-cut to Muskoka Falls. Instead of taking the more roundabout route over the new bridge at Bracebridge, they were in the habit of using a path through a neighbour's farm and somehow crossing the river at this point to join the road. The problem was that the river bank on the other side was too steep for Samuel to climb easily. With typical determination he set about making some improvements. "Some fifty steps [were] cut in the hard clay bank to the farm on the plateau by the river," writes J.J. Matthias in his memoirs. "These steps were cut with much labour by Grandfather Trethewey for his own convenience." Samuel's spirit of initiative had not deserted him.[7]

But although James had river frontage on the Muskoka, he seems to have made a curious choice of site, because the big falls where he might have built a mill were a little way upstream of his property, and in any case someone else was building a grist mill there in 1862. Possibly he worked for this miller during his short time living in Bracebridge. However this may be, the site did not satisfy the brothers for very long.

"Their location did not suit them. They were millers and operating millwrights," continued Matthias. "In order to escape the 'awful wilderness' of pine forest . . . James and Samuel Trethewey moved up the south branch and built a sawmill and grist mill on the falls that bears their name today." This new site in the nearby community of Muskoka Falls was to be their permanent home in Ontario.

This time there was no doubt that James had found a prime location.[8] The site he had chosen was at one of the dozen most impressive waterfalls on the entire Muskoka River. Draper Falls (later known as Trethewey Falls) came thundering down between wooded banks in a long set of rapids with a total drop of 35 feet. This valuable power source has since been maximised as the site of a 1,600 kilowatt hydro-electric station, built in 1929 and owned by Ontario Hydro.

Only ten years after emigrating, and still in his early thirties, James was now a mill-owner and large-scale land-owner. He had already fulfilled ambitions that he could never have hoped to realise back in Britain—ambitions which would have seemed like an impossible dream to his father. The saga of Trethewey enterprise had begun.

Once again, family life revolved around James's magnetic personality. Samuel and Rebecca accompanied James and Mary Ann to Muskoka Falls and lived next to them. Paul too was convinced to start a farm in the same area, and lived just a mile or two away.[9] Samuel senior, the "aged father" of the pioneer accounts, was with them as well, and probably continued to live with them until his death (about 1869.)

Here at Muskoka Falls James appeared to be thoroughly settled. He and Samuel built mills beside the river, opposite to James's home farm. James operated the grist mill and Samuel ran the one-man sawmill. Unfortunately the Crown still had the rights to all the pine at that time (other than for building or fencing purposes.) However, they probably found the hemlock on their land to be a useful source of income, since their neighbour on the next property had set up a tannery, which depended on a continuous supply of hemlock bark.

The subject of neighbours brings up yet another of the time-honoured pieces of Trethewey family lore—the legend that James and Mary lived here in a log cabin twenty miles away from their nearest neighbours. Regretfully, one has to shatter this myth. Several families were moving into the district at the same time as the Tretheweys, for the attractions of land in supposedly fertile Muskoka were being rumoured far and wide by 1862. As well as having two lots of relatives in the immediate area, James and Mary had at least a dozen neighbours within a radius of just a few miles. Pioneer memoirs tell us exactly who was living on the adjacent homesteads, and although each farm was somewhat isolated, there certainly was a sprinkling of settlers all over the district.[10]

Just the same, each family needed to be very self-sufficient. The 1871 census tells us that James and Samuel each kept a cow and farmed in a small way. James had 18 acres improved by then, and was raising a certain amount of wheat, oats and potatoes, as well as having 4 acres in hay. Mary, like the other wives, made butter and looked after the vegetable garden, according to the usual custom of pioneer living. It was typical of Mary that, in addition to her regular workload, she tackled all sorts of extra projects—for instance, buying herself a cobblers' outfit and making shoes for the whole family. But, above all, Mary Ann was a nurse. This was her training and this was her true vocation. In a community where the nearest doctor was many miles away, she must have delivered babies, set broken bones, helped out in sickness and responded to all kinds of medical emergencies. Throughout her life Mary Ann found immense satisfaction in her nursing career, which she was able to take up more fully when her children were older.

The personality of Mary Ann Trethewey made a deep impression on her children, and stories about this remarkable lady have been passed on from one generation to the next[11]

Mary Ann was not a person to be trifled with. This is clear from the story of her encounter with the suspicious-looking stranger who turned up at her door one evening when James was away from home. The man asked if he could spend the night in her barn, but Mary was suspicious of him, as parts of his story did not fit together, so she turned him down. She told him to go back to a neighbour's where she knew there was a father and two sons at home. The man only laughed at her when she said this, and told Mary that there was nothing she could do to stop him. This was a mistake. Mary promptly drew the little gun she always carried in her skirt and told him he had sixty seconds to get out of sight. He laughed again, and jeered that she couldn't even hit the broad side of a barn with her little toy gun. He was not so amused when Mary calmly took aim and fired, delivering an accurate flesh wound in his right arm, exactly as she had intended. The last she saw of him was a fleeing figure in full retreat down the trail the way he had come.

Mary's pearl-handled gun was a source of great attraction to her youngest son Arthur, and one day, so that he could take a good look at it, he managed to persuade the family to leave him at home alone while they went out. He lost no time in going to find the gun, and with reverent touch took the treasured item out of the top drawer of Mary's dresser. Unluckily, just as he was examining it, the gun went off. It did no harm to Arthur, but the damage it did to Mary's dresser drawer was considerable: the bullet had gone off at an angle to the drawer, making not one hole, but two. Something had to be done about this, and it seemed a good idea to patch up the holes with mud. Surely his mother would never see the difference! Needless to say, he under-estimated her powers of observation. The result was "another hot posterior," says Arthur's son Clarke, who tells the tale.

The Trethewey children were a healthy, high-spirited lot. Four more children had been born at Muskoka Falls—Elizabeth, in 1864, William Griffith in 1865, Richard Arthur (always known as Arthur) in 1867, and Emma in 1871. Their energy and zest for life led to a number of escapades, which Mary dealt with in the firm and direct fashion of the day. She was, in fact, a very strict disciplinarian, and probably needed to be, with so many strong personalities in her growing family.

The older children were sometimes asked to take care of the younger ones when Mary needed to make a day-long trip to buy her grocery staples. As she was concerned about the dangers of their going into the woods, she would instruct them all to stay safely inside the house while she was gone. Naturally, the older boys became bored with the limitations of a whole day indoors and soon began to think up various ways of amusing themselves. One favourite pastime was the gunpowder game. As soon as Mary was well on her way, the boys would go off to the barn to collect some gunpowder and some wheat straw. "A few grains of gunpowder, placed inside of a wheat straw, then lighted by touching a live coal in the open fireplace, made a very fascinating projectile," explains Clarke Trethewey. "The wheat straw shot about the floor like live creatures. They scared the poor cat out of its nine lives; it would climb the wall and hang by its claws from the ceiling." (Regrettably, scaring the cat was one of the objects of the exercise.)

But their misdeeds caught up with them one day when they decided that one of the longer wheat straws could do with a few extra grains of gunpowder. The straw took off like a bullet. It shot to the nearest wall, along to the bedroom door, around the door itself and right through a pair of Mary's shoes. Not just any shoes, but Mary's best pair, which she had only just finished making for herself! Retribution followed, and after this episode the gunpowder was always kept under lock and key.

To reach the nearest school the children had to cross the river beside their home. Mary would row them across in the morning, and in the afternoon when they came back, they would whistle and call to her, and she would row across for them again. One lovely spring day young Arthur was enjoying his lunch hour so much, scampering after rabbits, squirrels and chipmunks, that he couldn't resist staying out all afternoon. He finally made his way back to river bank to wait for his brothers and sisters, and fell into a deep, contented sleep. When he woke up, he could see by the sun that it was time to be home, so thinking the others would soon be with him, he called across to his mother. To his dismay, he saw the whole family looking at him from the opposite bank.

Arthur's punishment was psychologically devastating. "His mother did not say a word to him then or in the days that followed. He found himself in a world of his own, completely ignored by his entire family. When he could stand it no longer, he went to his mother, got down on his knees and begged her to punish him and get it over with." This story, told to his son by Arthur himself, gives us the clearest possible indication of Mary's implacable strength of purpose when she had made up her mind that her duty lay in a certain direction.

Her decisiveness and quick thinking in emergency were qualities which frequently came to the fore when she was called upon to act as nurse and midwife in this isolated community. But Mary's most prestigious achievement, as remembered by her descendants, was—surprisingly enough—in the field of politics. The settlers in Mus-koka had a grievance. Although they were allowed to cut the pine on their homesteads in order to build their homes and make their fences, the rights to all the rest of this valuable pine lay with the Crown, just as in the case of minerals. It seemed to them outrageous that they should not have the rights to the timber on their own property and that all the profit should go to the lumber companies. They held meetings among themselves to discuss what should be done.

It was agreed that they needed to present their case to the government in Ottawa, but the problem was that the men of the Muskoka Falls district could not take time away from their work to travel there. As Mary had been one of the most vocal protesters in their local debates, it was decided that she would have to be the one to go to the capital to represent their area. This was a compliment enough, but a greater honour was to come. In the discussions in Ottawa, her speaking ability so impressed the other delegates that they selected Mary Ann to be the spokesperson for the whole group. "Thus it happened," asserts her grandson, "that for the first time in the short history of Canada, a woman stood on the floor of the House, and pleaded the cause of the settlers."

This would, indeed, be a historic event to record for the Trethewey family, and a landmark too in the history of female representation in government. Was there a chance that the archives of the Library of Parliament might confirm the story and supply some background to it? Unfortunately, to uncover the details at this late date is a difficult assignment, and an extensive search of Parliamentary records by the librarian has failed to yield any results. The basic story—that Mary represented the settlers in some official capacity—has a great deal of credibility, but how much the tale has been elaborated on, it is hard to tell. Probably the exact circumstances will never be known. All that one can say is that had Mary been living today, she would have made a most eligible candidate for any legislature!

But one very sad event cast a shadow over their lives in the winter of 1870, and this was the loss of their oldest child, Emily, at the age of fourteen. During the November of that year a deadly form of influenza swept through the neighbourhood, taking its toll of almost every household. Everyone in James's family had the sickness; the children all had a high fever, James himself was delirious, and only Mary somehow remained on her feet by sheer willpower to care for them all. When Emily died, it was Mary's painful responsibility to ask the first neighbour who came near to bring a coffin, and then to lay her child in it herself. According to Clarke Trethewey, the house was strictly quarantined, and the door nailed shut, so the coffin had to be taken out through a window. Somehow Mary managed to get James to his feet, still delirious, to help her raise the coffin to the window ledge, but he never realised the fact of Emily's death until after he recovered. A few months after this tragedy Mary conceived her last child, a girl, to whom she gave the name of Emma, reminiscent of the daughter she had lost.

But already, by 1871, James was growing restless. In spite of all its advantages, he put the farm up for sale. The following advertisement appeared in the Muskoka newspaper at the end of June 1871:

> IMPROVED FARM AND VALUABLE MILL PROPERTY FOR SALE — The above farm comprises Lot No. 4 on the 9th concession of Draper, on which is a Saw-mill and Grist-mill, 1½ miles from Muskoka Falls, and 4½ miles from Bracebridge, being in a good locality. This site is one of the best in the district—a clear title will be given. Also in connection with the above, 3 lots, Nos. 6, 7 and 8, on the 9th concession, 6 acres pastured on the two last named lots; 3 acres cropped on Lot 6. $50 being the full amount required. For particulars apply to Jas. Trethewey, Muskoka Falls P.O.; or Thomas McMurray, Bracebridge.[12]

Apparently nothing came of this attempt to sell, but James was now thoroughly unsettled. In his entire life he was never to live on the same piece of land for more than about ten years at a stretch. Always the wanderlust hit him; always the compulsion to explore, or the urge to start up some novel venture. This time the object of his fantasy was the very new province beyond the Rockies, the province of British Columbia.

For James it had a twofold lure. In the first place—gold! Gold and British Columbia had been almost synonymous during the gold rush period of the 1860s and James's imagination had been more deeply stirred by this image than anyone realised. Mines and mineral exploration would one day become his obsession—and the obsession of his sons as well.

But secondly, and more realistically, James had an appreciation of the tremendous business opportunities that would open up in British Columbia as soon as it was connected by rail to the rest of the country. Promised in 1871 as a condition of Confederation, this railway did not become fact until 1885, but no one—and certainly not an optimist like James—had any idea it would take so long. He was anxious to be among the first comers, and so he hastened west as early as 1875.

His family did not go with him. The capable Mary was left in charge of the homestead while James went out to evaluate conditions in British Columbia. If he liked what he saw, he would send for the family as soon as the economy there was on the move. Surely, at this stage, they could none of them have imagined that it would be a whole seven years before they were all re-united.

The small group of Tretheweys who had emigrated together to Simcoe were now dispersed and never lived in such close proximity again. Samuel senior had died. Harriet and William had not come with the others to Muskoka Falls, but had moved to Brantford and later to Stratford. The younger Samuel seems to have lost his wife Rebecca towards the end of the 1870s and left Muskoka: some of his descendants now live in Seattle. Paul Trethewey did eventually come out to British Columbia like James, but the details of his life are largely unknown.[13]

James's Muskoka days were over now, and had not lasted more than a decade or so. But for his sons and daughters, who stayed on there with Mary and lived there throughout their youth, Muskoka with its rural delights would always be thought of as home, and would always be given that special place in memory that early childhood holds.

END NOTES

1. Helen Cambray to Nicky Cunningham, Feb. 24, 1983.
2. Land records, Land Registry Office, Barrie, Ontario.
3. Death certificate #478, Elizabeth Trethewey.
4. Census of 1861, Reel C1048, Lincoln County, Township of Louth, Dist.1, p.17.
5. The family was still at St. Catharine's on the day of the census, March 7, 1861, but was at Bracebridge when Samuel Dunn Trethewey was born on Nov. 18, 1861.
6. Land records, Land Registry Office, Bracebridge, Ontario.
7. J.J. Matthias, *Muskoka Falls*, article in unidentified newspaper, May 1928. Linney Papers, Box 4, file 9, Thomas Fisher Rare Book Room, University of Toronto.
8. Land records, Land Registry Office, Bracebridge, Ontario.
9. John Rogers, *Guide Book and Atlas of Muskoka and Parry Sound Disrtricts*, H.R. Page & Co., Toronto, 1879, 2nd offset ed. 1972, p.49.
10. Anon., *Passing of Thomas Galbraith*, article in unidentified newspaper, undated. Linney Papers, Box 4, file 7.
11. The stories quoted in this chapter are from Clarke Trethewey's notes on family history.
12. Advertisement in unidentified newspaper, circa June 1871. Thomas Fisher Rare Book Room.
13. Paul is said by Gertrude Wallace (his great-niece), in an interview recorded in the Mission Community Archives, to have built the first locomotive for the CPR. She stated that there was a plaque in his honour at one of the CPR stations.

4

James's Pot of Gold

The darkly forested banks of the Fraser River above New Westminster in the 1870s showed little sign of any human presence, thought James, as the steamer chugged its way slowly upriver. Giant firs and cedars closed in on either side, marching in endless ranks up the mountainside as far as the eye could see. Only a few small farm clearings or the occasional native village breached the great wall of green along the river's edge.

The townsites of Haney and Mission did not yet exist, so it came as something of a surprise to any first-time passenger when a thriving settlement suddenly appeared in sight on the river bank opposite the Matsqui flats. From the number of white-washed log buildings it was obvious that this was a community of some size, and the fields and orchards on the hillside above showed every sign of well-organised farming activity. But the focal point of the whole complex was a small chapel. This was clearly no ordinary community.

It was, in fact, the Roman Catholic mission known as St. Mary's Mission, and it was to be James Trethewey's first place of work in British Columbia.

The idea of one of their number settling in the midst of a papist community would no doubt have horrified James's uncompromising Methodist forbears—it was, after all, a Trethewey who had introduced Methodism into Roche and provided a house for the first services there. James's brand of Methodism was, however, more accommodating, and he announced himself more than willing to run the grist mill which the Fathers had recently built there. (In any case, he did not live at the mission itself, but lodged nearby with a Hatzic farmer named Joshua Wells.)[1]

James had arrived at a very opportune moment for the mission. The grist mill and sawmill were the latest developments in the Oblate Fathers' plans for self-sufficiency. It was only fourteen years ago that the young French priests of the Order of Mary Immaculate had gone to work with axe and hammer to put up the first crude log cabin on the site. Since then, they had added a surprisingly large collection of buildings. First came the chapel; then two school buildings (one for boys and one for girls)—for the chief focus of the mission was its residential school for native children. Barns, outbuildings, post office and store all followed, as the community grew. The latest additions had been a sawmill and grist mill. Assuming that the boys would eventually take up farming like the white pioneers, the priests taught them how to cultivate the land, to grow fruit and crops, to make hay, and—latterly—how to thresh wheat and grind flour.

James is often given credit for the initial construction of the grist mill, but here again, myth has been at work. The mill had already been operational for a year or two before James ever arrived in British Columbia. The Oblates themselves began building it in early March 1872—"A new flour mill is being constructed at St. Mary's Mission Mills. The charge will be $5 a ton," reported the *Mainland Guardian*.[2] The project then hung fire till the following year, when they tackled the job of constructing the dam for the water power.

"There was this crick, Mission Crick, and they built a regular dam away up in the bush to hold the water," remembered Cornelius Kelleher, a part-native orphan who went to the school. "The mission, of course, had the Indians whipsawing lumber for to make this flume and this penstock to turn the water wheel below. The flume was all of 18 inches wide, all ripped out by hand, and the same for the penstock that went to catch the water that drove the turbine. Them timbers that they put in under the grist mill and sawmill were 12 by 12's and no spikes in them days—or drift bolts either. All them tie beams and things was bored with an auger, and a peg drove in there to hold them together."[3]

When the grist mill first started up, a Chilliwack farmer named Shelford used to come across the Fraser to do the grinding—"Shelford is at his old game, viz. making excellent flour at St. Mary's Mission Mills"[4]—but when James arrived, he evidently lost no time in convincing the Fathers that he was the right man for the job. He was there on the spot; and he had every intention of making Mission his home for the foreseeable future. In fact, if Mission turned out to be one of the future railway towns—and the odds looked very good for the Fraser Valley route to be selected by the CPR—he had big plans for Mission.

Though Mission was undeniably his favourite spot, James soon began to take on work at other mills as well. With the luck of the Tretheweys, he happened to have arrived in British Columbia at just the right moment for someone in the milling trade. Although the province in general was in an economic slump since the dying throes of the gold rush era, the production of wheat was on the upswing. In the past, the farmers hadn't been able to compete with the cheaper American wheat, but in 1865 the government had stepped in and raised the import duty, so that local growers were finally able to make some profit. Quite a few flour mills had gone in during the late 1860s and early 1870s, and an experienced grist miller would have been in some demand.

Both of the other mills where James worked had been built at about the same time as the mill at St. Mary's Mission. One of them was in the immediate locality, just across the river at Sumas, but the other was in completely different country—the famous Cariboo, where prospectors had made their fortunes in the goldfields only a dozen years before.

At Sumas he ground flour for the pioneer Chadsey brothers, who owned hundreds of acres of good farming land—most of the land in Sumas, in fact. But although the mill was a great convenience, local residents were not altogether happy with the quality of the flour. Not that they were critical of James's milling techniques—"he was a good English miller," wrote Mrs. Isaac Kipp—but the wheat

No 2
People of 1873
23rd July 1873
Henry ? Edmond
Govt Agent

New Westminster 22 July 1873

To
H V Edmonds Esqr.
New Westminster

Sir

Having posted notices as required by law for the terms of 30 days stating my intention to apply to you for permission to record all the water flowing into the Fraser through what is called Mission Creek. The said Creek goes from the Fraser towards the mountains about 35 chains, where I ask permission to build a dam capable of containing water to the depth of 15 ft. Then, running north 45 chains where it divides into two streams, one a natural stream going Eastward & taking all the water coming from the hills north East. The other stream being a ditch along the foot of the hills going westward about two miles and taking all the water & streams coming from the hills north West. — I ask permission to have all above described water — recorded for the term of fifty years, said water to be used for farming & milling purposes for the use & benefit of St Marys Mission. No objections having been filed to prevent the issuing of said Record, I now respectfully ask that the same be granted to me

I have the honor to be Sir
Your humble & obedt servant
L. J. D'Herbomez O.M.I.

Letter from Bishop D'Herbomez requesting water rights to the creek before building the grist mill and sawmill. (Oblate House, Vancouver)

grown in the Fraser Valley had been something of a disappointment. "Alas! our wheat was too damp and soft to make good flour."[5] Many of the early farmers had come from southern Ontario, where wheat grew well, and they had not taken into account the different climate of the Fraser Valley. Still, at this stage of pioneer settlement, poor flour was better than no flour at all, so they had to make the best of it. Later, after the railway came through, James began to import better wheat from Manitoba.

The mill which appealed to James more than Sumas as a place to spend his time was the mill at Pavilion in the upper country. All his life, James was to find it stimulating to move to different surroundings. The pine forests of Muskoka had come as a refreshing contrast to the bare, wind-swept moors of Derbyshire; but later the forbidding grandeur of the Coastal forests and mountains had eclipsed the softer scenery of Muskoka; now, in turn, the bleaker country of the dry Interior began to hold its own fascination for the roving James.

But Pavilion had another major attraction—it was on the edge of the Cariboo, the richest gold region in the whole of British Columbia. No doubt James faithfully performed his duties at the mill for the manager (and later owner) William Lee, but while he was here in mining country, all his real interest was centred on the topic of gold and gold mines. It was not so very long since the Cariboo had become a sensation overnight, and the memory of it was still fresh in everyone's mind. Great quantities of coarse gold and even gold nuggets had been found in almost every stream bed—or so it seemed to James, as he listened to the old prospectors. It was certainly within the bounds of possibility that valuable deposits still lurked amid the rocks of the Cariboo, waiting to be discovered. Stories of lucky strikes and sudden fortunes began to fill his thoughts, and soon his mind was occupied with the pleasing fantasy of the bonanza that might await him on some prospecting expedition.

"His sole ambition"—according to Lee's nephew, R.D. Cumming—"was to discover and sell a gold mine and get rich quick overnight. He could talk of nothing but mines, and his ambition along that line was governed by the magnitude of any gold excitement that might arise."[6]

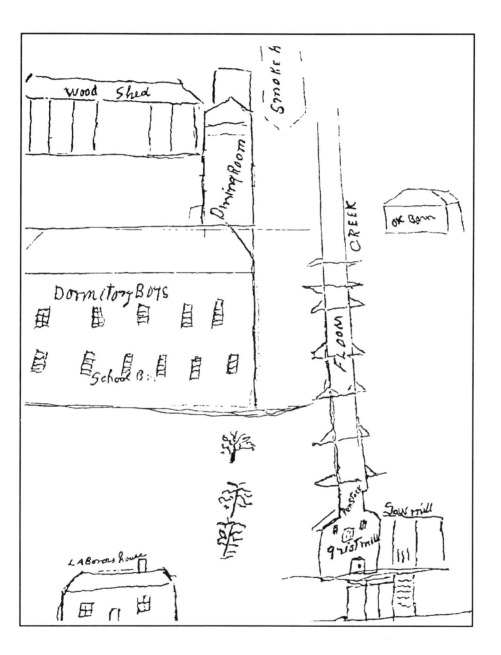

Portion of a sketch map of the St. Mary's Mission settlement, showing the grist mill and flume. Drawn by Cornelius Kelleher. *(#9234, Map Division, PABC)*

It so happened that in the middle of the 1880s (James was by now well settled in British Columbia) a tremendous mining furore flared up again almost in this very area, when propectors discovered the rich Bonanza Ledge at Cayoosh Creek near Lillooet. It rekindled all James's enthusiasm for the search.

He remembered that a year or two back, when he was out for a Sunday hike in the bush, he had noticed a very promising-looking ledge high up on the mountainside. It was some distance away, but he had made a mental note of all the landmarks that would lead him back to it. He had climbed the wooded slope opposite the mill, crossed an open valley, and then plunged into the timber again in the rough and hilly country beyond. Somewhere in here, up on a high cliff, he had suddenly spotted this ledge of quartz. It looked so attractive to his prospector's eye that he had carefully studied its position, and resolved to come back one day and stake it off.

He now became impatient to set out on a properly planned expedition to search out this eldorado. Mill-owner William Lee had more than a touch of gold fever himself, being a veteran of two famous gold rushes. He needed little persuasion to be Trethewey's partner on the trip. And so the two of them set off with pack-horse, provisions and plenty of faith, ready to make a fortune for themselves and all their relatives.

Lee's two young nephews were left in charge of the mill and store. "To our young minds it was more or less of a tragedy—two old men who had little future to worry about [they were then in their mid-fifties!]—and no means whereby they might spend and enjoy a fortune to be made out of a castle in the air—setting out and climbing trails made only by the feet of wild things and disappearing from sight into the practically unknown, perhaps never to return!"

The two seasoned prospectors did return, of course, at the appointed time. They were very tired and rather grim. They vouchsafed no information about their trip, and from the look on their faces it seemed wiser not to ask.

Over the next few days the truth began to emerge. They had tramped for miles and miles. They had had an uncomfortable night, sleeping out on hard ground, but in the end James was convinced that they had come to the very spot where he had glimpsed the famous ledge. What then was the problem? The problem was that the ledge of quartz had disappeared!

"Trethewey's alibi, when he had regained consciousness, was that an earthquake had changed the face of nature in the locality and had taken the ledge of quartz with it. He saw the very spot, but it was different. Uncle Lee laughed, after the tired feeling had left his bones, and said that Trethewey must have had a pipe dream . . . However, they never found the pot of gold at the end of the rainbow."[7]

It did not really matter. For James there would always be another rainbow and another pot of gold to chase. His life would be a succession of bright visions. He would have his modest share of gold, but the ultimate reward would never quite be his. It would be for another Trethewey to find that eldorado, for—incredibly—James's dream for his family really would come true: one of his sons would one day find that pot of gold.

By the end of the 1870s James had made up his mind that his future lay in British Columbia; it was time to plan for his family to join him. He must have returned to Ontario to discuss all this with Mary, for the census in April 1881 found him back at Muskoka Falls. He was almost a stranger to his younger children, and two of the older ones, Joe and Jim, were now married to girls from neighbouring families and had young children of their own. Elizabeth, too, was about to marry.

James stayed only long enough to make arrangements for the move, and by the late spring was off again, but not alone. With him was his oldest son, Joe, a go-getter like his father. James had had another of his inspirations. Instead of returning to British Columbia the routine way by train through the United States, why not travel through his own country and see the rest of Canada? So CPR construction ended at Portage la Prairie? Then so much the better—he and Joe would ride the trail and explore the country at leisure. They would travel the vast prairie, they would cross through the heart of the magnificent Rocky Mountains. The audaciousness of the idea only made it more attractive.

And this was how James came to have his adventure of a lifetime. What a story to tell his friends! And James evidently did tell it—he was undoubtedly a good raconteur—for it became legend among the children who were brought up at the St. Mary's Mission school. "The old man and his son Joe came over the Rocky Mountains long before the CPR," declares Cornelius Kelleher.[8]

With this trip completed and the rest of his family about to join him, another episode in James's life was now over. His years on his own in British Columbia were at an end. One cannot help harbouring a strong suspicion that this long period of freedom from family obligations had not been at all unwelcome to James—even a sort of glorious escape from everyday life to the allure of the unknown West. Spectacular scenery, pioneer adventures, the promise of gold— all had been invested with the glamour of novelty.

Now it was time to turn to the practical economics of life once more. With the CPR line about to come through Mission, James's mind was brimming over with plans to benefit from all the new commercial opportunities this would bring. He would organise the lives of all his family members so that each one of them had their chance to do well out of the railway era. He was confident that they would all rise to the challenge.

END NOTES

1. Cornelius Kelleher, taped interview with Imbert Orchard, 1963, Provincial Archives of B.C.
2. Mainland Guardian, Mar.6, 1872.
3. Kelleher interview.
4. *Mainland Guardian*, Nov.26, 1873.
5. *Chilliwack Progress*, June 25, 1958, reprint of notes written in 1920 and based on the diary of Mrs. Isaac Kipp.
6. *British Columbian*, Aug.2, 1947, article taken from the *Ashcroft Journal*.
7. Ibid.
8. Kelleher interview.

5

The Plan for Mission Junction

On August 1, 1883, the Trethewey family stood on the banks of the Fraser at Mission, watching the sternwheeler draw away and disappear round the bend of the river. The river shimmered in the heat of the summer afternoon, and clouds of mosquitoes swarmed above the water. It had not rained for weeks. The mountains were half lost in a veil of heat haze, and the country all around was black with the smoke of slash fires from the railroad clearance. The family's material possessions lay dumped out on the river bank in one miscellaneous pile—furniture, provisions and enough lumber to build a house—and around this extraordinary encampment wandered one slightly bemused milking cow and half-a-dozen agitated hens. James and Mary Ann were about to establish the family home in Mission.

The fact that they had no house or any form of shelter waiting to receive them did not trouble them at all—they were old hands at pioneering. Quickly they went into action to improvise sleeping-quarters for the night. With the help of their three teen-aged children they piled boxes together for walls, and over the top of this they spread cloths to make a roof. They would camp out in this makeshift shelter while the house was being framed.

Meanwhile the two carpenters, Lawson and Purdy, whom they had brought with them from New Westminster to build the house, had wandered over to the work-camp of the Chinese railroad workers and borrowed a few crotch sticks and some bits of old board. They propped these together to form a makeshift hut of their own. "We . . . spread our blankets on the ground under this wonderful structure," wrote Joseph Lawson to his wife, "and crawled under ourselves for 10 nights, not forgetting to light smudge fires, as they were very necessary."[1]

Luckily the hot, dry weather held out, and by the end of ten days, Lawson and his co-worker Purdy had the roof on, three sides covered in, and the lower floor laid, so everybody migrated to more comfortable resting-places at night. Their belongings were "partly in and partly out." Now that the urgent work was done, Purdy went home. "I am here to finish alone," reported Lawson. "It will not take long, as everything comes machined."[2]

Lawson, whose lively letters supplied so much graphic detail, was amused that such a strongly Methodist family as the Tretheweys should choose, of all places, a Catholic mission settlement for their home.

"This seems to me rather a quear [sic] place for a Methodist family to locate," he commented. "The Mistress is a Methodist, and the 'Mister' is not a bad Man, in fact he says himself 'that he is about as good as a Class leader to his Wife'—'and that he used to be *quite pious,* but somehow or other, he dosen't [sic] exactly know how, but since he came to this country, knocking about he's kind got slack some way.'"[3] (No doubt Mary brought him up to scratch again, as James and the others all featured in the list of the Methodist congregation in Mission a few years later.)

Their acre of land certainly *was* at very close quarters to the Oblate mission—immediately on the western boundary. But it was also in a prime commercial location. At that time in Mission's history this was the heart of the settlement. Everything centred around the mission and its activities. The post office and store were here; the wharf was here; and now Mission's first railway station had just been built in this same area, at the foot of the OMI property. There was no doubt James had chosen well. He congratulated himself on his foresight in arriving early enough to secure this first-class site.

But how far ahead into the future was James looking when he

first arrived with his family on that sultry August afternoon? Did he think no further ahead than the commercial prospects for that one little acre of land? Or was he already going over in his mind a far broader series of developments which would completely change the face of the district? Was James at that moment picturing the future town of Mission which would one day be built on a site quite separate from the Catholic mission community—the town which he himself intended to found?

At the moment it required a considerable degree of optimism to conjure up any vision of this kind. The Mission district was then almost as much of a raw wilderness as Muskoka Falls had been when he and Mary had come there to live. There were no roads, no settlements, no churches, no schools—only the Roman Catholic mission. Few farms had been started, and most of the land was covered in virgin forest. But once the railway was finished, it would only be a matter of time before some speculator jumped in and decided to develop a townsite. James made up his mind early on that he was going to be that person.

The Tretheweys' first step was to establish themselves in business, and in this early phase Mary Ann was to play the leading role. By now they were a couple that were no longer young. James was now fifty, with receding hair, a wild beard, and the staring eyes of a dreamer. Mary Ann was forty-nine—stout, solid and determined-looking, a woman of obvious fortitude and strength of character. It had taken faith and courage on both their parts to give up the security of their established home in Ontario and come out to these primitive surroundings. Mary Ann would, in fact, be the first white woman to live in the district, apart from the Sisters of St. Ann at the Catholic mission.

But far from being dismayed by this situation, Mary immediately warmed to her leadership role. She felt she could hardly wait to get started with all the numerous business activities she was planning for the spring of 1884.

From the moment she had first arrived in British Columbia in 1882 to join her husband, she had, in fact, been tremendously busy. The family had spent the first winter at Spuzzum in the Fraser

Canyon, where railway construction was in frantic progress and jobs were readily available.4 Mary's arrival was a boon to the slender medical facilities in this section of the line, and her services as a nurse were instantly in demand by the CPR. Accidents on the line were almost a daily occurrence while the dangerous work of blasting and grading was in progress along the precipitous edge of the Canyon. As a qualified nurse, Mary was welcomed with open arms.

She remained in the employment of the CPR even after moving to Mission in 1883. It did not matter to her how far up the line she had to travel to reach the scene of an accident—and sometimes she would go as far as Kamloops, which was the end of this section of the work. She was ready to set off at a moment's notice, and she was prepared to use whatever sort of transportation happened to be available: hand-car, freight engine, or caboose. Carrying her worn leather bag, which contained bandages, needles and splints, as well as overproof brandy for an anaesthetic, Mary was a familiar figure travelling the rails in those pioneer years.5

Although Mary continued on call as the nurse for the CPR, now that she was in Mission she had more ambitious ideas for making use of her nursing skills. She planned to start a small maternity home on her own premises—on a small scale it would be Mission's first nursing-home.

But this was only one of her ideas. Besides this, she decided to run a small hotel enterprise, with meals and lodgings for travellers passing through. Most important of all, however, would be the general store which James would construct for her and which she would run with the help of the younger family members, Arthur and Emma. All Mary's latent entrepreneurial talents would finally have scope in this new setting.

She was anxious to get started with her plans as soon as possible, so as soon as winter was over, James built a small annex on to the house for use as the store—nothing ambitious, just "a little side room, lean-to", as Cornelius Kelleher remembered it. Mary immediately launched a series of advertisements in the *British Columbian* of 1884:

MRS. TRETHEWEY

—GENERAL—

Groceries, Provisions and Dry Goods.

———

General Agent for British Columbia for the Lamb Knitting Machine.

———

Good Accommodation for Travellers and Tourists.

———

Within five minutes' walk of the Railway Station,
ST. MARY'S MISSION, B.C.

Mrs. Trethewey is a duly qualified and certificated nurse and accoucheur, and is prepared to give the best attention and accommodation to invalids and ladies during confinement at her home as above, the situation of which is one of the most salubrious and delightful on the Lower Fraser. A skilful physician will be in attendance, if required. [6]

Somehow Mary managed to juggle all these different enterprises, and even an extra one which came her way only a few months after the store opened. This was the coveted post office operation. The Tretheweys' *good* luck here was the direct result of *bad* luck to another businessman, William Perkins.

Perkins, who had a little store in Hatzic, had taken over the post office from the Oblates in late 1883, but he had only had it a year when the store burned down (due to his own carelessness, rumour went.)[7] As a result, the post office had to be transferred immediately to the Trethewey store, and two months later, on January 1, 1885, James became the official postmaster. Of course, since he was so often away, busy with his milling contracts, Mary was to all practical purposes the postmistress, as well as the manager of store and hotel.

Her business expanded rather than decreased as she got older. To begin with, her operations were small. This first store of hers just held a few basic grocery supplies and necessities for the home, like pots and pans and brooms. Her hotel business too must have been quite modest in scope— the "tourists" whom she wished to attract by her advertisement must have been rare specimens indeed in those early days. "Travellers"—yes. It is on record, for instance, in the Public Accounts for 1883-1884 that Constable Guest called in there for a meal along with his apparently docile prisoners, Ah Hack and Ah Luck—all for a cost of 50 cents.

The knitting-machine which Mary Ann rather surprisingly mentioned in her advertisement was the outcome of one of the many sidelines to which she devoted her overflowing energy. Like other pioneer women, she had always been in the habit of knitting clothes for the family. Then, during her winter in the Fraser Canyon, seeing the railway construction gangs at work with their picks and shovels she had realised that here was an obvious market for the sale of warm knitted garments. Mary had set to work to produce a steady output of knitted gloves and socks, which were snapped up as soon as they were off the needles. As a result, she was now the agent for the Lamb knitting machine.

But first and foremost Mary was a nurse, and it is clear that she loved the work and had a real vocation for it. For her first four years in Mission she was the only nurse in the district. Her nursing-home undoubtedly flourished—"Never lost a patient," she was to advertise ten years later! The fortunate patients who recuperated here must have benefited too from the peace and quiet of the riverside scenery, for the situation was every bit as "salubrious and delightful" as Mary had described it in her advertisement.

For the first five years or so of their residence in Mission, James and Mary Ann must have been the leading business people in town. They had the store, the post office, the hotel premises and the medical facilities. No one else in Mission at this stage controlled a comparable number of vital services or had the same standing in the community as the enterprising Tretheweys.

Besides this, James had quickly become the owner of a large and central portion of land. All the evidence points to the conclusion that James must have had the idea of a townsite in mind right from the very start. He would have been well aware that townsites had re-

Do You Remember Mission When —

So far no one has turned up a picture of the first public school in what is now Mission City but Miss Edith Catherwood has discovered a faded photograph of a sketch of a small cabin flanked by fir trees together with some notes on the early days written by her father, the late J. A. Catherwood, dated Jan. 1st, 1928. The sketch (reproduced above) is believed to be of the school which opened Oct. 1st, 1885 in a little log cabin approximately where the Branch 57, Canadian Legion building now stands. It opened with 10 pupils and the teacher for the first month, the notes reveal, was a Mr. McDonald. Then Mr. Catherwood took charge about Nov. 1st, 1885 and continued for four years.

The Trethewey log cabin rented for use as Mission's first school in 1885. Drawn by John Catherwood, who taught there. *(Mission Community Archives)*

cently been registered at nearby Haney in 1882 and Hammond in 1883, and James was not slow to recognise an opportunity when he saw one. In any event, within the first year or two of the family's settling in Mission James had managed to get hold of one of the best pieces of developable land.

It was a good central acreage—an L-shaped portion wrapping around the present downtown Mission west of Grand Street—and besides this, it had the advantage of being right on the northern edge of the CPR tracks.[8] If a new railway station went in there to serve the townsite, then perhaps the Tretheweys would build hotels to accommodate railway passengers and the CPR men . . . James was never short on ideas. Full of enthusiasm for his new project, he quickly went ahead to satisfy the Crown Grant requirements for land occupancy, clearing trees and putting up some kind of crude dwelling.

The little log cabin which James Trethewey built on the site happens to have a unique place in Mission's history—it became the first school in the central area. It was only a stopgap measure, since the school trustees were about to build on other land, but as nothing else was available at the time, they arranged to rent the cabin from James. It opened on October 1, 1885, and for a few months this little shanty was where the first classes in Mission were held.[9]

In developing his ideas for a future town, James found a kindred spirit in his son Will, who was now just entering his twenties. The older boys, Joe and Sam, were too busy developing their farms in Dewdney (east of Mission); Jim was still in Ontario; as for Arthur, he was too young as yet to enter the world of higher finance. Besides, every one of these four brothers preferred a life with a strong element of physical activity. But Will was out of a different mould. Not for him the rugged life of the lumberman or the toilsome life of the farmer. William Griffith Trethewey had the instincts of a business-man right from the beginning; the executive life-style of the trader and promoter was more to his taste, and his commercial aptitude was obvious at an early age.

Will became James's great partner and ally in his development plans for the townsite. He qualified as a notary, and he teamed up with his father in promoting his business plans and negotiating for more land to add to the townsite area and make the project more viable. The acreage they badly wanted was the acreage east of Grand Street, linking up to what they already had, but this was held by another party. However, as Will wanted to take advantage of the Crown Grant land scheme, in the meantime he filed for some land with river frontage just south of the present Mission Hills shopping centre.[10] It was a rather swampy piece of land, but it was still a useful piece of real estate, adjoining both the river and the railway. Unfortunately, it did not join up with James's piece. It was to be another four years before the vital acreage they needed was to come on the market.

But now Mission began to boom in a way that may have surprised even James himself, for a wonderful development was about to take place. The CPR was planning to construct a line running south to the United States, and every town in the Fraser Valley was competing to be chosen as the junction point. Finally the good news was out—Mission would be the junction and Mission would have the first bridge to span the Lower Fraser.

A state of euphoria prevailed among the Mission settlers. As an important railway junction, Mission was surely destined for great things in the days ahead! The Tretheweys now felt confident that this would guarantee the town a lead over all other business competitors for the next few years at least. Even the major centre of New Westminster had no bridge as yet. It was not unreasonable to regard Mission as having a potential future as one of the leading cities on the Fraser River.

James and Will had only one reservation about this future development. The CPR was not planning for the bridge to be planked to carry road traffic, and this would be a big drawback to local trade. James immediately began to organise a pressure group to appeal to the government for the planking to be part of the bridge construction project. All through 1889 he was actively chairing meetings on his side of the river, while the Matsqui settlers did the same. Finally Will, with his notary training, drew up a petition to the Premier:

"We petition . . . that the new proposed C.P.R. Bridge be built for the accommodation of Traffic and foot passengers. It is true we have Railways and Steamboats, but we want a road to some market," he wrote hopefully.[11] They gathered many signatures, but nothing ever came of their request, and—incredibly—Mission had to wait nearly forty years before the bridge was ever planked.

In spite of the doubt that still clouded the bridge issue during 1889, James and William felt that they should not wait any longer to launch their townsite. They may, in fact, have had no option but to do so, whether or not they judged the moment to be ripe, because an American speculator named Reidt had already forestalled them and registered a town plan of his own. He had bought up Will Trethewey's swampy piece of lowland; he had registered the plan in June 1889, and at once put the land on the market, duly laid out in streets and lots. Had this development ever amounted to anything, Mission would be known today as "New Seattle".

But it does not appear that there was any great rush to buy up these rather unappealing lots on the Mission flats, and in any case Reidt soon had other competitors to reckon with. During the four months that had elapsed since Reidt unveiled his plans, the Tretheweys had been working furiously to rush their own plans and surveys through all the official channels. Finally, on October 21, 1889, they too had a townsite to offer to the public—the Trethewey Estate in the town of Mission Junction.[12]

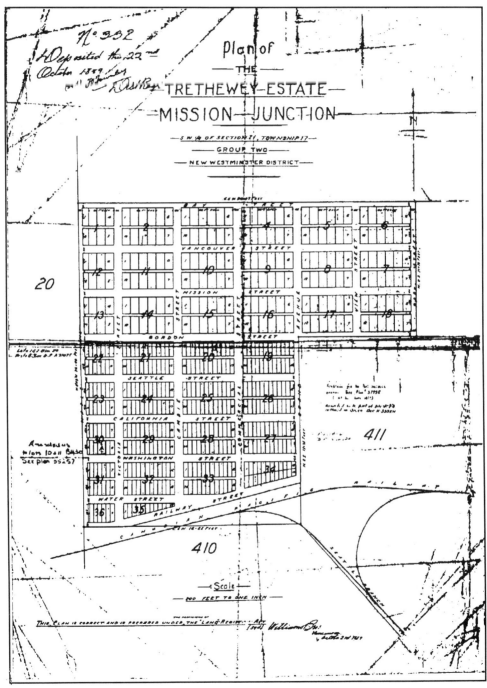

The Trethewey plan for Mission Junction, 1889. (Mission Community Archives)

The Trethewey Estate was James's hillside property, running from the present 7th Avenue down to Railway Street and from Cedar Valley Road to Grand Street. Abutting on the new railway station, it was a prime piece of real estate, and lots began to sell quite quickly.

But the Tretheweys had still not completed their plan for Mission. While all this activity was in progress, they had been frantically negotiating for the purchase of the other vital piece of property, the acreage on the other side of Grand Street to the east. This, oddly enough, was held by the Oblate Fathers at the mission, not because they had commercial ambitions, but because they held the property in trust for the orphan Cornelius Kelleher, whose father Mortimer had owned it since the 1860s. Finally, on December 30, two months after the Trethewey Estate was launched, the whole master plan fell into place. Will Trethewey triumphantly became the owner of the second piece of land,[13] and the Tretheweys were now in control of the whole area which is downtown Mission today.

After all these years of anticipation on James's part, why was it that when the big auction of lots in the Mission townsite was finally announced in 1891,[14] it was not the Trethewey family at all who were the developers and promoters of the whole scheme, but an American named James Welton Horne?

Horne was at that time Vancouver's wealthiest citizen, who had made his first fortune out of the creation of another town like this— the town of Brandon, Manitoba. With less well-judged reasoning, he thought he saw the same possibilities here in Mission. He certainly had the money—more capital than James could ever lay hands on; and he no doubt made James and Will an offer they couldn't refuse. So in mid-1890 Horne took over all the land that the Tretheweys had assembled—and more besides—and embarked on a massive advertising campaign to sell the town.

As it turned out, the Tretheweys were probably wise to have taken the course they did, for Horne's investment certainly failed to live up to expectation. Too many of the buyers at the 1891 land sale proved to have been speculators and not genuine future residents. Besides, the population was too small to attract immediate development and was unlikely to grow much, because the Council could not afford to build roads. Obviously Mission City was many years from being the metropolis of Horne's dreams.

The Tretheweys were to be even more thankful for their decision a few years later, when the great flood of 1894 swept across the Mission flats, submerging all the buildings near the wharf in 6 feet of water and ruining the lower town. All these lots were immediately devalued.

By this time James was long gone from Mission, and totally taken up with his next project, which was in the Chilliwack district. His family, however, were slower to move away and join him, for all of them were doing well in the new town of Mission City. As usual, every one of them had eventually gravitated into James's orbit. Jim and Libby had left Ontario and were running a hotel in Mission, Ontario House, (where the Bellevue is today.)[15] Elizabeth and her husband Joseph Taylor also had a small hotel, Albion House, just west of Jim's place.[16] Sam and Joe were happy on their farms, and with their lumbering interests. Emma had married a local farmer, Richard Brett and was established close to her brothers in Dewdney. Even James's own wife did not accompany him just yet, but stayed on in Mission, where all her interests lay!

Mary Ann—definitely a career woman by inclination—was by no means ready to give up her nursing and storekeeping when James left for Chilliwack. She even went ahead and expanded her business. Since the post office and store at her home were too far out of town now that the town centre had shifted, perhaps she did not have much choice. One did not have to be clairvoyant to predict that, if she took no action, some other merchant would soon put up premises and take away her trade. At all events, in 1891 she decided to put up a new commercial building on a site that was nearer to the centre of things. Arthur was to be the builder.[17]

Her new premises were not to be compared with the modest quarters she had had before. Elegant balconies, curlicued fretwork, and fine woodwork graced the large new building which she erected on Horne Street (then the main street in Mission.) Luckily—or perhaps shrewdly—she built it at the higher end of the street, north of the tracks, well above the flood level, and when most of lower Horne Street was destroyed in the flood of 1894, this was one of the few buildings to be immune from damage. The old leather-bound stock-book from the store still survives, and it shows the enormous range of goods she carried there—everything from farm tools to furniture, from chamber-pots to silverware. It was a hardware store, drugstore, jeweller's, clothier's, stationer's and furniture store all rolled into one.

But gradually the family closed down their businesses in Mission and district, and most of them went to join James, who, as usual, had great things all planned out for everyone. The last one to leave (except for Emma) was James's own wife, who, instead of heeding her conventional duty, insisted on continuing her career in Mission until the last possible moment. It was only around 1896, at the age of sixty-three, that Mary reluctantly gave up the work she loved, and departed for the life of retirement and undesired ease.

END NOTES

1. Joseph Lawson to his wife Catherine, Aug.12, 1883, Provincial Archives of B.C.
2. Ibid.
3. Ibid.
4. John E. Gibbard, *Early History of the Fraser Valley, 1808-1885,* unpublished M.A. thesis, University of Britsh Columbia, Vancouver, 1937, p.262. Information supplied to him by James's and Mary's daughter Emma, though there are a few inaccuracies in the account.
5. Clarke Trethewey, unpublished memoirs.
6. *British Columbian,* advertisement running from June 25-Sept.27, 1884.
7. Cornelius Kelleher, taped interview with Imbert Orchard, 1963, PABC.
8. Letters patent for SW¼, S21, T17, exclusive of portions of L411, G1, New Westminster.
9. *Fraser Valley Record,* Feb.5, 1958, sketch and notes by J.A. Catherwood, the first permanent teacher.
10. Crown Grant 346, L 412, G1, New Westminster.
11. Petition from the Mission settlers to the Hon. John Robson, Dec.28, 1889, PABC.
12. Plan of the Trethewey Estate, Mission Junction, Williams Bros (Land Surveyors), Oct.21, 1889.
13. L411, Bishop D'Herbomez to W.G. Trethewey, Dec.30, 1889, Absolute Fee Books 15.123.

14. *Vancouver Daily World,* May 20, 1891, report of the great land sale that took place on May 19.

15. SW¼, S21,Bl.34, L18 & 19, James Trethewey to Jas. E. & Elizabeth J. Trethewey, Feb.4, 1890, Absolute Fee Book 15.123.

16. SW¼, S21, Bl.34, L23 & 24, James Trethewey to Elizabeth Taylor, Nov.6, 1889, Absolute Fee Book 15.125.

17. *Daily Columbian,* Dec.18, 1891, p.1.

6

The Chilliwack Interlude

It says a great deal about James's personal charisma and powers of persuasion that—yet again—several of his family adopted his suggestions and followed him to his latest place of residence. Once again James had a new enterprise brewing in his mind, and once again he had key roles planned out for his sons.

The new locale had the same attraction as Muskoka Falls—water power.

Elk Creek was a small settlement at the foot of a massive mountainside—Mount Cheam, whose distinctive, scalloped silhouette dominates the skyline of the Central Fraser Valley. The mountain rises abruptly from the Chilliwack prairie to a grandeur of 7,000 feet, cresting into four main peaks, known to oldtimers as "The Lucky Four". The forest drapes the lower slopes in heavy swags of green, and through its dark thickets sparkle the silver ribbons of many waterfalls plunging down to join the streams below.

One of the most majestic of these cascades was Elk Creek Falls near the foot of the mountain. As a source of water power it was one of the finest in this part of the Valley, and James had often wondered why its potential had so far been overlooked. This was the feature that drew him now. The time had come, he decided, to build a mill of his own again, just as he had in Muskoka.

After fifteen years based largely in Mission, James was on the move once more. He had stayed long enough in one place, and he was

restless. Now he felt the urge to savour the excitement of new surroundings, and experience the familiar thrill of starting up a new
project. In any case, there was no point in remaining in Mission with
all his ideas played out. He needed a new goal. Once more, the watchword was: go ahead!

Only a few months after selling the Mission townsite, James was
into the new venture. "A short time ago Mr. W. Prest sold 160 acres
of land on the big prairie to Mr. Trethewey of Mission," announced
the *Vancouver Daily World* in November 1890.

James was soon enthusiastically mapping out a plan for himself
and his sons. First, he would build his grist mill. Then he would build
a sawmill, which would operate from the same water system, and his
sons would follow him to Elk Creek and start in the lumber business.
At the same time they would all have large and prosperous farms, for
the flat land at the foot of Mount Cheam was rich alluvial soil—
first-class land for agriculture.

As usual, everything worked out very much as James had
planned it.

By this time he was no longer working at any of the three grist
mills which he used to contract for. The Oblates' mill at Mission had
been dismantled in the mid-80s when the railway line cut through
the site. The Chadsey mill was now used chiefly for coarser grains.
As for the mill at Pavilion, the truth was that the owner was now
looking for a younger man who would be willing to adopt the new
techniques.[1] Rollers were now beginning to replace the old grinding-
stones, for the public was demanding a finer, whiter type of flour,
which could only be produced by the system of rollers. James had
been trained in the old style of grinding with millstones, which produced a dark, coarse flour. Though this would be much appreciated
today with the current trend towards healthier, unrefined grains, the
housewives of the early 1890s were starting to regard it as a crude
and unappealing product. However, James apparently preferred to
stay with the method he knew.

The machinery he installed at Elk Creek was machinery he was
very familiar with, because it came from the Oblates' old mill at St.
Mary's mission.[2] By the summer of 1891 he was ready to move it

across the river, and in the usual co-operative spirit of pioneer times all his new neighbours in the Elk Creek community offered their help with the move. "The farmers are ready to turn out and convey the machinery from the steamer landing to the mill site, and otherwise assist in the project gratis," wrote the local correspondent of the *Chilliwack Progress.* This faithful source of information duly reported that the "genial proprietor" of the mill had just turned out his first batch of flour on the Monday before Christmas, 1891.

Once the grist mill was running, James turned his attention to getting the sawmill built, and probably oversaw the project himself, as the two sons who were going to operate it were still tied to their jobs in Mission. The 100 hp turbine waterwheel was shipped out from New Westminster in March 1892, and by June the first lengths of lumber were already rolling off the production line.[3]

James junior (Jim) was to be the sawmill's "pushing proprietor", (as the newspaper rather inaptly described this very unpretentious Trethewey), and his youngest brother, Arthur, was now in partnership with him. Both of them, on leaving Mission, bought acreage on Prairie Central Road near the mill. A few years later they were unexpectedly joined by their brother Sam after his farm at Dewdney was ruined by the flood of 1894, and for the rest of the '90s he lived near them on Chilliwack Central Road. To some extent he was associated with their sawmill business, but news items in the local paper make it clear that his preferred activity was actually prospecting and that he found work at a mine on at least one occasion. Even Will, the notary, invested in 20 acres on Prairie Central Road, though it remained strictly an investment, and he had no thought of settling there in the wilds.[4]

So now, once more, James had most of the family gathered about him, and he resumed his role of family patriarch and counsellor. It obviously gave him genuine satisfaction to promote his children's interests, to advise, encourage, assist, and even create business opportunities as far as he was able. It has been said of his grandson, Roy Brett, that he had an almost magical ability to inspire confidence in his children, and one feels that this quality may well have been inherited from James, who so clearly had the gift of inspiring all his family to think in terms of success. Unquestionably, though he may have been an absentee father in their youth, he had the strongest possible sense of family cohesiveness and solidarity.

Mary stayed on in Mission for at least another two years. She sold the new store and post office in 1893, but she still went on advertising her maternity home even in 1893. Prominently throughout that summer this notice appeared in the *Daily Columbian*:

PLEASURE & HEALTH RESORT

Ladies and gentlemen desiring to gain health and strength will find a country home at the residence of Mrs. M.A. Trethewey at Mission City, B.C., who has had long and successful experience with ladies during their confinement. Never lost a patient. A physician of lengthened experience in attendance. Special attention and all the comforts of home given to ladies in confinement. Terms reasonable.

She was still living in Mission in 1895, listed as a member of the Mission City Methodist Circuit, and possibly in 1896 too, for she was not received by the Cheam Circuit in Chilliwack until 1897. In recent years she had been depending on the help of another qualified nurse, a younger woman named Annie Munro, so fortunately Mrs. Munro was able to take over as the district nurse when Mary Ann finally left.

By the time Mary rejoined the family, the two milling operations were running very smoothly indeed. Jim and Arthur were temperamentally congenial and worked successfully together, as they were to do at intervals throughout their lives. Sam, who joined them for a time, seems to have been something of a loose cannon. He was undoubtedly a hard worker, like all the Tretheweys, but with his volatile personality, which contrasted in every way to Jim's and Arthur's, he might not have been the ideal partner in this particular enterprise. "Arthur and Sam fought like cat and dog," remembered one family acquaintance with amusement.

Letter from Jim and Arthur Trethewey, owners of the Elk Creek Sawmill, 1897.
(Matsqui-Sumas-Abbotsford Museum)

In any case, Sam had become infected with the mining craze that suddenly swept through British Columbia in the 1890s, and he spent much of his time dabbling in mining ventures. The lucrative Silverton prospects and the Mount Baker mines were two of the places that attracted his interest, according to the local newspaper, which kept an eagle eye on the comings and goings of Chilliwack residents. Joe too, a born promoter, was constantly roaming the province in search of mineral prospects, though he maintained his ranch at Dewdney.

With his usual discernment James had picked one of the most abundant sources of water power in the Central Fraser Valley. "The location is one of the best sites to be found anywhere," one reporter pointed out, "having a never-failing stream of water falling from a perpendicular height of over 200 feet, which is to be used as motive power for the mill."[5]

Timber was plentiful in the forests in their own area, and the brothers hauled it down to the mill by teams of horses. Horses were often the accepted currency of payment for the lumber, for money was scarce, and barter was extremely common. Writing of this economically depressed period, Clarke Trethewey gives it as his opinion that there was "no more money in circulation in rural British Columbia than there had been in Muskoka." Because of the barter system the family would eventually accumulate more horses than they needed, so once a year they would make a trip to the big annual horse fair held in Stanley Park each fall, and trade the horses in for money or goods—whatever they could get.

The horrendous flood of 1894, the worst flood of the Fraser River in recorded history, did not affect the Tretheweys directly, as they were on comparatively high ground and some distance from the river. They were, in fact, able to shelter other families. But everyone in the Valley had some flood adventure to relate afterwards and the Tretheweys were no exception. On the actual morning when the dykes gave way, the Trethewey brothers happened to be dangerously close to the approaching flood waters. They had set out that morning for Chilliwack with a wagonload of lumber, but they had only gone a mile or so when they began to realise that the level of water in the ditch was steadily on the rise. Before long their worst fears were confirmed: in the distance appeared a wide lake of water, relentlessly spreading out over farms and fields, and moving slowly towards them. There was no time to lose. Quickly they unhitched the horses and turned back the way they had come, abandoning the wagon by the roadside.

But as they hurried along, they suddenly heard the sound of crying, and looking up, they saw three frightened little baby bears stranded on the snag of a dead tree. The mother bear had taken refuge up a larger tree and was calling to them to come and join her. Water was swirling round the bottom of the snag, and every time the babies ventured down the tree and reached the water, they took fright and scurried up again. There was only one way the Tretheweys could think of to rescue the cubs. Reluctantly, they shot the mother and took the babies home with them.

The little cubs became great pets, and two of them were adopted by the flood refugees when they returned to their homes. Arthur could not resist keeping the third cub, and it became very attached to him. Unfortunately baby bears have a habit of outgrowing the domestic environment, and eventually Arthur had to part with his friend. When he went in to the Stanley Park horse fair later in the year, he took the little bear with him and gave it to the zoo. The following year, when he went to the horse fair again, his pet still recognised him. It followed him around all day, not letting him out of its sight. When Arthur wanted to go home, he was obliged to call the keeper to put the bear on a chain, and he then made his getaway, though not without a pang of guilt.

Although Clarke says that money was scarce in these years, the Tretheweys obviously prospered, for all through that decade they initiated one major project after another. And now it was not merely *one* enterprising Trethewey who was thinking up the ideas and launching into speculative investments. *Five* Trethewey sons were now among the leading entrepreneurs in the Valley, and they were just as active as their father, and just as imaginative in their approach.

James's sons were now men in their thirties. Temperamentally they were all very different, but they had one thing in common—

ambition. They pursued their goals in different ways, but each one was programmed from birth to be an achiever, and each one made his mark in the Fraser Valley and beyond. This was the period in which they first began to try out their own strategies. Gradually, as the 1890s went by, they began to detach themselves from James's overpowering personality and the influence of his ideas, and find themselves as individuals. Though James's name continued to figure in some of their joint ventures, the young Trethewey men now came into their own as the active principals who were running the show.

The story of the Tretheweys in the 20th century is the story of these five remarkable sons and their equally remarkable descendants—strong, colourful figures all of them, fiercely individual, yet at the same time fiercely protective of family solidarity.

Elk Creek was James's last home in the Fraser Valley. Though his sons moved away at the end of the decade, selling the sawmill to their sister Emma's husband, Richard Brett, James and Mary Ann went on living there for a few more years. James even continued to run the grist mill at times for the benefit of the local farmers. Finally, in the early 1900s, health problems forced them to move to Vancouver, so as to be closer to medical facilities. In the meantime, life continued to have plenty of zest for James, as in his late sixties he eagerly identified with his sons' new plans and unhesitatingly put his money into some of their more ambitious ventures.

END NOTES

1. *Fraser Valley Record,* n.d., article by R.D. Cumming, nephew of the miller Lee.
2. *Daily Columbian,* Aug.17, 1891.
3. *Chilliwack Progress,* Mar.17 & June 2, 1892.
4. Chilliwack Assessment Rolls.
5. *Chilliwack Progress,* July 9, 1891.

Arthur Trethewey and Susan Gowan on their wedding day, 1891. *Trethewey family archives*

Arthur and Susan and family, c.1916. Top row (left to right): Robert, Annetta, Clarice, Arthur, Emma, Leslie. Bottom row (left to right): Charlie, Susan, Clarke. *Trethewey family archives*

General view of the Abbotsford millsite.

Loggers employed by the mill company. Back row: fourth from right, Matt Higginson. Front row:———, Mark Jackson, Jack Call, Dan McEwan.

Matsqui-Sumas-Abbotsford Museum

Many of the Sikh community worked at the Abbotsford Mill.

Nash S. Gill

The log dump at Mill Lake.   *Matsqui-Sumas-Abbotsford Museum*

Huge timbers produced by the Abbotsford mill for the Welland Canal
 project.   *Trethewey family archives*

Climax locomotive pulling into the millsite at Mill Lake.
                                              Matsqui-Sumas-Abbotsford Museum

Joseph Ogle Trethewey.   *Trethewey family archives*

Trethewey House, Joe's Abbotsford residence, built 1920. Now a heritage site.
Don Freayh.

The ranch house at the Chilco Ranch, owned by Joe 1910-1922.

Joan Campbell

Joe with his step-daughter Erna (left) and daughter Cora (middle) on the Gang Ranch Road, 1919.   *Joan Campbell*

Samuel Dunn Trethewey and Elizabeth Morrow on their wedding day, 1889.
Heather Coupland

Sam's home on Castleman Road, Chilliwack. Rosanna, Ernest and Howard at left; Sam and Elizabeth by the door.   *Chilliwack Archives*

James Everett (Jim) Trethewey and family at Elk Creek, 1895. Standing at back, (left to right): Isaac Spring, Olive, —, —, —, William Hall, Muriel. Seated (left to right): Mary, Elizabeth with Everett on lap, Jim.

Trethewey family archives

Sniped log in the process of being skidded. Jim on left.

Trethewey family archives

Jim logging at Newton.

Trethewey family archives

Examples of Jim's wood-
work.   *Donna Pound*

Elizabeth Taylor and the children of her three marriages. Standing at back: Violet and Paul. Seated (left to right): Jim, Elizabeth, Arthur, Albert.

Trethewey family archives

Emma Brett (née Trethewey) in her later years.   *Trethewey family archives*

The Brett family, (left to right): Emma, Earl, Roy, Richard, Beatrice, c.1907.
Trethewey family archives

7

The Providence Mine

I t was Joe who happened to spot it—the gleam of silver in that otherwise ordinary fragment of rock below the bluffs of Harrison Lake.

It was an almost accidental discovery—except that to Joe, as to his father, it was second nature to look at every outcrop of rock in terms of possible mineral value. He had come across it while he was in the process of doing some horse-logging on the Trethewey timber limits on the west shore of Harrison Lake. A stray fragment of rock caught his eye, a piece of "float" that had broken away from the main lode of ore higher up the cliff, and he stopped to examine it more closely. The more he studied it, the more his excitement grew. He had a strong hunch that this particular specimen was worth looking into.

He showed it to his father—that old hand at prospecting—and asked his opinion. Though James never had found his "pot of gold", it still did not take much to excite him where minerals were concerned, and he volunteered to have the specimen assayed. To everybody's jubilation it was found to carry values of $134.74 in silver and gold.[1]

This was the birth of the celebrated Providence mine, which became the richest mine ever to be found on Harrison Lake.

It happened in 1896, only a short time after the Tretheweys first arrived at Harrison Lake to set up a logging camp. Jim and Arthur were still running the Elk Creek mill and logging around East Chilliwack, but just recently they had decided to branch out and acquire some first-class timber limits on Harrison Lake.

It was not the first logging to take place there, for the Martins who had the sawmill at Harrisonmouth had been bringing logs down the lake for the past ten years. But judging from the publicity which the Tretheweys' camp attracted, theirs must have been the first large-scale logging operation ever to be seen on Harrison Lake. It caused immense interest, and all the pleasure excursions cruising up the lake that summer featured the logging camp as one of the highlights of the trip. "Tretheweys' camp, which can be visited" was one of the sights of the lake.[2]

The Trethewey timber limits were about halfway up the west side of the lake, close to streams which are difficult to identify from today's map. According to the description in the *B.C. Gazette* of 1896, Jim's and Arthur's limits were just north of a stream called Black Creek. There was also a stream named White Creek, and this was where Joe too had obtained timber limits just a month after his brothers.

But if timber had been at the forefront of Joe's thoughts at the beginning of the year, it quickly receded in importance when he made the "providential" mineral discovery that was to change the course of his life—the discovery of the Providence mine.

Joe already had a fair amount of experience in prospecting. James's mining obsession had rubbed off on all his sons, and as the eldest son, Joe had been exposed to the full strength of his father's convictions. As early as 1891 he was reported as bringing back "rich specimens of quartz" from the upper country (the newspaper accounts of the day always liked to strike an optimistic note.) He was ready to take risks and he was lucky. "Everything Joe touched seemed to turn to gold," said one family member.

Out of all the mines on Harrison Lake the Providence mine turned out to be the most lucrative and productive, though at the time, when all the hype and flamboyance of the various claims was confusing the issue, it was difficult to assess where the true values lay.

The year 1896 was a year of intense but secret activity on the

No. 12   Incorporated 1897, under the Laws of the
          Province of British Columbia
          "Companies' Act, 1890," and Amending Acts.   —200— Shares.

PROVIDENCE
MINING & DEVELOPING COMPANY
LIMITED LIABILITY.

Vancouver, B.C., *March 25th* 1897

This Certifies that *E. Dorothy Linday Phillips*

is entitled to —200— *Shares, fully paid-up,* numbered *19,001 to 19,200* inclusive, in the *Capital Stock* of the **PROVIDENCE MINING AND DEVELOPING CO., LIMITED LIABILITY.**

Transferable only on the books of the Company and upon the surrender of this Certificate. In testimony whereof the said Company has caused this Certificate to be signed by its President and Secretary the day and date above written.

James Trethewey , President
W. J. Trethewey , Secretary.

Share Certificate for the Providence Mine, 1897.   (Provincial Archives of B.C.)

part of the two or three serious prospectors on the lake. Not a word of it reached the pages of the *B.C. Mining Record* during that year, nor did the Mining Report in the *B.C. Sessional Papers* make any mention of discoveries in this part of the province. Even the local Chilliwack newspaper seemed unaware of anything unusual happening up the Harrison other than the logging at the new Trethewey camp. But covertly the prospectors were up there in the hills, feverishly staking out their claims, testing their samples of ore, and jockeying for the choicest spots before the news broke and the big rush started.

That October Joe was sure enough of what he had found to purchase the whole 160 acres that included his claim.

Over the winter the news began to leak out, and at the first sign of spring a full-scale mining boom suddenly made the quiet waters of Harrison Lake a scene of frantic activity. "The region around Harrison Lake is swarming with prospectors and . . . some jumping of unregistered claims is likely to take place," announced the *Chilli-wack Progress* at the beginning of March, 1897. "A large number of locations have been made." And two weeks later: "A group of prospectors with their outfits is becoming such a familiar sight on our streets as to attract little attention."[3]

Countless claims were registered all around the lake. Mostly they belonged to small investors with minimal equipment and capital, but the Trout Lake mines on the eastern side of the lake were a bigger proposition altogether and attracted as much publicity as the Providence mine during 1897. All the fanfare about the Trout Lake mines mysteriously faded away at the end of the first season, and no more was heard of them, for their promoter, John Brown (owner and manager of the resort hotel at Harrison Hot Springs), now had a much more interesting prospect to pursue in the form of the ill-fated Fire Mountain mines at the head of the lake.

Joe, on the other hand, made a substantial profit from the Providence mine. So did his family, for it should come as no surprise to learn that one of the trustees of the company was none other than James himself, keen as ever to make good with a mine. Joe took the lead in all developments, but he brought in his younger brother Will and a business associate of Will's, Lemuel G. Munn (the Sea Island Cannery owner), as partners. Will was also the secretary of the company. As usual, the family hung together at important moments.

Finally the news of the mining boom hit the newspapers, but the Tretheweys had managed to keep their plans dark until the very last moment. They registered the company in March 1897, just as the news was beginning to make headlines in the local press. As a good Methodist family of speculators, they had given the new company a very suitable choice of name—the Providence Mining and Development Company. (Later, when Will had a spectacular mine of his own, he too was to talk of Divine Providence and the Guiding Hand.) By the end of the month Providence mining stock was for sale at 15 cents.

The Providence claim was on a wooded slope running down to the water, about seven miles above the northern tip of Long Island, at today's Davidson Creek. Mountains filled the whole skyline on either side of the lake. Across the lake soared the icy pinnacle of Mount Breakenridge, streaked with glacial blue; while behind the mining camp rose the endless green ranges of the high Coastal Mountains, clothed in a dense dark forest that was yet to be explored. A few miles to the north, on the same western shore, stood the Indian land-mark of the Doctor Rock, a strange figure etched in a cleft of the rock and believed by the native people to control the sudden storms that sometimes tore the surface of the lake. Farther north still, at the head of the lake, was the ghost town of Port Douglas, eerie with its aban-doned buildings from the old gold rush days, and home to only one or two isolated families. The last remains of the town were to burn down the following year due to the carelessness of some miner tak-ing shelter there.

The mineral values were contained in three main veins just 400 yards apart and almost parallel. As early as 1896 the Tretheweys had taken out some surface ore and sent a carload to the Everett smelter for testing. Even this shallow sample of ore had shown good returns of both silver and gold. Encouraged by these promising results, Joe made up his mind to go ahead, and the following season he went to work in earnest, sinking a 50-foot shaft and drifting 300 feet into the mountain. By July they had 25 tons of rock ready to send to the smelter, and Joe was feeling buoyant.[4] It was common knowledge in mining circles that "the owner, Mr. Trethewey, has wagered a suit of clothes with a prominent mining man that the shipment will give gross returns of $100 a ton"![5]

The outcome of this wager must be left to the imagination, but there seems little doubt that good profits came in, for at the begin-ning of the 1898 season the company invested in new plant, includ-ing a 4-drill compressor—$5,500 of machinery in all—and pushed ahead at a great rate with the development of the first two veins. They sank another shaft and they tunnelled farther into the moun-tain. Huge piles of ore lay on the dump—165 tons, it was said.[6]

It seems curious, on the face of it, that just as the mine was reaching such high yields the Tretheweys should have decided to sell their interest, but it was consistent with their usual policy: make sure of a good thing. This was what they had elected to do when they sold the Mission townsite, and this is what would happen again when Will sold his fabulous silver mines in Ontario. The Tretheweys' gambler instincts were always tempered with a strong element of prudence. When their enterprises reached a certain stage of development, they tended to weigh up rather carefully the relative advantages of holding on or selling out. Often they opted for the certain profit, and this was evidently the route their business judgement dictated in the case of the Providence mine. At the end of 1898 the Trethewey interests were taken over by Joe's partner, Lemuel Munn and another investor named Adams.[7]

One consideration that may have influenced their thinking was the unwelcome knowledge that some of the tunnelling would soon have to go very close to the lake itself, and even under the lake, with all the attendant risks. These were complications they could do without. Munn and Adams carried on at the site for another two years, but after this all activity seems to have died away. Problems had indeed arisen when the new company had started tunnelling towards the lake, and in any case these leads had not proved very productive, so it would seem that the Tretheweys probably enjoyed the best profits. It was rumoured in later years that altogether 350 tons of ore had been shipped out from the Providence mine, and Joe was supposed to have walked away a rich man with a sum of $20,000.

By now Will was just as much of a compulsive prospector as James or Joe or Sam. As well as being a partner in the Providence mine and an extension called the Silver Bell, he had also been a trustee of the Harrison Lake Star Mining Company Ltd. (This was another extension claim up the mountain.) Besides this, he was a principal in the Harrison Lake Mining, Developing and Prospecting Company Ltd. His regular work was still in Vancouver, where he was now a successful patent attorney, but at the back of his mind was always the vision of that elusive mother lode hidden away somewhere in Canada's vast wilderness. Others were making fortunes in the Kootenays and the Klondike; why not a Trethewey? Perhaps even Will himself would have been surprised if he could have foreseen the future and realised how quickly his vision was about to come true.

END NOTES

1. L.K. Hodges, *Mining in British Columbia*, a 1967 reprint of *Mining in the Pacific North-West*, published by the *Seattle Post-Intelligencer*, 1897.
2. *Chilliwack Progress*, June 3, 1896.
3. Ibid, Mar.3 & Mar.17, 1897.
4. B.C. *Sessional Papers*, Report of the Minister of Mines, 1898.
5. *B.C. Mining Record*, July 1897.
6. B.C. *Sessional Papers*, Report of the Minister of Mines, 1899.
7. *Daily Columbian*, Oct.12, 1898.

8

Fiasco at Harrison Mills

The ink was scarcely dry on the sale documents of the Providence mine when the Tretheweys flung themselves with their usual enthusiasm into another enormous undertaking. This time it was not a mine but a mill.

The Martins, who had the big, fairly new sawmill at the mouth of the Harrison, were in a mood to sell. One of the sons was anxious to return to the more civilised lifestyle of Ontario, and "old man Martin", as he was known to the locals, was in frail health and nearing the end of his life. The Martin mill was much larger than the sawmill at Elk Creek, and with the mill went the Martins' magnificent stands of timber on Harrison Lake. All in all, it was a proposition not to be missed.

James, of course, was ready and willing to make another major investment, and by now Jim and Arthur had enough experience to take on the management of a larger mill. In November 1898 the news was made public in the local paper: "The Tretheweys have bought the Martin mill as well as the timber limits in connection with the mill. They intend building a new mill and extending business."[1]

A new mill?—The Martin mill was only six years old and well equipped for its time. But although it was an advance on their previous operations, the mill was still not large enough or modern enough to satisfy the Tretheweys' present ambitions. What they had in mind now was a far larger-scale operation and a far wider market. They would build a new mill, and it would be the most up-to-date and the most efficient that they could afford. As usual, the watchword was: "Go ahead."

It was a site that had enormous potential. The timber was superb, and the supply apparently unlimited. From the earliest times of settlement the forests of the Harrison had been recognised as some of the finest in the province. Huge firs and cedars, and the great field maples too, flourished in prodigal abundance in these luxuriant rain forests. White pine, which had a high commercial value, was also in plentiful supply. "It is especially abundant on the upper part of Harrison's River and is of surpassing beauty," ran the description in one of the early guide-books. [2]

From the point of view of transportation the site could not have been better. The Martin mill stood in between the railway line on one side and the Harrison River on the other. By water they had access to the markets along the Fraser River. By rail they could reach the desirable prairie market—and this was the development which was now uppermost in their minds and was one of their main reasons for the move. They were well aware that it would take outside capital to expand the business in this way, so they immediately went through the process of forming a company, which called itself the Harrison River Mills Timber and Trading Company Ltd. and which took over the sawmill and the six timber limits in November of 1899.

Interestingly, there was now a new element in the management structure, since for the first time in their lumbering activities the Tretheweys were bringing in partners other than family members. These new partners were all prairie men, who would provide the contacts the Tretheweys needed to get into the prairie market. T.A. Cuddy, the secretary-treasurer, was a lumberman from Winnipeg, while two other major shareholders, Thomas Jackson (later Mayor of Chilliwack) and Franklin Boyd, were also from Manitoba. James, the family patriarch, was still at the helm in the role of president. Arthur was vice-president, and Jim was one of the directors.[3]

The reason for Jim's subsidiary role was probably that he was out of action at about this point, due to a serious illness. For the first little while, he and Arthur had run the mill jointly, but before long Jim was suddenly taken ill. It was diagnosed as a severe attack of rheumatic fever, and he was sent to the Vancouver General Hospital for treatment. For some time it was doubtful whether he would survive, but slowly he recovered, though it was eleven weeks before he was fit to be discharged. In his convalescent stage he took treatment at the well-known Harrison Hot Springs spa, which was just a few miles away, at the foot of Harrison Lake, and he always believed that the healing effect of the hot sulphur springs had had a great deal to do with his complete recovery. Eventually he shook off all the ill effects of the rheumatic fever and, in fact, lived to the greatest age of all the brothers. In the meantime he withdrew from any active part in the business.[4]

Construction of the new mill started almost as soon as the company was formed. The contractor was Jim's brother-in-law, James Spring, for the Tretheweys always liked to keep things in the family if they could, both then and later. Huge in size compared to the original Martin mill, the new mill building measured 40' x 330'. It was equipped with the most efficient and up-to-date machinery and even that admirable modern feature—a large electric light plant. In a 10-hour day the sawmill was capable of turning out from 40,000 to 50,000 feet of lumber. The two dry kilns had a capacity of 150,000 feet.[5]

Undoubtedly it was the largest and most modern sawmill in the whole district, and it is believed to have been one of the largest on the entire West Coast at that time.

It took only eight months from the time of forming the company to the time when the mill was fully operational: the first lumber came off the saws in July of 1900. The prairie market was now the Tretheweys' chief priority, and they shipped almost their whole production to the prairie provinces, though they did maintain a lumber yard in Chilliwack.

They acquired a new work-boat too, a sternwheeler named the *Defender*, which towed the log booms down from Harrison Lake to the mill. Occasionally the *Defender* was chartered out to local organisations for the more frivolous purpose of holiday excursions.

The Chilliwack baseball club hired it out, for instance, for their Victoria Day outing in May of 1902, when they made the popular voyage up the sparkling length of Harrison Lake to the wooded bay at old Port Douglas, and pronounced the boat "very satisfactory." "It will be used again, no doubt," noted the reporter.[6] The captain of the *Defender* was another of Jim's brothers-in-law, Isaac Spring.

With large numbers of mill workers and their families moving into the district and swelling the population, the little settlement at Harrison River began to change its character as a direct result of Trethewey initiative. From being just a quiet farming area with a mill as a minor feature, it suddenly turned into a mill-based community with a village centre and a real community life. Many new buildings went in, and thanks to the job creation brought about by the new mill, Harrison River at the turn of the century became a much livelier and more prosperous place. Some idea of the extent of the operations can be found in the B.C. Directory's description of the district as it was in 1901 soon after the Tretheweys came:

> "At the railroad station is the Harrison River Mills Timber and Trading Company's sawmill, turning out 50,000 feet per day. They employ in the timber and at the mill 175 whites, Chinese and Japanese. Around the mill is a village including two stores, a hotel and the butcher shop."

(A school was soon to follow, especially as a shingle mill too was just being built on the opposite side of the Harrison by other investors.)

But Trethewey enterprises did not remain static for very long, and only two years later, in 1903, further changes were afoot. A rumour began to circulate to the effect that the Tretheweys were about to sell out and that "a large company of experienced millmen" would be taking over the sawmill. The secretary, Boyd, issued an immediate denial, categorically stating that the report was not true—the mill "was not sold, nor likely to be."[7]

Like many other denials of this sort, his statement was only partially correct, for in reality all sorts of negotiations *were* proceeding and a radical change in the organisation of the company was very definitely in the offing. It was not to be an outright sale—merely the transfer of a half-interest to another company, the Rat Portage Lumber Company. This was a strong and well established prairie company which owned a whole chain of lumber yards on the prairies, as well as a box factory in Winnipeg. As usual, the Tretheweys were never content with merely maintaining the status quo; always they had to be augmenting and improving their holdings. The rationale behind this latest proposal was to entrench themselves even more firmly in the prairie market.

By July all the paper work was ready. The selling price was $125,000. The documents had been signed, the cheque made out, and everything was proceeding as planned, when suddenly disaster struck. Fire—it was every mill-owner's worst dread and it was all too common in that era. Now it happened at Harrison River: the Tretheweys' brand-new mill went up in flames.[8]

The fire started in the early evening in the dry kiln near the main mill. All hands quickly turned out to throw barrels of water on the flames, but a strong breeze was blowing and soon the flying sparks had set the main mill alight too. In the hot dry July weather the fire took hold quickly and flames raced through the building before anything could be done to save it. The fire advanced rapidly across the site, swallowing everything in its path—the piles of lumber, the mill-workers' housing, even Arthur and Susan's own home. Finally the railway station too fell into ashes as the flames swept through.

It was a truly devastating blow for the mill company, for they only had insurance for $30,000, and the damage was estimated at a minimum of $80,000 and more likely $100,000 to $125,000. The whole situation with the Rat Portage company now needed re-thinking. Three months after the fire, the announcement came. The Rat Portage Company, instead of taking the half-interest as previously arranged, would completely take over the Tretheweys' company. (Strangely, the business still functioned under the old name of the Harrison River Mills Timber and Trading Company for another four years.)

Neither of the Trethewey brothers had any further association with the mill itself after this. Jim moved to Haney to start up a small mill of his own. Arthur, however, did not leave the district just yet, but carried on with the logging side of the operation, living at Harrison River and supplying logs to the Rat Portage for the next few years.

The company resumed operations quite quickly. After only about a six-month cessation of activities, they brought in a portable mill early in 1904 and immediately afterwards rebuilt the sawmill. Jim's brother-in-law, James Spring, who had built the mill that burned, was the contractor for the new mill too. He was not in good health and he had had to come all the way from Los Angeles to carry out the contract, but he did it as a special favour to Jim. He was less enthusiastic over the project when he realised that Jim was no longer involved; however, he stayed to finish the work. Unfortunately, Spring was a sicker man than anyone had realised. On the way back to California his condition began to deteriorate, and he died before he was able to reach home.[9]

The Tretheweys' mill had been regarded as ultra-modern, but it was completely outclassed by the huge and elaborate set-up which the Rat Portage Company introduced into Harrison Mills. The new sawmill was capable of producing twice the daily output of the old one. Lavishly equipped with every modern device, it was a model of gleaming efficiency with the most state-of-the-art machinery that then existed. Everything was large-scale and everything was of the best. The village itself suddenly burgeoned from a straggling riverside community into a neat little company town. Two streets of houses went in for the millworkers and executives, and many other buildings were either constructed or renovated for use as bunkhouses, boarding-house, company store and office, hall and poolroom. The whole new town was weirdly raised up on posts and pilings to protect it against the annual floods when the river overflowed its banks each spring. With its strange ungainly appearance, this curious village on stilts was one of the major sights of the river.[10]

One can only guess at the feelings of the Tretheweys as they watched this proliferation of construction and reflected upon the vast influx of capital being poured so lavishly into their own cherished project. Although perhaps they did not waste an excessive amount of time and emotional energy in dwelling on their own misfortune and the results of the fire, they would not have been human if they had not experienced a pang of envy to see another company in their place, fulfilling their dreams.

But there was to be yet another twist to the story. The worst irony of the whole situation was something totally unexpected—the extraordinary collapse of the Rat Portage enterprise after a mere two seasons of operation! No expense had been spared in equipping the mill; years of preparation had gone into the project. Yet after finally starting up in early 1909, the mill shut down at the end of 1910—never to reopen.

Again, one speculates on the feelings of the Tretheweys when they heard of the astounding demise of this well-financed operation. Surely some sense of bitterness must have soured their thoughts as they pondered over the incredible waste of such resources and such a site. Over and over again, they must have discussed the situation among themselves, analysing the mistakes and misjudgements that might have led up to the disaster. They could hardly have avoided comparing the failure that had occurred with the success which they themselves might have made of it—and which the site undoubtedly deserved.

By the time of the Rat Portage mill closure, any Trethewey association with their group had long been at an end. For a time Arthur Trethewey had been supplying the Rat Portage with logs from his timber limits at 20-Mile Point on Harrison Lake, where he and his partners, Bill Hanna and John McEwen, had their logging camp. For this contract they had been using one of the early donkey engines, for the Tretheweys made a point of being up-to-date—or even ahead of others—with their machinery. Finally in 1907 he had sold these timber limits to the Rat Portage (as well as other timber limits in the Chehalis Valley) and moved away from Harrison River. [11]

After severing his connection with the Harrison district, Arthur moved to New Westminster to consider his next step. Extraordinary events had been taking place within the Trethewey family, and the future needed careful deliberation. New choices suddenly presented themselves. New possibilities loomed on the horizon.

If it had not been for this sudden turn of fate, possibly the lives of all the five Trethewey brothers would have continued to run on the same relatively steady and prosperous lines, their business affairs subject to moderate gain or occasional reverse, but on the whole moving comfortably along in a fairly predictable and successful pattern. Without doubt all five of these energetic brothers would have done well, yet they might have lacked the capital to develop their ideas to best advantage.

Now, out of the blue, came a development that no one had seriously foreseen—the wild card that changes everything in the game. It was as sudden and unexpected and shattering as winning a lottery: Will discovered the silver mine that was to make him a multi-millionaire.

ENDNOTES

1. *Chilliwack Progress,* Nov.7, 1898.
2. T.N. Hibben, *Guide to the Province of British Columbia,* 1877.
3. *B.C. Gazette,* 1899, Vol.2, p.2015.
4. Mildred Kitching (daughter of James E. Trethewey), interview with the author, 1992.
5. *Daily News Advertiser,* July 22, 1903.
6. *Chilliwack Progress,* May 28, 1902.
7. Ibid, Apr.29 & May 6, 1903.
8. Ibid, July 22, 1903.
9. Kitching interview.
10. Fenn Pretty, taped interview with the Agassiz-Harrison Historical Society, 1979.
    Photographic records, Kilby General Store Museum.
11. *Chilliwack Progress,* Oct.16, 1907.

9

The Cobalt Millionaire

I t was May 10, 1904, and it was a day that William Trethewey would never forget.

He had arrived in the mining camp only the previous day. It had been a tedious trip from Toronto to Cobalt, dragging out to three days of travel, though it was only a distance of about 300 miles. He had had to take three different trains and then a steamer up the river, and even after disembarking at Haileybury he had still had to tramp a muddy trail for five miles before reaching the little tent town at Cobalt (or Long Lake, as it was called then.) Instantly he could see that all around him were claims that would make their owners rich men.[1]

Will was an experienced mining man, like all the Trethewey family. He had made a certain amount of money out of mining in British Columbia, but so far his assets resulted more from his shrewd dealings in real estate than from mining.

What brought him to Cobalt now was the result of a chance meeting. In late 1903 he had struck up an acquaintance with Dr. Willet Miller, the provincial geologist for Ontario and a former professor of mining at Queen's University. Because of Will's interest in mining, he soon developed a habit of dropping in regularly to look at Miller's latest geological specimens. One day just as William was on the point of leaving Montreal for a business trip out west, Miller happened to remark: "By the way, they have found something in the

Nipissing country which is very promising."[2] (This was an under-statement, for Miller had actually been astounded to see huge chunks of silver as large as cannon balls, casually scattered around so-called copper veins.)

At the sight of Miller's specimens of rock with their obvious traces of native silver, Will's prospecting instincts went into immediate alert and he promptly forgot all about his intentions of returning west. Although, as far as he knew, silver had never amounted to much in Ontario, he could not resist the idea of having a look for himself and he decided to make a trip to the site as soon as the snow was gone.

The place he was heading for was a wilderness area around a stretch of water called Long Lake close to the Quebec border. No settlement existed there—only a few tents pitched amid the mud and stumps where one or two claims had been discovered in 1903. Although Professor Miller had been broadcasting the news of this rich mineral district in newspaper articles all through the winter, it had been received with general scepticism as just another exaggerated rumour. No one had any conception that this isolated tract of woodland was about to become the silver mining capital of Canada.

As soon as spring arrived, William had sped off to Toronto to get his miner's licence and to outfit himself for mining. On May 6 he started out for Long Lake. Even on first arrival Will could see at a glance that these were rich strikes. He was amazed to find so little excitement among the prospectors, in spite of the fact that half a million dollars in ore had already been taken out. "They were just sitting back and doing nothing," he marvelled later, "with $200,000 sitting up there and looking at them right on the surface of the vein." [3]

His first move was to try to purchase one of these claims, but nobody was willing to sell, so he decided to prospect for himself. His first day's exploration was unrewarding. So was the morning of his second day, but at four in the afternoon of May 10 he decided to go off on his own and have a look in a direction which no one else seemed to think of any value. Others had been in there before him, of course, but had written it off as a worthless spot.

He passed over several low ridges until he saw one where the signs looked more promising, and followed this to the foot of a rocky bluff. Here the trail ended in a tangle of trees and fallen timber, which rested up against the side of the cliff in such a way as to form a low dark tunnel. It was also very swampy. But instead of skirting round this damp and difficult bit of bush, as other miners had done, some unexplained instinct told him to take the less obvious route beneath the spiky barrier of branches.

An early newspaper account tells the rest of the story with the flourish it deserves: "Stooping down, he crept along, the cavern growing darker, till suddenly he came out into a crevice in the rocks which let in the waning evening light, when lo, before him lay tons of decomposed rock and float, the accretions of half a century, revealing to the practised eye a wealth of mineral that for a moment took away the breath of the beholder."[4]

To a professional prospector like himself it was clear that right before him was the fortune of a lifetime. As much as $200,000 worth of silver ore was in full view. "I walked almost straight to the old Trethewey mine," William told a newspaper reporter a few years later.

Now his problem was to establish ownership. "I had no axe with me, and there were fellows down at the camp who would have made a wild rush up there if they had known, and I might have lost my mine. So I hid it as well as I could by throwing sticks and moss over the rock where I had chipped it."

In a state of extreme suspense he came back to his tent and quietly had his usual tea, all the time turning over in his mind the problem of how to get back to stake the claim without attracting anyone's curiosity. In the end he decided that he would pretend that he needed to take an axe and chop down a tree.

"I started out with my axe on my shoulder slowly enough until I got out of sight of the camp, and then I only hit the ground at the high places," he said in describing that memorable day.[5] He put in a post with his name and licence number, then walked a little farther along the bluff. Incredibly, there was yet *another* potential mine clearly showing on the cliff face! This was the famous Coniagas mine. All in a few short hours Will had discovered two of the most outstanding claims ever to be developed in the district of Cobalt.

But even with all his circumspection in keeping the news secret until he had staked his claim, William still ran into problems over establishing his rights to the mine. With the stakes so high, there was no shortage of unscrupulous characters in the camp who were only too ready to jump a claim, if they could find a way. As the story goes, an attempt of this kind was made soon after the discovery of the Coniagas, when one of the miners in camp fraudulently carved his own name and an earlier date on a log that was lying near the claim. Although this was not a legal method of establishing a claim and probably would not have held up in court, it was enough to give Will a considerable scare.

Fortunately he had a witness, Alex Longwell, who had helped him to stake the claim. Since Longwell was at that time working for a wealthy investor named Colonel R.W. Leonard, Will offered Colonel Leonard a half-interest in the Coniagas in return for the promise of his and Longwell's support, if it ever came to to a legal case.[6]

Will's family quickly rallied round as well. His elder brother Joe hurried out to Cobalt to give him all the help he could in establishing the claim and fighting the case. As it turned out, they were spared the ultimate legal hassle, as the claim was never challenged in any court of law, but Will felt so much indebted to Joe for his support that he gave him too a share in the Coniagas. The one-eighth interest which Joe received was sufficient to make him a wealthy man— by far the wealthiest of the four brothers who remained in British Columbia.[7]

So rich was the ore in these mines that huge slabs of silver lay bare on the surface of the vein, just waiting to be stripped off the surface—"like boards off a barn", as one awestruck onlooker described it. "But this is better than the mines of Solomon!"[8] exclaimed another. When the first rich carload of ore came trundling out from Will's mine five months later, his fortune was made. In terms of worth he had become a multi-millionaire almost overnight.

The Trethewey discoveries were the signal for crowds of other investors to come flocking into the area, which was now widely glorified as "the richest silver camp in the world" with "wonders which fairly beggar description". Many other outstanding mines were to be developed here during the next few years.

In view of the growing celebrity of this new mining district, Professor Miller decided that it deserved a place-name with more panache and descriptive flair than the rather banal "Long Lake". One of the typical signs of a silver vein was its coating of a beautiful pinkish bloom known as 'cobalt', and this was the imagery which gave Miller the inspiration of using the name of "Cobalt" for the town. It was Miller too who thought up the name of "Coniagas" for Will's other mine, concocting this word out of the chemical symbols: Co for cobalt, Ni for nickel, Ag for silver, and As for arsenic.[9]

William Griffith Trethewey was thirty-seven years of age at the time of his expedition to Cobalt. He was already a successful businessman of many years' standing, whose commercial instincts and talent for invention had displayed themselves early in life.

As a youth of seventeen, during his first summer in British Columbia, he had worked at a shingle mill in New Westminster, and he had worked hard and well. But although his father and uncle were both in the milling business, this was definitely not the sort of life that he envisaged for himself. All his native instincts were the instincts of a businessman and trader.

He fell in eagerly with his father's plans to put together the land for the townsite of Mission, and must have been left in a good financial position after the sale of the land to J.W. Horne. At the age of twenty-five he applied to become the first notary public in Mission. He set up as a land agent too, quickly acquiring a reputation as the "rustling real estate dealer" of Mission City.[10]

In 1892 he had married Charlotte Helen Mackenrot, known in the family as "Lottie". Her home was in Vancouver, where her father was a carpenter, but she probably met Will in Mission when visiting her sister, who was married to the bakery owner, James Plumridge. It was a successful marriage. Lottie was a girl of fastidious tastes, who would be more than equal to her eventual social position as the wife of a multi-millionaire—her grandchildren remember her as a very gracious lady with high standards of behaviour—while temperamentally she and the affable Will were well suited to each other.

Though his eye might have wandered to other ladies in the course of his life, Lottie remained for him the loved and respected centre of his life.[11] They were to have three children, Frank, Ruth and Bertram.

William made money easily right from the start. He did well in real estate and his notary business, and he also must have profited from his share in the Providence mine.

But besides his flair for business, he had other talents. Will was a natural inventor, with the aptitude for mechanics that ran in the Trethewey family. Like his grandfather Samuel with the hydraulic engine, and his father James, who had once invented a cooling machine for treating meal, Will was full of creative ideas, and he launched into the problematic process of developing his inventions.

The first device which he patented was the W.G.T. Labelling Machine. Designed for industrial use, this machine had the capability of labelling cans at great speed—120 cans per minute. It would retail for $350. Many fish canneries were being built along the Fraser River during the 1890s, and this was evidently where Will foresaw a market for his invention, for he tested out one of his prototypes at the Sea Island Cannery owned by his acquaintance Lemuel Munn.[12]

Locally his machine attracted a certain amount of publicity—the newspaper deemed it "an important invention"—and Will was optimistic. With two partners, Charles Gardiner Johnson and I.N. Bond, he formed the W.G.T. Labelling Machine Manufacturing Company Ltd., registered in 1895.[13] It seems likely that the machine did come into use in some of the Fraser River canneries, but whether he profited as he would have wished is questionable. In later years he hinted to one newspaper reporter that, like many other inventors, he had been the victim of exploitation.

No sooner had he developed the labelling machine to his satisfaction than he had another invention on the market. "Use the Trethewey and Munn lamp chimney holders," urged one advertisement, "which will save your lamp chimneys from breakages and yourself a lot of trouble and money." This little device was for sale at a modest price of 10 cents, and was available at the Chilliwack merchants', Ashwell and Sons, during 1896.[14]

But the invention which brought Will the most acclaim and

the most money was a mechanism so ingenious that it came to be adopted through the entire system of the Canadian Pacific Railway. It was a new type of air brake coupler, known as the 'patent automatic car pipes coupler'. The idea had come to Will as a result of his early years in Mission, where as a youth he had spent many fascinating hours watching the box-cars being shunted back and forth along the tracks. "He figured there must be a better way of making this coupling for these cars," says Alan Trethewey. "I understand that he designed a coupling that was flat. Instead of being upright and fitting together upright, he cut them out of wood and made this coupling that was flat."[15] Hopeful of having a winner here, Will took his invention to Montreal in 1901and introduced it to the head officials of the C.P.R.

They agreed to give the coupler a trial run, and Will rode the train on that suspenseful journey. To his intense relief, everything functioned perfectly. "It went through without a break or hitch of any kind," reported the *Chilliwack Progress,* "and the trainmen were most enthusiastic about it."[16] What chiefly appealed to the CPR was its enormous saving of steam and labour, and they accepted the device without delay. It was something to be proud of, for it was described at the time as "the most important invention in railroading since the introduction of the Westinghouse air brake." Will sold the rights to Westinghouse, and apparently made a very substantial amount of money from the deal.

By the time of the coupler invention Will had long since abandoned the little country town of Mission for the business world of Vancouver. He had moved to Vancouver in 1894 to promote the labelling machine, and had worked there ever since as a patent attorney with the firm of Rowland Brittain. With his latest success his life changed again, and he went to live in Montreal to oversee the development of the coupler. He never again returned to British Columbia except to visit.

By some accounts it was the coupler invention that gave Will his major stake in the Cobalt mines. Others suggest that it was actually his latest real estate dealings that made the mine development possible.

Will had certainly done very well out of his land speculations on the prairies. The Edmonton area had been attracting investors ever since the announcement that the Grand Trunk Pacific Railway was about to be constructed, and Will had decided to have a look and see what was to be had. He had invested in a property known as the Groat estate, and he had invested very shrewdly, because he was able to turn it over at a considerable profit only a year or two later.[17] He had, in fact, already put together a "moderate fortune", according to one account, before ever setting foot in the mining town of Cobalt.

Will had his mines in production by the end of his first season in Cobalt, making use of all the most up-to-date methods—typical Trethewey style. "I put in the first little steam plant that went into Cobalt, and there was a dynamo for electric light. We shipped the second car of ore that ever came out of the camp on October 1, 1904."[18]

Back in British Columbia, James senior must have been ecstatic to learn of Will's fabulous discovery. Incredibly, his lifelong dream had become a reality, and at last a Trethewey had found that "pot of gold". Although his pleasure might have been tinged with a slight shadow of regret that he himself had not enjoyed the euphoria of fulfilment, there is no doubt of the rejoicing that must have gone on within the whole Trethewey family.

Caught up in the general excitement, Will's younger brother Arthur rushed out to Cobalt too, in hopes of finding a claim of his own. Sadly, Arthur had no luck at all, and when he had to return prematurely to look after his business interests at Harrison Mills, his finances were in depressing contrast to his brother's new wealth. Will's kind heart would not let him see his brother go back disappointed. It is believed in the family that Will insisted on giving Arthur a very generous sum of money, which may have been in the region of $9,000.

Living in a daze of elation and excitement as the carloads of precious ore rolled forth to the smelter, Will nevertheless was an experienced enough businessman to keep his head and consider how best to capitalise intelligently on this once-in-a-lifetime opportunity. He had seen enough of mining ventures to realise that it was all too easy to see the profits sunk uselessly into dwindling veins and barren tunnels. It had always been Trethewey policy to cream off the obvious profit and sell while their project was still sound and viable, and this was what William did after only three seasons.

It must have been an agonising decision to part with his interest, when the mines all around Cobalt were still proliferating vast quantities of silver, but at that time no one quite dared to believe that the veins would go very deep. "Mr. Trethewey himself was frankly pessimistic, and sold out early," wrote a newspaper reporter four years after the event. "Without exception the operators of the early days were afraid of their own good fortune. Trethewey was averse to the establishment of a post office here, because he believed there would never be enough people to warrant the continuance of one."[19]

In any case, Will knew that he faced heavy expenditures in the near future. He would have to invest in a concentrator now that the surface ore had been stripped, and it was entirely unpredictable whether the Coniagas and Trethewey veins would continue to yield. Prudence got the upper hand, and he made the decision to sell.

In the fall of 1906 he sold his interest in both the mines for figures which were astronomical in their day. The Trethewey mine alone brought in the sum of $1 million, the buyers being Jack Bickell (a Toronto stockbroker and grain dealer), and Colonel Alexander Hay (an English investor.) As for the wonderful Coniagas, Will's holding in this netted him a figure well over the million mark, if rumour is to be believed—and this was merely for a half-interest. The buyer was his partner who had the other half-share, Colonel Leonard.[20] Besides the proceeds of the sale, Will had, of course, already taken out vast amounts of ore from his three years of surface mining, amounting by his own admission to as much as $600,000 worth of silver.[21]

The Trethewey family today suspect that, judging from Will's subsequent lifestyle, all these figures are conservative, to say the least, and that he may in actual fact have made as much as $10 million from his discoveries in Cobalt.

James Trethewey did not live quite long enough to witness the outcome of the sale of these mines. He died on May 24, 1906 (his wife outliving him by a bare two years), and was accorded the large and lavish funeral that befitted the father of a multi-millionaire. Will ordered the tallest and most conspicuous tombstone he could find for James's gravesite in the family plot at Mountain View cemetery in Vancouver, where it towers over the others around it—the family tribute to the memory of a remarkable pioneer.

END NOTES

1. *Globe,* Oct.3, 1908, p.3
2. Ibid.
3. Ibid.
4. Undated newspaper clipping, a Vancouver paper, circa 1910.
5. *Globe,* Oct.3, 1908, p.3.
6. Phillip Smith, *Harvest from the Rock,* an excerpt from a forthcoming book, printed in *The Northern Miner Magazine,* April 1986.
7. Information passed down in the family to Alan Trethewey.
8. *Cobalt Daily Nugget,* Mining Industry Edition, Sept. 1910, p. 15. Smith, Harvest from the Rock, p.33.
9. Smith, *Harvest from the Rock.*
10. *Daily Columbian,* Jan.18, 1892.
11. Joy Fairbarns (née Trethewey) and Dick Fairbarns.
12. *British Columbian,* Jan.2, 1895 & *Chilliwack Progress,* Feb.6, 1895.
13. Memorandum of Association, notarised Jan.30, 1895.
14. *Chilliwack Progress,* June 17, 1896.
15. Clarke and Alan Trethewey, taped conversation, 1989.
16. *Chilliwack Progress,* July 24, 1901.
17. Undated clipping, see above.
18. *Globe,* Oct.3, 1908, p.3.
19. *Cobalt Daily Nugget,* Sept. 1910, p.2.
20. Smith, *Harvest from the Rock.*
21. *Globe,* Oct.3, 1908, p.3.

10

After the Discovery

From Muskoka farm boy to Toronto millionaire—it was the traditional North American success story, and William went on to enjoy his riches in the time-honoured way, accumulating handsome mansions, fine estates, luxury cars and yachts, and all the usual gratifications that go with such a state of affluence. At the same time, he proved himself a very community-minded person, frequently using his money for the benefit of others. He and Lottie did not forget their families either. Arthur Plumridge, now ninety-five, whose mother was Lottie's sister, remembers one handsome gift received at their home in Mission. "Aunt Lottie in Toronto once sent my family a piano," he recalled.

Will was generous to his friends as well. The Trethewey family believe, for instance, that it was Will who offered one of the Hollingers the funding to finance the Hollinger gold mines, lending a sum of something like $100,000.00 just as a favour to a friend—no shares or strings attached. This mine became one of the largest gold producers in the world.[1]

He was now quite in demand for newspaper interviews, and all reports agreed that his basic personality remained unchanged by his rise to wealth and social position. He came across to his interviewers as a level-headed, straightforward and friendly type of person, with no trace of pomposity or pretentiousness. "There is no condescension about his welcome," wrote one reporter. "It is whole-hearted, and the way he grasps the visitor's hand is a sure indication that he cherishes a brotherly feeling for all men. The face is frank and open, the eyes shrewd. His hair is light and curly, brushed well up from the forehead. There is no 'side' about him, and the visitor feels perfectly at ease from the outset."[2] He had an air of relaxation about him. "He grows younger and adds avoirdupois every day," commented another, "like the man who has bidden farewell to care and worry."[3]

His attitude to his fortune might be summed up in his own words: "It was the Lord's money thrown right into my hands. I just found it, that's all."[4] This most revealing comment tells us a great deal about Will and his basic values. It was a surprising credo for a self-made millionaire still in the first flush of success, and it was certainly not what his interviewer had expected to hear—he found it "the most singular expression" in William's whole recital. In this unpretentious piece of philosophy we clearly hear the moralistic voice of his long line of Methodist forebears, preaching the message of Providence and the divine purpose, but we also seem to sense Will's own recognition of the responsibility of wealth.

Certainly Will had no reservations about enjoying his state of opulence to the full, and he now established a gracious family home, Glen Lince, in the fashionable Rosedale district of Toronto. He had a business office in the city and travelled to it in his large new automobile, which he enjoyed driving himself—unlike many rich men of his day, who employed chauffeur-mechanics. Apparently he drove with considerable verve, once attracting a $20 fine for speeding on Dundas at the reckless rate of 21 miles per hour.[5]

He and Lottie would give elegant dinner parties, with Lottie presiding regally at the head of the table, every bit the gracious lady, her dignity only disturbed by Will's habit of getting out his gold toothpick after the last course had been served. Will, who was rather a tease, would throw his large white table napkin over his head and employ the toothpick under cover so as not to offend her gaze.[6] Like the rest of the Tretheweys he loved a practical joke—"he had a wicked sense of humour," says one of the family—and so did his two sons, Frank and Bertram. Will once brought in a special variety of walnut to go with the port at one of their dinner parties; the boys thought it would be a very good joke to open up the nuts, extract the contents, and then seal the shells together again all ready to serve at dinner—their parents quite unsuspecting. The sight of the guests' faces when they cracked open their nuts was too much for Will. Poor Lottie was mortified, but Will could not help it—he went into paroxysms of laughter.

But although he enjoyed entertaining a limited circle of good friends and acquaintances, he had no ambition to enter the social swim of fashionable Toronto. "He is not a society man; his name rarely, if ever, appears in the social column," commented one reporter. He preferred to occupy his time more productively on personal projects which he believed would ultimately be of benefit to the community in general.

When he bought property at Weston on the northern outskirts of Toronto (400 acres before World War 1, and 200 more after the war), he did so not only for the pleasure of owning a private estate, but with a view to setting up a model farm and improving current agricultural practices. The keyword was to be efficiency. He believed in a very heavy use of fertiliser, and invested a great deal of money in the early years in enriching the soil. He also believed in the use of machinery as far as possible, and now—free from any financial limitations—he thoroughly enjoyed himself in producing all sorts of mechanical contrivances in his own workshops. His family remember one such invention which he called the "Canadian Corn Cover". Intended to protect the corn from rain and frost, it was no doubt an ingenious idea, but it failed to catch on in the general market.

Each section of the operation was intended to be complementary to another, so as to eliminate all unnecessary wastage. To deal with surplus crops, for instance, he built a cannery which processed peas, beans, tomatoes and fruit on the premises. This turned out an end-product of such superior quality that it was all pre-sold and never required a marketing agency.[7]

Will was now known as the "millionaire farmer" and his experimental farm attracted a great deal of attention at the time. "There is not another farm on the American continent quite like the Trethewey farm," it was claimed at the time.[8] Whether it ever proved its point by becoming economically viable is another matter: in the pre-war years he was grossing a healthy revenue of about $60,000 a year from the whole enterprise, but still not recouped his initial investment, nor did he expect to for some time, he said. With the war and other circumstances intervening, it is doubtful that he ever did.

Will had a piggery at the farm. Unfortunately, one batch of pigs became infected with cholera and was ordered to be disposed of. Will accepted the inevitable, but he thought of a novel way of going about it. Having been brought up in pioneer country, he was a keen hunter and outdoorsman, so he decided to make the pig-kill into a shooting event. He had a long wide burial trench dug at the foot of a ravine, and he and his sportsman friends stationed themselves with their guns a little distance from the trench. Then the pigs were taken to the top of the cliff and herded over the edge. Will and his party, waiting below, shot at them as they fell into the trench. It was a Trethewey version of the traditional buffalo kill.

The field above this ravine is famous in the history of Canadian aviation, because it was the scene of one of the two earliest air meets ever to be held in Canada. The year 1910 was memorable in aviation for these two thrilling air displays. The first one happened in Montreal, the other took place on Will Trethewey's estate at Weston. The first plane ever to be seen in the skies over Toronto took off from Will's field, which he had been delighted to offer for this historic occasion.

It was a three-day meet featuring five airplanes—two Wright biplanes and three Blériot monoplanes—and one of the pilots was the famous Count de Lesseps. There were plenty of thrills to excite the crowd. Everyone broke into applause when de Lesseps reached a height of 1000 feet, but he then went on to astonish the onlookers still further by reaching a height of 2000 feet as he soared into the skies above Toronto! Wild cheers greeted him upon his return, and the crowd carried him on their shoulders to the grandstand. Here Will presented him with a gift of $500 in honour of his 28-minute flight. Later, another pilot surpassed this achievement with a height of 3000 feet, thereby setting an altitude record for the whole meet.

Gusty winds for the first two days made some of the stunts even riskier. At times the steep nose-dives only missed a crash by a matter of moments. One plane actually did crash. It had become warped by rain during transit, and on the first day failed to get off the ground at all. On the second day it had just reached a height of 600 feet when a control wire snapped, and the pilot ended up in the branches of a pine tree. His plane was wrecked, but he fortunately escaped without injury. Another of the highlights was a simulated bombing attack on an earthwork fort in front of the grandstand. An aircraft flew over the field, dropping sandbags on the fort, while dynamite charges planted in the ground were exploded with realistic effect by the personnel of the 2nd Field Company, Canadian Engineers—an early anticipation of modern warfare.[9]

After this event, the field was always referred to as the de Lesseps Field.

Curiously, after all the thought and effort that had gone into the planning of his model farm, William apparently lost interest in it after only six years. He retained title to the land, and presumably appointed a manager to the farm, but he himself was far away—he had gone to live in England.

It is hard to account for this mysterious move to a country he really did not know, for he himself had not been born there, and it was not even a part of England where his family had ever lived. His descendants are under the impression that Lottie may have been quite influential in the decision, having fallen in love with the English countryside when she and Will had travelled there on a holiday.

As well, one suspects that although Will and Lottie were not attracted to society life as such, their social position had inevitably changed as a result of their new wealth, and they must have been considering a much greater range of possibilities in their life-style. It was in 1911 that William began to fancy the idea of a pedigree and a coat-of-arms, and contacted the College of Arms in London, who produced both the coat-of-arms and the extensive genealogical information which has only recently been improved on.[10]

This new interest in status and ancestry was surely indicative of the way his thoughts were turning, as he mingled with a class of Torontonians many of whom came from an Old Country back-

Samuel was employed by the Roche Rock mining company, which took its name from this unusual crag on the edge of the village of Roche. On top are the ruins of the ancient chapel. *D. Sleigh*

The village of St. Dennis, where Samuel grew up.

The old mine office and spoil heap of the Watergrove mine outside Foolow, where Samuel was an engineer for 10 years. *John Swan*

A typical engine house at one of the old Cornish mines just north of Roche. *D. Sleigh*

The Muskoka homestead of James and Mary Ann, as it looked in 1991.

D. Sleigh

The lower end of Trethewey Falls, seen from the power station, 1991.

D. Sleigh

Holmsted Place, Will's English residence, as it looked in 1992.   *D. Sleigh*

Ornate frieze in the bathroom of Holm-sted Place.
D. Sleigh

Stained glass window in the entrance hall, Holm-sted Place.   *D. Sleigh*

ground of large estates and historic mansions. The thought of a baronial hall began to strike William as a very desirable thing for a gentleman to have, and with his new-found wealth it was a dream he could easily gratify if he so wished.

The English manor house where Will and Lottie took up residence at the end of 1913 had all the attributes which they could have desired. With its creeper-clad walls, its high gables and its tall Elizabethan chimneys, it was picturesque enough to satisfy the most romantic imagination, and its interior appointments were no less impressive. Coffered ceilings, elaborate fireplaces, and acres of hand-carved panelling were standard throughout the reception rooms, except for one whose walls glowed sumptuously with richly-coloured leather. As for the main bathroom, it was a true masterpiece of luxury with its marble walls, tessellated floor, and silver-plated fittings. It was all a far cry from the simple log home of his boyhood back in Muskoka Falls.[11]

Each of the eleven bedrooms had its own style of decor: there was a Sheraton bedroom, an Adam bedroom, Hepplewhite, Chippendale, Queen Anne, William and Mary, and so on, demonstrating a fine Victorian eclecticism in this melange of periods. The antique furniture and the suits of armour apparently came with the house, which was bought "handsomely furnished".[12]

Holmsted Place, as it was called, stood among the woods and fields just west of Cuckfield in Sussex. It was an old estate, founded from the wealth of the 16th century ironworks, but the house itself was a 19th century replacement of the original home. It was a Victorian interpretation of the Tudor style, featuring the characteristic half-timbering on the gables, the tile-hung upper storey and the tall brick chimneys. At the same time it drew freely upon any other elements which would create a romantically pleasing effect.

Across from the mansion were the long brick stables with a clock-tower surmounted by a metal weather-vane. This weather-vane seemed to Frank and Bertram to offer an irresistible target for their .22 rifle. From the upstairs bathroom window the vane was within easy range, so they spent a happy afternoon taking pot-shots at it—aiming all too successfully at their target. On this occasion

Will was not amused, and the boys were belted for the damage they had caused. The holes in the weather-vane could still be seen when it was inspected in the 1970s.

One of the chief attractions of the property to William was the fact that its 317 acres included a good home farm which, by the time he sold the place, was comparable in scope to the one he had in Weston. He raised wheat and other crops, and he also ran a flour and feed mill and a bacon-curing factory—operations which he may possibly have initiated himself, since they came within his area of expertise. He certainly attempted to improve the farm in every possible way, putting down "several thousand tons of fertilisers", just as he had at Weston. He appears to have added another 200 acres to the property, comparing the 1914 figures to the 1923 statement of assets.

Another feature of the place was the state-of-the-art workshop which William built, with the metal-working tools on one side and the woodworking tools on the other. In this congenial retreat he spent many happy hours with his inventions. His particular dream was to finalise the construction of a new type of steam tractor, but according to his son Bertram, this was one ambition which he never quite brought off.

Only a few months after Will and Lottie moved to England, World War I broke out. In some ways the lifestyle which they had anticipated would have remained unchanged, for they were in an unthreatened rural area, where traditional rural pursuits went on in the usual way. Will would have had his hunting and shooting—"the property forms a complete little sporting estate", says the Harrods catalogue— and his projects on the farm would have taken on an even greater importance than he had originally imagined.

But besides his agricultural contribution to the war effort, he felt that he should do as many other owners of large houses were doing at that time, and offer hospitality to soldiers returning from the front. Extra beds were installed in the elegant period-piece bedrooms, and Will and Lottie kept open house for Canadian soldiers who would otherwise have had nowhere in England to spend a comfortable leave. They were treated like honoured guests, had their shoes shined and were looked after in every possible way. In these luxurious and peaceful surroundings many Canadian soldiers were able to enjoy a few days of complete relaxation and a brief respite from the stress of battle fatigue.

Since war had broken out so soon after their move to England, for the first four years of their stay Will and Lottie never had a chance to enjoy the privacy of their estate or to experience the full pleasure of English country living, but after 1918 they began to resume a fuller lifestyle. They went cruising again on their private yacht. This had been sent over from Canada early in 1914, when they went on a two-month winter cruise of the Mediterranean—their last pleasure trip before the war.

In his time Will owned two beautiful yachts. One of these was a graceful ocean-going vessel called the *Vergemere,* which had a length of 120 feet and required a crew of twenty. The *Vergemere* seems to have come into his possession before the war, but he only acquired the *Semiramis* in 1924. This was a somewhat smaller boat, a diesel-powered motor sailer with a length of 94.3 feet, and was used on the Great Lakes or along the east coast. (After Will's death the *Semiramis* is said to have met a rather ignoble fate when it was sold to a wealthy buyer in New York, who reputedly turned it into a freighter for rum-running during the Prohibition period.)

Heavy taxation after the war began to make the Holmsted estate an expensive luxury to maintain. Finally Will decided that this phase of his life was over and he would return to Canada to his native roots. He put Holmsted Place up for sale early in 1923, entrusting the transaction to the most superior firm he could think of—the famous Harrods of Knightsbridge, who conducted the auction on February 27 of that year. Son Frank and daughter Ruth went back with their parents, but the second son Bertram remained in England for the rest of his life.

Will spent his remaining years, which were to be few, at his Toronto home, still organising the Weston farm and planning improvements. In 1925 he sub-divided a portion of the land and constructed "a magnificent roadway" through it at a cost of $60,000, dedicating it to the townships of York and North York and naming it Holmsted Drive. Good roads had always been one of his major concerns.[13]

He had just begun to build himself a new large mansion on the Weston property when he fell ill, the victim of a deadly form of the disease known as sleeping sickness, which he contracted on one of his travels. To try to regain his health he and his family left on the *Semiramis* in December for a cruise to the South. On the way his condition worsened, and by the time they reached Sarasota he was so ill that he was finally obliged to go ashore and enter hospital. He died there in Florida on March 6, 1926, not quite sixty years of age, a man still in his productive years with many plans unfinished.

Lottie survived William for about ten years, living for at least part of that time in the new house at Weston with Frank and his wife. This house and a portion of the estate were bought by Martha Eaton of the well-known Eaton family some time after 1937, though the Eatons no longer own it today.[14] The Trethewey name is still remembered in the road that runs through the district, Trethewey Drive (the former Holmsted Drive), and also in a 5-acre municipal park, donated by Frank Trethewey in the year of his father's death, and named Trethewey Park in memory of the family.

END NOTES

1. This story was told to Alan Trethewey by his father, J. Edgar Trethewey.
2. Undated clipping from a Toronto newspaper, c.1910.
3. Undated clipping from a Vancouver newspaper, c.1910.
4. Ibid.
5. Phillip Smith, *Harvest from the Rock*, excerpt printed in *The Northern Miner Magazine*, April 1986.
6. The anecdotes concerning Will are from Beth Norgrove (his grand-daughter), Joy Fairbarns (another grand-daughter) and Dick Fairbarns.
7. Undated clipping from a Toronto newspaper, c.1910.
8. Ibid.
9. *The Barn Stormers*, photocopy of pp.72 & 73, no author, no date. From Trethewey family files.
10. As a Christmas greeting to his relatives in 1911, Will sent out a little booklet

containing a family tree and some notes on family history. It was bound in crimson leather and on the cover was the Trethewey coat-of-arms—three leaping goats in crimson on a green background. The information (which contains a few small errors) was derived from oral history, family Bibles, and research work done in England by his cousin, Reginald Trethewey. Will wrote to him in October 1911: "Dear Reg, Herewith I send you a copy of Cousin Wm's letter with his family history and some extracts from *Magna Britannia,*which are interesting.Now, if you can put this tree in form for the printer, I would be glad to rush it on and have it ready for Christmas."

The following year, Will also received a very extensive pedigree of his earlier ancestors, authored by Everard Green, Somerset Herald, F.S.A., College of Heralds, March 1912, and based on Colonel Vivian's 1887 history of Cornwall.

11. The descriptions of Holmsted Place are based on a visit by the author and on the Harrods' auction catalogue, *Holmsted Place, Cuckfield,* Feb.27, 1923.

12. *Province,* Jan.7, 1914.

13. J. C. Boylen, *York Township, an Historical Summary, 1850-1954,* The Municipal Corporation of the Township of York & the Board of Education of the Township of York, 1954, p.57

14. Information from the Trethewey family.

11

Arthur and the Abbotsford Mill

After Will's amazing stroke of luck at Cobalt, things were never quite the same again for the Trethewey family. Directly or indirectly, every one of Will's brothers benefited from his discovery. Joe's 1/8-share in the Coniagas enabled him to finance the Trethewey mill at Abbotsford, which Arthur so badly wanted to acquire. This in turn provided executive positions for Sam and Jim at certain points in their careers, and was later to furnish a variety of jobs for the young men and women in the next generation.

But besides these tangible consequences of the Cobalt discovery, there was the effect it had on the thinking of the Trethewey family. The impact must have been enormous. Incredibly, the vision of eldorado which had fascinated the Tretheweys for the past three decades had actually come true for one of their own. It was no longer just a wild fantasy—some flickering mirage—to believe that a mining speculation could bring riches on such an extravagant scale. The Trethewey fixation on mining had been justified. Will's success was to have a profound effect on the whole family and would colour their outlook on life for at least two generations to come.

Undoubtedly all four of his ambitious and hardworking brothers had qualities of drive and personality which would have made them leaders in their community, whatever the circumstances of their lives. But with the added backing of Joe's money to finance the Abbotsford mill they were given the opportunity of maximising their talents and taking a leading part in the development of the Fraser Valley. At the time of the silver discovery in 1904 Arthur's work was still centred at Harrison River in the logging and towing business. Then came the sensational news of Will's two mines. Arthur was by no means immune to the family obsession with mining, and the urge to go out to Cobalt and look for a claim of his own became too strong to resist. He followed Will and Joe out east, and spent several months in 1904 and 1905 with them at Cobalt.[1]

However, it was not very long before problems arose at home. Arthur was urgently summoned back to Harrison River to protect his interests in the sale of the Harrison River Mills Timber and Trading Company. His stay in Cobalt had lasted less than a year. He had had no luck with any of his claims, and it is doubtful that he ever went back before Will sold the mines in 1906. Just the same, family members are under the impression that Arthur came out of the affair with a substantial sum of money, as Will would not allow him go away empty-handed. Figures are apt to become inaccurate over the years, but the sum in question may have been in the neighbourhood of $9,000.

How was Arthur to invest this windfall? For a while he settled back into the more humdrum occupation of logging, but other ideas were stirring in his mind: he had not yet finished with mining! He had come away from Cobalt awed by the wealth he had seen in that silvery underground world. The old Trethewey fascination once more exerted its lure. Undeterred by his previous lack of success, he turned his back on the steady but unexciting business which he knew best—the lumber industry—and made another plunge into the speculative world of mining.

All of his brothers—even the prudent Jim—occupied themselves with mining ventures from time to time in their lives, so perhaps it was not surprising that Arthur too was a prospector at heart. The vision of the huge slabs of silver ore coming out of Coniagas by the carload was still very fresh in his memory, and the glamour of all that was happening at Cobalt was enough to make an optimist out of anybody. In a move that reveals the more adventurous side of his character, Arthur rashly put his money into new mineral claims—not precious metals this time, but more utilitarian minerals such as iron, copper and coal.

Arthur went into this venture with Jim, his old working partner from their sawmilling days. They located some promising claims on Texada Island up the coast of British Columbia, and they developed these up to the stage where they needed more capital to continue. Hoping to find something that would pay off quickly, the brothers hit on the idea of going up to the Queen Charlotte Islands, which were known to be so rich in copper that any claims were likely to be extremely productive.

Up to a point this theory was correct: there was indeed plenty of copper, but, according to Arthur's son Clarke, this very abundance proved to be the difficulty. "It was so rich they couldn't mine the damn stuff," Clarke maintained. "They just couldn't get it out. Pretty near solid copper." (Later generations of the family have thought this a curious statement, and one which they find hard to believe.) In any case, on these blustery islands there were other problems too: "The wind blew so damn hard, it would blow an ore car down the track and off into the chuck. So they had to tie the bunkhouses down with cables." According to Clarke, the Texada mines had to wait another sixty years before they proved economically viable.[2]

Although these were the only two places where Arthur managed the operation himself, he did also interest himself in one other set of claims at this time. Vaguely described as being in the Rocky Mountain trench, they were in an area believed to be rich in coal. Arthur provided the funding for this exploration, which cannot have been wildly successful or more would be known about it in the family.

After these experiences Arthur apparently relegated the business of mining investment to the sidelines, though he still dabbled in it from time to time. (In 1910, for instance, he applied for a licence to prospect for coal and petroleum in the district of Matsqui.[3] His wife Susie was still buying mines even after Arthur's death.) However, he now turned to a more reliable form of making money and one in which he had proven expertise—the sawmill business. He had heard of a very interesting proposition, and if Joe would only back it, he thought it had immense possibilities.

In the little village of Abbotsford, beside Abbotsford Lake (as it was then called), was a fair-sized sawmill belonging to the Abbotsford Lumber Company. (This should not be confused with the Tretheweys' much later use of the same company name.) The owners, Alexander Johnston and James Cook, had started up in the 1890s with a smaller mill which stood by the tracks on Railway Street. In 1903 they had incorporated, and in 1907 they had moved to the site at Abbotsford Lake and built this bigger mill, capable of 50,000 board feet a day. They had even installed 2½ miles of logging railway to reach their timber limits south of Abbotsford.[4]

It was this nice-looking set-up which caught the eye of Arthur Trethewey in 1909, after his decision to return to the sawmilling business. It was an ideal site because it had access to several railway lines (south to the United States and east to the prairie markets), but it was a costly proposition, and it meant an investment of an impressive $375,000. The only way in which Arthur could hope to raise this sort of money was to try and interest his brother Joe, who was now a man of considerable wealth from his share of the Coniagas. Joe *was* interested. As far as the plant was concerned, it was obviously a sound investment, and he had sufficient faith in his younger brother to give him the major backing he needed—in fact, putting up the bulk of the required capital. "Joe was always willing to help someone," says Clarke Trethewey.

Arthur himself put up a large amount of capital, and the rest came from three other men who were minor shareholders—Frank Boyd and John McEwen, who had been associated with Arthur at the Harrison mill, and G.D. Brymner, a banker in New Westminster. They incorporated on April 22, 1909, and took over the Abbotsford Lumber Company. Since they wanted more scope in their operations than the original company had aimed at, they did not use the same name, but called their new company the Abbotsford Timber and Trading Company Ltd.[5]

Arthur and Susan moved to Abbotsford the following year, and settled into their permanent home, a large house on the Yale Road on the hill just west of McCallum. "It had two rooms which were made into one large room and this room was used for all the parties, and the whole town attended," remembered Clarke. "One did not have to send out invitations; it was just understood that there would be a party and everyone came, it being Easter, Thanksgiving and other holidays."[6]

Because of their role as the biggest employers in the district, it was expected of the family that they would take a leading part in community life, and Arthur and Susan wholeheartedly lived up to this obligation, as did their older children. Arthur was a school trustee, for instance, but he was also a lacrosse enthusiast and cheerfully acted as referee for many of the games in the Fraser Valley League.

Susan took on the usual role expected of females in that era. She was active in church affairs, sometimes cooking two 5-gallon crocks of pork and beans for the Presbyterian church socials, but as time went by her life in Abbotsford expanded to much more than this. With her competence and her strong personality—perhaps rather like her mother-in-law, Mary Ann, in this respect—Susan came to be regarded in the community as someone to turn to for advice or for help in times of sickness, a tower of strength in any emergency. Her own family was to need this strength later when her husband's health began to fail.

Already, the year after he took over the mill, there were signs that Arthur was not as strong as the rest of the family. Perhaps he had been driving himself too hard in getting the company organised and the mill operating smoothly, but the outcome was that he had what was described as a nervous breakdown, but which was probably the beginning of a physical disease that involved a degeneration of the nervous system. He appears to have recovered from this, or more likely his symptoms went into remission; at any rate, he was able to resume the reins and manage the business efficiently himself for the next few years. Although Joe was the majority shareholder, it was indisputably Arthur's mill in the sense that he was the manager and decision-maker and chief authority on the spot, while Joe would only look in at the mill a couple of times a year.

Arthur was an excellent administrator with a good understanding of the employee's point of view. His whole attitude to the question of labour relations had been coloured by an incident which took place during his first year in British Columbia when he was a boy of fifteen and he and Will were packing shingles at a mill on Burrard Inlet. That season at the shingle mill back in 1883 was an episode never forgotten by either of the brothers, for it turned out to be a disillusioning lesson in human nature. Arthur and Will had been quick to learn the technique of bundling shingles and soon had quite a reputation for their speed as shingle weavers. They had quickly increased their earnings from 80 cents a day to 4 dollars a day, so they were looking forward to a fair-sized sum of money at the end of their nine months' stint, which ended on December 24. But when they went to collect their pay, the owner coolly told them that they were too young to have such a sum of money in their possession and refused to pay them a single cent. Arthur's son, Clarke, describes what happened:

"They walked to New Westminster and arrived there Christmas Eve. Someone took them in a boat across the river and they found an empty shack and spent the night in it. It had been taken over by skunks, and when it was dark the skunks were out in full force to reclaim what they considered to be their stamping-ground. Both boys had a .22 rifle and shells for it, so they spent the night lying on their stomachs shooting at the eyes of the skunks who prowled about the shack. It was a Christmas Eve to remember.

"As soon as it was daylight they started to walk to Mission on the south bank of the river. Late on Christmas Day they reached the spot on the south side of the river across from Mission. Someone rowed them across the river and they were home Christmas night, cold, hungry, tired and broke, after nine months of very hard work."

This episode left Arthur with the determination always to treat his own workers fairly when the time came, and he did not fail to live up to the high standard he had set for himself. He had the knack of bringing out the best in his employees, though he was tough when he had to be. His son spoke of him with respect: "He was a man among men and his employees stayed with him for years. He was well liked by the workmen, as he was most honest and fair with them. He was also a great judge of character and surrounded himself with honest and capable men."

One incident made a lasting impression on Clarke: "When I was young, I was with him a great deal around the mill and I noticed he would always talk to everybody, even the section man, and I said to him one day, 'Father, why do you always talk to all these people?' He said, 'My boy, every one of these people, no matter how lowly they are, has an idea, and if I don't talk to them, I'll never know what that idea is.'"

Compared to the colourful Joe and the erratic Sam, Arthur was considered a sober sort of character, but the general impression was that his naturally genial personality had been heavily overlaid with the views and beliefs of his strong-minded wife. "Susan was pro-Temperance, so Arthur did not drink," says one acquaintance. There was never any liquor in the house except for a small bottle of brandy in case of sickness. Susan was a devout Presbyterian, so Arthur was too.

As a young man he had been of a more carefree nature. "I'm sure my father was a gay blade,[7] the same as the rest of the folks," theorised Clarke, "because Emma has a letter that he wrote my mother, and my mother was a very religious woman, and he thanked her for bringing him to Christianity. That kind of straightened him out. He worshipped the ground my mother walked on."

Arthur had met Susan in 1890 when he was still an assistant at his mother's store in Mission and she was a young teacher at the newly-opened Hatzic school west of Mission, where she was teaching eight grades in one room.[8] A year later, on June 6, 1891, they had married—Susan then twenty years of age and Arthur twenty-three. Their surviving children were Annetta, Frances, Leslie, Clarice, Charles, Robert, and Clarke. Susan was perhaps over-strict with her children, but her high standards made a deep impression on each of them, and they felt that any success that came to them in later life was due to her early influence.

While Susan was the tough disciplinarian of the family, Arthur's sense of humour sometimes softened his approach to juvenile pranks —the Trethewey men never could resist a bit of fun. Clarke remembered one occasion when he had been misbehaving himself by putting sand on the railway line so that the speeder would jump the tracks. It was very amusing, he thought, to hide there and watch the speeder suddenly shoot up the bank and the two occupants come flying out from the impact! Of course, eventually he was found out and he overheard his parents discussing his fate. Arthur said: "Oh, Susie, let the kid have his fun; he's only a boy, don't give him a licking all the time." Clarke happily thought: "Oh gosh, I'm just as free as a bee. I'm going to go back with this one," but he had overlooked his mother's uncompromising nature. As soon as his father had gone to the office next morning, Clarke had the usual punishment administered. "I didn't get by with it." Nobody did with Susan.

Trethewey projects were never static for very long. Arthur's first priority, once he was owner of the mill, was to put in an electrical plant, just as he had done at his Harrison River mill. He probably installed this in 1910, the year after the Tretheweys took over. Gradually he made other improvements—a steam drag-saw which cut logs to any length required, and a new fast-feed planer which produced faster work with a finer finish. The capacity of the mill increased to 75,000 board feet a day: it was even known to reach 90,000 when need arose. He pushed the logging railroad farther and farther into the dense woods which then covered the Clearbrook and Huntingdon areas, until he had 7 miles of track in use. (Part of this trackage, which was standard-gauge, would be moved from time to time when a new district was to be logged.) Arthur had never owned the Harrison River mill long enough to put in a shingle mill, but he now did so at Abbotsford, around the year 1914. A 3-machine mill, it worked by steam power and could turn out 100,000 shingles per day.[9]

The Abbotsford mill was a success right from the start. Good management was basically the secret of the Tretheweys' success, and they soon built up a reputation for prompt and efficient delivery. As well as this, they had shown good judgment in investing in a mill which had an exceptionally good location, being close to no fewer than three different railway lines. Spur lines to each of these gave them access to the C.P.R., the Great Northern and the B.C. Electric., and made it possible for the company to ship to a wide variety of mar-

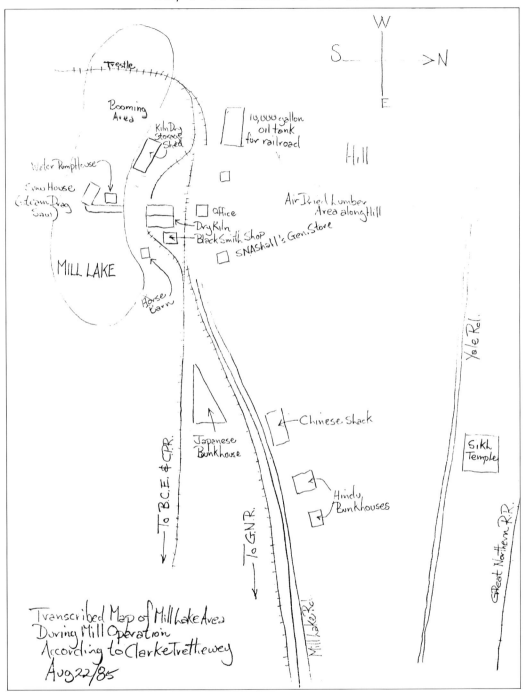

Sketch plan of the A.L.M.D.CO. *grounds, 1920s. Drawn by Clarke Trethewey. He has omitted the shingle mill (bottom right of lake) and sawmill (adjacent to kilns).*
(Matsqui-Sumas-Abbotsford Museum)

kets. They had the advantage over many other mills in this respect.

The mill stood beside a small lake which was then known as Abbotsford Lake or Matsqui Lake, but later took on the name of Mill Lake, by which we know it today. This side of the lake is now a pleasant residential neighbourhood with a spacious park donated by the Trethewey family, but when the mill was running, the whole area was one big industrial site. It had dry kilns and a horse barn, blacksmith shop and general store near the lake itself, with an area for air-dried lumber along the hillside below today's Fraser Highway. Over to the east, along today's Mill Lake Road, stood the bunkhouses of the Japanese and Chinese mill-workers. At the west end of the lake (south of the present Sevenoaks shopping centre) was the spot where the logging railway crossed the lake over a trestle and had its log dump.[10]

Each day the company's Climax locomotive trundled its burden of logs down to the booming-ground at the lake. Fir and cedar were the woods most in demand in this era (hemlock came into its own later.) In the days before World War I the greater part of the production—60% of it—was turned into railroad timber, and the company developed a reputation for this. However, they handled a great variety of other work too.

Hard as it is to visualise today in the modern city of Abbotsford, one of their early orders in 1910 was to supply lumber for the wooden sidewalks on Essendene Street. Another early contract was for lumber to build the factory of the Kilgard Clay Company. Their most outstanding contract in later years was in connection with the construction of the Welland Canal in Ontario: timbers of exceptional length were needed, and it was the Trethewey mill which was called upon to supply this major contract.

The Tretheweys had a good reputation as employers, and their employees stayed with them a long time. Hank Pennier, who worked for the company in 1930, writes: "Some of the men had worked there for 35 years. Hell if you worked there only 20 years you were just a new man."[11] They looked after the families of their employees too. In 1916 there was an accident in the woods when a young man of eighteen, Ray Combs, was killed as the result of a guy line snapping and striking him on the back of the head. "There was no such thing as the Compensation Board at that time," remembered his sister. "The Lumber Company took full responsibility for the accident." Arthur immediately arranged for compensation, which in this case took the form of deeding to the family the 10-acre parcel which they were in the process of buying from the lumber company. The father and two sons-in-law continued to work for the Tretheweys for several years.[12] Later the company was one of the first in the province to bring in Workers' Compensation for its employees.

By 1912 the Tretheweys were already employing as many as 90 men, and this number steadily increased, until by 1919 their workforce had swollen to a figure of 260. A large proportion of these men were loggers, but unlike most loggers of that era they usually lived at home, not in a logging camp, and commuted to the logging areas each day from Abbotsford and district.

The mill attracted a large number of Sikhs to Abbotsford to work at the millsite, and there is still a large community of Sikhs living in the district to the present day. Their original wooden temple was built in 1910 on a site near the mill (on the north side of the present South Fraser Way), which the Trethewey family believes may have been donated by Arthur and Joe. They probably gave the lumber for the temple also. There is no documentation for this, but the story goes that at quitting time each day the Sikh millworkers were allowed to take some lumber away with them to use on the project.[13]

The early growth of the town of Abbotsford was undoubtedly due to the Trethewey mill. For over two decades the Abbotsford Timber and Trading Company was by far the largest employer in the whole district, so much so that almost every job in the village of Abbotsford was either directly or indirectly dependent on the mill and its prosperity. Until the early 1930s Abbotsford was very definitely a mill town. To the oldtimers of Abbotsford the memory of the village in those days is perhaps more vivid than the reality of the modern town today. "In my mind's eye," says Margaret Weir, "I still visualise Abbotsford with the locomotives rattling into town with logs for the mill, and the whistles tooting. Nobody minded the noise or smoke because it meant prosperity for the town."

Edgar in the workshop of his Maple Ridge home.

Trethewey family archives

One of Edgar's rock pictures on display at Trethewey House, Abbotsford.

Trethewey family archives

Fleet of logging trucks, Port Douglas, 1958-9. Trethewey Logging Co.
Trethewey family archives

The log catchment area, Port Douglas. Trethewey Logging Co.
Trethewey family archives

The log jam that blocked the Fraser River. Trethewey-Wells Timber, c.1964.
Trethewey family archives

Close-up view of the log jam.   *Trethewey family archives*

Powerline installation by Catre Hi-Line, near Hope, 1980
Trethewey family archives

The Kananaskis Highway project, near Banff, 1974.
Trethewey family archives

But all these years of hard work and successful planning had taken their toll, for Arthur's health had been steadily declining ever since his breakdown in 1910. Round about 1912 he began to suspect that he was suffering from a chronic disease, though at first he could not believe that it could be anything serious. Slowly the weakness in his limbs began to take hold. The doctors found it hard to diagnose and were still describing it as severe rheumatism the year before he died, but in the view of the family today what he was actually suffering from was multiple sclerosis.

In spite of his physical weakness, Arthur's mental energy remained unimpaired and for several years he was perfectly well able to continue running the mill, although he could not get around the site in the way that he had been accustomed to. However, his growing periods of disability began to perturb his partners Boyd, McEwen and Brymner, who seem to have felt that Arthur might soon be incapable of handling the responsibility of management. In 1917 a crisis arose. The three men decided they would make an attempt to take over the company without the consent of Arthur and Joe. Indignant at what they considered an act of disloyalty after an association of so many years, Arthur's family quickly rallied to prevent the company from being seized.

If the three partners had counted on a walk-over, with only a sick man to oppose them, they were seriously under-estimating the opposition, for they had the indomitable Susan Marilla Trethewey to contend with. Arthur gave Susie a blanket power of attorney to bring a lawsuit against the three, and had full confidence in her ability to represent him in the case. He knew what he was about, for Susie handled the entire proceedings with her usual steely determination, and her attorney went on to a decisive win. Arthur decided not to take matters any further, as he and the others were all Masons together, but he and Joe immediately took steps to buy out the interests of the three, a procedure which dragged on into the middle of 1918.[14]

Sadly, it was now clear to Arthur that in his weakening state of health he could no longer hope to keep up the management of the mill, for physically he had become almost completely incapacitated.

Had his oldest son Leslie been at home, he, though only twenty-two, might have been able to deputise for his father, but it was the last year of the war and Leslie was away in France with the Canadian army and could not get released. Arthur's only option was to sell his interest to his brother Joe, who was still the principal shareholder and president of the company.

When Joe was forced to take personal control, he at once regarded it as an opportunity to use the company as a vehicle for pursuing his cherished mining interests, which still occupied an important place in his mind. Although he had been pre-occupied with the Chilco Ranch for the last few years, he had never abandoned his taste for mining development, and now he was extremely anxious to make the most of company resources to pursue this form of investment. Under his authority the company was completely re-organised and given a new name—the Abbotsford Lumber, Mining and Development Company Ltd. (incorporated on December 31, 1918.) This was done expressly with a view to branching out into mining activities and other investments, and during the 1920s the company's mining division did proceed to invest in several claims in the northern parts of the province, as Chapter 12 describes.

Arthur's health went steadily downhill in the months that followed, and it became increasingly obvious to those around him that he was entering the last stage of his illness. He died in the early hours of October 10, 1919, having lived only to the age of fifty-one. With his kindly and honourable personality, Arthur was much mourned by his family and friends and all the men who had worked for him.

Arthur's death had been expected, but no one could have foreseen that within two years Susan too would have passed away, and at the same early age of fifty-one. Susan had gone to live in Vancouver, where some of her children were attending school, but in November 1921 she had gone down to Butte, Montana, to buy some mines, for her taste for business was just as keen as ever, even after Arthur's death. She was back in Vancouver for Christmas Day, and the family was gathered round the dinner table enjoying the festivities, when she suddenly collapsed. It was a massive heart attack, and it was a fatal one. For Clarke Trethewey, then aged fifteen, the trauma of his mother's death was a memory that remained with him for the rest of his life, and in old age he was to make the poignant remark: "To me her passing was the greatest loss and shock I have ever experienced."

END NOTES

1. *Chilliwack Progress*, Feb.22, 1905.
2. Clarke and Alan Trethewey, taped conversation, 1989.
3. *Abbotsford Post*, Oct.7, 1910.
4. *B.C. Gazette*, Vol.1, 1903, p.200.
   Canadian Lumberman and Woodworker, April 1907.
5. *Western Lumberman*, May 1909, p.13.
   B.C. Gazette, 1909, p.1793.
6. Clarke Trethewey conversation.
7. As the context implies, Clarke is using the word "gay" in its original sense of "light-hearted".
8. *B.C. Sessional Papers*, 1891, Education Report. Susan obtained her Third Class, Grade B, Certificate in July 1890
   B.C. Sessional Papers, 1892, Education report. She taught at the Hatzic School for 10 months until June 1891.
9. *Abbotsford Post*, July 19, 1912.
10. Sketch plan by Clarke Trethewey, Matsqui-Sumas-Abbotsford Archives at Trethewey House.
11. Henry Pennier, *Chiefly Indian*, Graydonald Graphics Ltd., West Vancouver, 1972, p.66.
12. An account by Ethel Gosling (née Combs), 1991, concerning her brother Ray's accident.
13. It should be noted that George Johnston, son of Alexander Johnston who originally owned the Abbotsford mill, claims that it was that his father who donated the lumber for the temple. Alexander had sold the mill by then, but could have had another mill somewhere else.
14. Historical notes by Clarke Trethewey.
    Pacific Coast Lumberman, May 1918.

12

"Joe had the Midas touch"

In 1955, when Joseph's grandson Alan was sunbathing on the beach at Waikiki with his wife Vivian, he struck up a conversation with a retired banker from Vancouver. On hearing the name Trethewey, the banker's face lit up at once, and he remarked wistfully: "I knew old Joe very well and I would give anything to have him here on this beach right now. He would sure turn this place upside down!"

This was the effect Joe had on those around him—stimulating, perhaps rather overpowering, certainly controversial, but always charged with vitality and the love of life. "Arthur was staid; Sam was rollicking; and J.O. was more than that!" says one Abbotsford resident who knew them in the 1920s.[1]

The eldest of the brothers, Joe was always a trailblazer, ready for any adventure—a larger-than-life character who plunged into all sorts of enterprises with intensity and zest and, in business affairs at least, won more often than he lost. Lucky in money matters, he was unlucky in love: his three marriages lacked any real depth of relationship, nor did he ever forge strong bonds with his children either. Perhaps his personal tragedy was that, though generous with material possessions, he was unable to give sufficiently of himself to those most closely related to him.

His was the dominant personality to emerge in his own generation, the leading spirit among his brothers and sisters, and after his father's death in 1906 Joe stepped naturally into James's position as head of the family, someone to turn to in time of need. This role was reinforced by his position of affluence, for he was easily the wealthiest of the brothers who remained in the Fraser Valley. "Joe always had the Midas touch," says one family acquaintance. "Everything he touched seemed to turn to gold."

His early years in British Columbia had been concerned chiefly with logging operations. He had settled on his ranch in Dewdney in 1884[2], and had kept this original homestead for many years after he had ceased to live on it except occasionally. Unhappy memories were associated with his home at Dewdney, for this was where he had lost his wife Mary in tragic circumstances only two years after they had settled on the land.

It was November of 1886, and Mary had given birth to her fifth child, Joseph Edgar, only a month before. She had three other little children at home, though she had lost her first-born while they were still living in Ontario. She was physically run down from the strain of bearing five children in six years and she was also finding it hard to endure the loneliness of pioneer life. It is almost certain that she was suffering from post-partum depression.

One evening Joe was so concerned at his wife's state of mind that he asked his fifteen-year-old sister Emma to stay in the bedroom with Mary while he walked all the way to St. Mary's Mission to ask for his mother's advice. Emma, tired out, fell asleep on the bed with Mary. When she woke up, Mary was gone. Her body was later found half a mile away in Nicomen Slough where the big creek runs in, and this stream has been known by local people ever since as Suicide Creek.[3]

Joe had no way of caring for a new baby and three pre-school children at home, so he was forced to split up the family and find foster homes for them all. What happened to the oldest child, William, in these years is not known, but the other three went to live with families in Maple Ridge. Edgar, the baby, was cared for by the parents of Jim's wife, while his sisters Margaret and Mae were fostered by a Hammond nurseryman and his wife, George and Edith Henry.[4]

After this, Joe seems to have spent very little time in Dewdney at all, although he continued to use this as his home address in any directory listing. In reality he was always away on trips connected with the lumber business, which was how he chiefly made a living in these years. He described himself as a "wood supply contractor" in the census of 1891.5 But Joe was his father's son, and at heart he was a confirmed prospector: the vision of that "pot of gold" was as real to him as it was to James. As he travelled the province in connection with the timber contracts, he found it very easy and convenient to combine these expeditions with a little prospecting on the side.

It was in this way that he stumbled upon the Providence mine and its rich yield, described in Chapter 7. The discovery of this mine was a turning-point in Joe's career, transforming him from a moderately successful minor entrepreneur into a businessman of substantial means, able to indulge any of his special interests. The ranching business had always had a genuine appeal for Joe, as it had for Sam, and he now went into it on a more ambitious scale. For the next quarter of a century ranching became his great passion in life, occupying the greater part of his time, and over the next few years he purchased a series of ranch properties, culminating in the famous Chilco Ranch.

The first of these was in Richmond, where the soil was some of the finest in the Fraser Valley. It was easy land to cultivate, consisting as it did of a deep river silt deposited by centuries of flooding, as the spring freshets washed over the land each year. Much of it was, in fact, natural grassland with only a light covering of brush. Early maps show notations of "good red top Grass Prairie" and no larger timber than "small willow brush".

Another great advantage of the Richmond acreage—and one which no doubt influenced Joe's decision to purchase—was the fact that the B.C. Electric Railway ran through the area, with Cambie station at the northwest corner of his property. This part of the line had been built largely for the benefit of the Steveston fish industry, but it was equally important to the farmers, who used it for sending goods to market and were given special rates for farm produce.

Joe was on the Richmond farm at the time of the 1901 census, and his household was now a very large one. All four of his teenage children from his first marriage had rejoined him and were with him in his new home, but as well Joe had a new young family from his recent second marriage. In the mid-90s he had remarried to a widow five years younger than himself—Sarah Jane McNeil—and he had fathered two daughters, Myrtle and Cornelia (Cora), aged 4 and 1 at the time of the census. Besides this, he had a stepdaughter, Lily (age 17 in the census), who was the only child of Sarah's first marriage. Also in the household were two farmhands, a carpenter, and a Japanese man-servant.[6]

The next ranch property that Joe bought (in 1904) was really intended for Edgar, to start him off with a good farming property of his own. It was on the outskirts of Maple Ridge on the flats beside the South Alouette River, with the Golden Ears mountains rising spectacularly into view beyond the fields. Edgar lived there after he was married, and Edgar's son Richard had the farm after him. Today it belongs to Richard's daughter Sharon and her husband Kenneth Stewart—so that the land has now been in the ownership of the Trethewey family for a span of 90 years and four generations.

It was the sale of the Coniagas mine in 1906 which enabled Joe to buy the Chilco Ranch and vast acres of additional rangeland. It was the Coniagas that turned him into a man of real wealth, as opposed to mere prosperity. Such was the euphoria of this splendid sale that Joe promptly launched into the biggest celebration of his life. "He returned [from Cobalt] to Vancouver," says Clarke Trethewey, "and gave a three-day party at the Grand Central Hotel, which was owned by Tommy Roberts, probably the most famous gambler in Vancouver. . . . I met a man who attended that party and he said it was probably the biggest party ever held in Vancouver. This was a gala affair with no restrictions, and champagne flowed freely." No one who attended this marathon party ever forgot it.[7]

A bath in champagne has always been considered the classic example of the ostentatious display of wealth—the ultimate experience—and it was completely in character that Joe should wish to gratify this form of self-indulgence. Joe's bath in champagne has become part of Trethewey family legend, but unfortunately no one quite knows what he was celebrating or when. All that anyone can recall is that the incident took place at a hotel in Ashcroft.[8] Given this locale for the famous bath, it seems more than likely that the occasion of it was his purchase of the new ranch in the Chilcotin.

Everything Joe did from now on, he did on a large scale, and when he purchased the Chilco Ranch in 1910[9] it was with with the full intent of building it up into something far larger It was, in fact, to become one of the most famous ranches in the history of the Chilcotin, a byword for its immense size and lavish set-up, second only to the celebrated Gang Ranch.

The ranch had been started twenty-five years before Joe had it, and it consisted of a fairly modest-sized spread of 500 acres with about 40 miles fenced. But only a few years later, Joe had more than quadrupled this acreage: by buying up Crown land and adding other ranch properties, he had become the owner of about 22,000 acres of first-class rangeland. He had also put in 50 more miles of new fencing.[10] The fact that he was able to put this much capital into the acquisition of the ranch, at the same time as becoming principal shareholder in the Abbotsford mill company, gives some idea of the wealth poured into the family coffers by the amazing Coniagas mine.

The Chilco Ranch was centred at Hanceville, a distant outpost of the Chilcotin, described in 1897 as "the most westerly inland settlement of the province." Even today, though Hanceville is an easy 60-mile drive on a good road running west from Williams Lake, it is still fairly remote from the outside world, and the paved highway soon peters out into gravel beyond this point. Endless miles of open range country fan out towards the Coastal Mountains, with meadows of bunch-grass offering lush grazing for the cattle, and little thickets of woodland to shelter the herds in winter. The Fraser cuts through these meadows in a deep canyon of brown clay, and into the canyon flow the turbid waters of the Chilcotin River, from which the Chilco Ranch takes its name.

Joe's plans right from the start were lavish and ambitious. As his rangeland grew, so did his herd, until the original herd of 500 cattle (mostly Herefords and Galloways) had been increased to about 800. Joe had always had a great fancy for horses, and on the ranch he was able to indulge his preference freely, stepping up the number of his horses from 50 at the time of purchase to about 225 a few years later. It is said that this number rose to as many as 500 in the course of time.

Horse-breeding was one of Joe's great interests. When he first started, all he had was a stable of work-horses, the sturdy Clydesdales, but he soon brought in a number of fancier breeds, and some first-class stallions, which carried off prizes in shows all across Canada. He was also interested in improving the quality of the regular ranch horses, and went to the trouble of importing five Hamiltonian studs from Ireland to cross with his own animals. The experiment was very successful, because it produced a more effective range animal, whose natural gait was a fast trot rather than a gallop, which suited the cowboys far better in their work.

Joe liked a bit of excitement in his life, and he was fond of fast-paced horses for his own riding, but in 1920 a serious accident put an end to this activity. He and his third wife, Reta, were driving up to the ranch one day, with his wife at the wheel. It was a bad road, and somehow Reta lost control of the steering. The car lurched heavily and turned over on its side. Joe, who was thrown out on impact, came to to find himself lying by the side of the road with a badly broken leg and the bone sticking into the muddy ground. Reta was trapped inside the car. Joe was a man of powerful physique, and he possessed willpower to match his physical strength. Crawling back to the wreck, he summoned up all his determination, and with one tremendous effort he managed to heave the car back on to all four wheels and free his wife. At the time when this incident took place, he was sixty-two years of age. Reta was apparently unhurt, but Joe unfortunately suffered a permanent leg injury as a result of the accident and was never able to ride a horse again.[11]

After this, instead of horseback riding, one of his favourite sports was to take out his democrat wagon and rush all over the countryside shooting coyotes. "He would go hell for leather across the range and shoot the coyotes on the run," remembered one oldtimer. Other times he would go off in the democrat on his own to shoot a steer for beef. A 3 or 4 year-old animal might weigh as much as 600 pounds, but it was nothing to Joe, with his great physical strength, to gut the steer and load it into the wagon single-handed—a feat which even his friends found hard to credit.

At times his craving for action and excitement led him to try out forms of amusement that were less than admirable. One of his cruder ideas of sport was to put about five of his stallions together into a corral and watch them fight, which seemed to him fairly good fun until—predictably—one of them finished up with a broken leg. That was the end of that particular form of diversion.

The big event of the Chilcotin year was the annual race-meet at Riske Creek. It was a local institution from about 1900 to 1920, and it was attended by every rancher in the district (though no "Siwash", as the aboriginals were then called, were invited.) Many of the residents in the area were from well-off British families, who imported expensive stallions, kept polo ponies, and had been brought up in the tradition of horse-racing. They may well have been the originators of this popular social event, which extended over two or three days. It was purely a sporting occasion, with no betting, and it had a very varied programme. Though horse-racing was the main theme, it was also lively with other sports like polo, foot-races and high jump events. No rodeo in those days—another hint of its British origins. Joe would certainly not have missed being present for this gathering—the highlight of the ranchers' year.[12]

But although he found plenty of recreation in the Chilcotin lifestyle, he took his ranching seriously and, like Will, who was concurrently developing his farm at Weston, Joe made a great many improvements as he expanded the ranch. To facilitate his building projects he put in a small sawmill, which could turn out 10,000 board feet a day if necessary. He also embarked on a huge irrigation project. This was a tremendous undertaking, as it meant bringing in water all the way from Big Creek, and the artificial channel which he had to cut was as much as 20 miles in length—and all this without the benefit of today's sophisticated machinery. With this very comprehensive system in place, he was able to water up to 1000 acres of land, and grow dense, prolific crops of alfafa and grain. Fortunately most of the acreage was not dependent on irrigation. Some of his meadows had natural access to streams, and most of the acreage consisted of a top layer of fine black loam, which retained its moisture because of the clay sub-soil.[13]

Although much of his time was spent at the ranch, Joe's restless energy took him all over the province looking after his business interests in mining and logging. He was constantly on the move, his own projects at the forefront of his mind, his personal relationships a poor second. Joe's second marriage was now on the decline. To Sarah it had been a disappointing relationship. Although he was a kind and generous man, too soft-hearted to turn down anyone asking for a favour, he had little talent for family life. He hated to be tied down, and was apt to treat his home as a convenience, disappearing for extended periods, only to turn up again quite unexpectedly.

Gradually the marriage came to mean less and less to both of them, until eventually they ended up leading separate lives, with Sarah making her home in Vancouver. When Sarah died of cancer in 1913, at the age of forty-nine, she spent her final days at the Vancouver home of her married daughter, Lily Coulthard, and it is said that Joe was not present at the funeral.

Her younger daughters—Myrtle and Cornelia (Cora)—were both teenagers at the time of their mother's death. They received an expensive private school education (as did all his children once he became affluent, for Joe was never grudging with money). One of Cora's adolescent memories is of visiting Joe at the Vancouver Hotel and finding him sitting around on the floor with his poker-playing cronies, the place knee-deep in stacks of money, and Joe stuffing great bunches of the winnings into his pockets. Although she and Myrtle were perhaps not close to their father, Cora wanted him to be remembered as a gentle person and one who was liberal to anyone in need.

But the final cause of the rift between Joe and Sarah was not merely a matter of incompatibility, it was an infatuation for another woman. Reta Belle Massen came to the ranch as Joe's housekeeper not long after he had bought the property.[14]There was twenty years between the two of them, but Joe was unable to resist the charms of the fascinating Reta. Tall and slender, with golden-dyed hair, she exuded sexuality and vitality—and these were qualities which struck a spark in Joe, for they were so much akin to the fun-loving side of his own temperament, which had been repressed for so long in his first two marriages.

Reta is something of a mystery woman in the Trethewey family. Nothing is known of her background, other than that she came from Toronto—the daughter of Salvation Army parents—had been married before, and from that marriage had a lovely teen-age daughter named Erna who was with her at the ranch. Little is known either of the circumstances which led up to her marriage to Joe in the summer of 1913. At the beginning of that year Sarah Trethewey was entering the final stages of her illness; Reta Massen was in the final months of a pregnancy. On February 21, as Sarah lay dying of cancer, Reta gave birth to a son, Joseph (always known as Joey.)[15] Two weeks later, Sarah was dead and Joe was a widower once again.

He married Reta four months later at a ceremony in Vancouver on July 31, 1913.[16] He immediately adopted little Joey, but many rumours abounded on the question of paternity. Some said that a ranch foreman was involved, others maintained that Joey was obviously the son of Joe because of a physical likeness. Certainly he was given the Trethewey name of Joseph; yet in Joe's will, though Joe refers to Edgar and William as "my sons", he describes Joey only as "Reta's son".

Joe and Reta lived mainly at the Chilco Ranch until Arthur's death in 1919, when Joe was obliged to take personal control of the Abbotsford mill. Perhaps reluctantly, he decided that Abbotsford must become his permanent home in the future. He kept the ranch on for a few more years, but increasingly his time was spent in promoting new developments for the company. In any case, one cannot imagine the vivacious Reta restricting her scope to an isolated frontier-style cattle ranch indefinitely. In 1922 he sold the giant ranch to an S. Logan of Vancouver.[17]

Reta suddenly exploded into respectable Abbotsford society as the third Mrs. J.O. Trethewey. Soon after moving to Abbotsford, Joe built her a beautiful new house on a site which overlooked Mill Lake. This was the residence now known as Trethewey House, which the Trethewey family donated to the Matsqui-Abbotsford Recreation and Parks Foundation in 1980 as a heritage property.

Though it could not be described as a mansion in size, it was certainly the most impressive house in Abbotsford at that time for quality and finish. It was a 4-bedroom home, built in the Craftsman style, sturdy, square and massive, redolent less of an elegant urban sophistication than a robust and solid rusticity. The hallmark of the architectural style was the emphasis on natural materials. Rounded field-stone was used on the chimney and porch, and interesting wood detailing marked the brackets, exposed rafters and corbels. Heavily gabled, massively constructed, scorning the fancy ginger-bread fretwork of the previous decade, it looked exactly what it was—the substantial home of a prosperous lumber baron.

The interior decor was not exceptional, according to acquaintances who visited the house in those days. Neither Joe nor Reta could be called aesthetic in their tastes, nor was Reta particularly concerned with decor, so the furnishings tended to be conventional and of good quality, rather than memorable or striking. What Reta loved to do was to have parties, and although she mostly liked to take her guests to Vancouver night-clubs, she did appreciate the house in Abbotsford as a locale in which to entertain—preferably in a big way.[18]

It did not matter whether Joe was at home or not; Reta would hold her parties regardless, the drink flowing freely, flouting the strongly temperance section of Abbotsford society. "Let's go upstairs and make babies," she was heard to say at the height of one of these festivities. Needless to say, all the rigidly Methodist and Presbyterian side of the Trethewey family totally disapproved of the ebullient Reta, though she would probably have got on very well with the flamboyant Sam, who was the relative they saw the most of, since he was now the superintendent down at the millsite.

Business at the mill was booming after the war, as the returned ex-servicemen came flocking back to settle in the Valley and build homes for themselves. And if the local market was strong, it still represented only a fraction of the output of the mill, for the bulk of the company's sales were to the prairies and eastern Canada. As many as 230 men were now employed almost all the year round. It was white labour only in the logging camps, but the Japanese worked the booms, and the Chinese and the East Indians piled lumber and worked at the millsite.

Joe and Sam began an active program of expansion and modernisation at the millsite. They built cottages down by Mill Lake for the married employees, they brought in new machinery, they added another dry kiln. They also innovated the use of tractors instead of horses for hauling lumber, though they did keep on a number of work-horses.[19]

But Joe's chief interest, when he took control of the company, was in furthering his mining ambitions, and in the early 1920s he began to invest in a number of mining properties on the company's behalf. It was mining potential which first turned his attention to a remote spot called Alice Arm, on the coast of northern British Columbia. Alice Arm lay in a mountain valley at the far end of one of the inlets north of Prince Rupert, and the only reason for the general public ever to have heard of it at all was that it had recently come into prominence on account of the famous Dolly Varden mines. These were possibly the largest silver reserves in all of British Columbia, and Joe was fascinated by the prospects in this geological area. Though he never lived to develop them as mines, he acquired two claims, Bunker Hill and the Speculator, and began a process of exploration. At the same time, he developed a profitable logging operation at Alice Arm.[20]

Though mining had gone on there since the turn of the century, no one had ever logged this valley before. The forests were known to be rich in spruce, which was now very much in demand for aeroplane manufacture, and Joe was anxious to tap this new market. In the spring of 1923 he put in a logging railway on the mud flats east of the Alice Arm settlement, and for the next three years he logged the timber on either side of the Illiance River. The best logs went down to the mill at Prince Rupert, while the lower grades were sent down to Pacific Mills at Ocean Falls to be used for pulp and paper. His son Edgar, not long married, went up to Alice Arm with his wife to take charge.[21]

Some time before 1925 Joe also invested in some valuable timber limits on Vancouver Island—an "astronomical" extent of timber, according to Alan Trethewey—which would apparently have brought Joe sensational profits had he lived to log these tracts. As it was, when his heirs came to dispose of these limits two years after his death, the Depression had just taken hold of the economy and their true value was never realised. Even so, the total selling price was over a quarter of a million. Interestingly, these limits were in the same region on the west coast of the Island at Gold River and Nootka Sound that the well-known Tahsis Company was later to operate so profitably.

According to Abbotsford rumour, Joe's idea in buying these tracts was to move the mill over to Vancouver Island once the local timber had run out. Speculation of this sort caused much unrest around the town, and not without cause. The report was probably quite well founded, for it would have been completely in character for Joe to have been contemplating a radical move of this kind and take advantage of changing conditions. Whatever the truth of the rumour, Joe never lived long enough to carry out any such plan, and the Trethewey family was never in a position to realise the potential of the splendid Vancouver Island timber holdings.

As Joe's will would later reveal, he was making an impressive amount of investment in other fields besides the lumber industry during the 1920s. He had two mining claims at Alice Arm (Bunker Hill and the Speculator); he had the majority shares in the Sunrise Hazelton silver mine just north of Hazelton; and he had also been investing in claims in the Kamloops district and the Omineca district, all of these dating to 1923 or 1924. Through the Abbotsford Lumber, Mining and Development Company he also held mortgages on various hotels, including—most notably—the popular and elegant Harrison Hot Springs Hotel with a mortgage to the value of $115,000.

As usual, all these interests kept him coming and going, and involved lengthy absences from home. Reta would go with him to Alice Arm on some of his trips, but it was not really her sort of life-style. She enjoyed the good life, the holidays, the parties, the jewellery, the clothes—"she knew how to spend his money for him," says one observer—and it was felt that the wealthy background perhaps appealed to her more than her much older husband. Temperamentally she and Joe had much in common, sharing an extrovert, fun-loving, liberal outlook on life, yet the affection was not there. People liked her, and to her friends she was kind and very generous, opening her home to anyone who was sick or in need of help, but to Joe she was uncaring. "She'd put the boots to the old man and he'd sleep on a couch in the office at the mill," recalls one of Joe's employees.

Although they were not living apart or officially separated at the beginning of 1927—this is obvious from a glance at the social column in the local newspaper—an estrangement did undoubtedly occur between them before the time of Joe's death in October of that year. This estrangement may have been hastened by the fact of Joe's terminal cancer, whose onset may have forced him to re-evaluate his relationships and make his decisions accordingly. By the late summer his condition was deteriorating fast. He took treatment at the hot sulphur springs at Harrison in August, but there was to be no cure, and a few weeks later Edgar was summoned back to Abbotsford to be with his father during his final days. Joe died on October 22, 1927.

In the last months of his life there is no doubt that he turned against Reta completely, and when he made his final will, three weeks before his death, he took very good care that Reta would not inherit his fortune, but only a carefully regulated amount, doled out in the form of an annuity. He spent his last days not in his own home with his wife at his side, but cared for by his daughter Mae at her home in Vancouver, nor was Reta with him even at the end.[22] His obituary still refers to Reta as his "wife", but his death certificate, filled in by Edgar, describes him as "divorced."

Although Joe had not left Reta by any means penurious, having already given her the house and land, and other real estate, as well as the annuity, she nevertheless contested the will. She succeeded in winning an extra $7000 lump sum, as well as further benefits for her son Joey. She then departed for South Africa for a few years, came back and lived in Vancouver for a while, and finally sold the Abbotsford house in 1936[23] to an Abbotsford merchant named Raoul Des-Mazes. Reta spent the rest of her life in California, dying there about 1960, and her name was never mentioned again in the hearing of the older generation of the Trethewey family.

END NOTES

1. Margaret Weir, interview with the Matsqui-Sumas-Abbotsford Historical Society, 1982.
2. Land assignments, GR436, Box 142, 9479, Provincial Archives of B.C.
3. *Colonist*, Nov.16, 1886, p.3.
4. Census 1891, April 29, Maple Ridge area.
5. Census 1891, City of Vancouver, Reel T6291, p.31.
6. Census 1901, Richmond area, Reel T6429, Sub-div.2, p.9.
7. Clarke and Alan Trethewey, taped conversation, 1889.
8. Cornelia (Cora) Trethewey in conversation with Alan Trethewey, 1991.
9. *Ashcroft Journal*, June 18 & Sept.24, 1910. Joe buys the ranch from Claude R. Wilson.
10. Photocopy from an unidentified book, 1912. Descriptions of Chilcotin ranches.
11. This story and others from Walter Bambrick, as told to Bruce Watt, 1991.
12. Program of Chilcoten Races, June 3rd. and 4th. 1912.
    Descriptions in the *Ashcroft Journal*.
13. Photocopy from 1912 book.
14. Cora Trethewey.
15. Vital Statistics Records, California. Birthdate Feb.21, 1913.
16. Marriage certificate, July 31, 1913.
17. George Terry, *History and Legends of the Chilcotin*, from material provided by community clubs, 1958.
    References in the *Ashcroft Journal*.
18. Margaret Weir in conversation with Alan Trethewey and the author, 1992.
19. *Pacific Coast Lumberman*, May 1920, p.44.
20. *Alice Arm & Anyox Herald*, Oct.7, 1922; Jan.10, 1925; Apr.3 & Oct.2, 1926.
21. Ibid, Mar.31, 1923
22. Cora Trethewey.
    Province, Oct.22, 1927
23. Agreement for sale, Joseph Massen Trethewey to Maria DesMazes, Nov.13, 1936.

13

Sam: a Likable Maverick

I t was the winter of 1918 or 1919, and Abbotsford was in the grip of a big freeze. Mill Lake had frozen solid: the ice was so thick that you could drive a car on it. In the centre of the lake someone had lit a large bonfire among some of the logs that were caught in the ice, and skaters were pausing to warm themselves by the glow of the fire.

Sam Trethewey had come down to the lake in his car, and seeing two ladies he knew, Mrs. Hutchinson and Mrs. Shore, he greeted them courteously: "Good morning, ladies! Would you care for a little drive on the ice?" It seemed like a delightful idea and they accepted with pleasure. But no sooner were they seated when Sam suddenly roared off at top speed and began a series of terrifying manoeuvres. First he would rev up, then just as abruptly he would put on the brakes, sending the car into a wild spin. It slipped and it skidded and it lurched uncontrollably against the logs that were frozen into the lake, until the women were afraid that at any moment he would dislodge one of the big logs and open up the ice. For them it was a nightmare ride. For Sam it was a typical piece of mischief that he thoroughly enjoyed.[1]

Samuel was the strange, engaging maverick of the family. All through his career Sam was to be found doing the unexpected—veering from one enterprise to another, flouting convention, forever looking for fresh stimulus to energise his life. It was not in his nature to spend his whole life at one occupation, as Arthur and Jim were content to do. Like Joe, Sam needed perpetual change and renewal to bring colour to his life, and he alternated between several of the Tretheweys' favourite types of work.

The Tretheweys typically were a mixture of lumberman, miner and farmer/rancher. They were vigorous, open-air men who loved an outdoor life and physical activity. Though clever in their engineering abilities, they favoured practical work over academic education. Though generous and kind-hearted, they had little understanding of more introspective, sensitive personalities. You worked hard and you enjoyed life—these were the rules they lived by. Samuel Dunn Trethewey and his brothers were all out of this same mould, but the same basic ingredients produced five very different characters.

Like his brothers, Sam was known as a lumberman, and a very experienced one, but by the time he was forty he had tried several different types of occupation. He had felled trees where the new city of Vancouver was to stand; he had created a farm at Dewdney; he had gone prospecting for minerals at Silverton and Mount Baker; and he had worked with Jim and Arthur at the Elk Creek sawmill. All this time he had never given up the Dewdney farm, so he had this to go back to when his brothers sold the Elk Creek mill in 1901. He and his wife made Dewdney their home again for the next two years.

Like Joe and Jim, Sam had married a Muskoka girl. All through his early years at Dewdney he must have been cherishing tender memories of Elizabeth Ellen Morrow, a girl from Muskoka Falls who had been in her early teens at the time he left. When he went back for a visit to his home district and saw her again, love was evidently rekindled, and in 1889 the two of them were married. Elizabeth was a week short of eighteen at the time of the wedding, and Samuel just on twenty-eight.

During their time at Elk Creek they had become very attached to the well-developed Chilliwack district with its prosperous farms and attractive, well-built homes. Life on the isolated Dewdney ranch seemed dull and stagnant, now that they had returned. Even the nearby town of Mission was drab and undeveloped. "A walk up Horne Avenue is enough to depress the most convivial nature and cause prospective settlers to look elsewhere," wrote one discouraged visitor.² In March 1903 they sold the Dewdney farm and returned to the brighter prospects of Chilliwack.³

They went back to the East Chilliwack district where they had lived before, though not to Elk Creek itself, but Camp Slough just a few miles away. After his years of logging in the forests around Elk Falls, Sam must have had a very shrewd idea of the quality of the available timber, and no doubt the appeal of this district lay as much in its lumbering potential as in his own personal liking for Chilliwack. Sam now devoted all of his not inconsiderable energy to mills and milling, and for the first time, he became a mill-owner in his own right.

During the next seven years he gradually acquired as many as three small sawmills. The first of these was one he built in Maple Ridge, if the reporting in the *Chilliwack Progress* in 1903 is correct.⁴ Described as a "lumber and shingle mill near Port Haney", it is recorded in Sam's name throughout the decade, though nothing is known of it in the family. The only brother remembered as having a mill in that area was Jim.

Sam and Jim were definitely the joint owners of a mill at Camp Slough two years later. They built the mill early in 1905 and advertised its opening in the following terms: "James and S.D. Trethewey, who have built a new sawmill near Camp Slough (Trethewey place), will be prepared about 1st May to supply all kinds of dressed and rough lumber, mouldings, etc."⁵

Jim's partnership with Sam in the Camp Slough mill is a fact which has never been brought to light in previous historical accounts, and the reason it has been forgotten is probably because the arrangement only lasted for a short time. It was an unlikely partnership in any case, given their very opposite temperaments, and it was almost doomed to failure. Sam's methods of running a business were distinctly unorthodox. In a fit of temper he might flare up and fire some trusty longtime worker, only to dismiss the whole episode a moment later with a cheery: "Relax, you're rehired!" He was also known to fire a man one day and then the next day call in at the man's house, enquiring innocently why he had not come in to at work that morning. This was not at all the style of his more placid brothers, Jim and Arthur.

"Sam was without doubt the most colourful member of the Trethewey family," says Clarke Trethewey, who spent many weekends in his uncle's home as a teenager after his parents' death. "He loved life and everything in it. He had a violent temper when he lost his patience, yet was a most gentle and tender person when the occasion demanded it. He lived every day as if it was his last and he experienced every emotion that life could hold for anyone."

In his capacity for extracting the most out of life Sam was like his brother Joe, but Joe had a basic intensity and forcefulness and judgement which took him to the top, while Sam's impulsive and unbalanced personality bordered on the eccentric at times. Yet Sam's openness had a touching quality about it—"You couldn't help liking Sam," said one Abbotsford resident—and he was warm and approachable in a way that Joe never could have been.

No one knows exactly what transpired between Jim and Sam at Camp Slough. They advertised as the Trethewey Brothers for a period of about ten months, but by April of 1906 the advertisement was in Sam's name only, and Jim was living in Haney. It is possible that Jim may never have received his share in the mill when the time came to sell, as Sam is believed to have put everything in his wife's name and altogether may have behaved in a rather devious way. "He was a scoundrel," claimed Jim's son, Everett.[6]

The mill flourished, and around 1908 Sam even took on another mill, buying the sawmill of the Muirhead brothers in the same district. He was doing well in the face of considerable competition—the *Progress* commented on the "the hive of mills now in the valley"— when in 1909 disaster struck. The main mill at Camp Slough burned to the ground. Only the fact that it was raining that night mitigated the extent of his losses at all, for at least it made it possible to save the outbuildings, but all the lumber was destroyed.[7]

It was a bad blow, but not as bad as it might have been, because it happened to coincide with other major events that were taking place within the Trethewey family. This was the very year in which the brothers had made their big investment in the Abbotsford mill. Having completed the deal only six months earlier, they were already in the process of planning for expansion and development, and they could use someone of Sam's energy and capability to take charge of some of their new initiatives. They offered him the opportunity to come in with them, and Sam accepted thankfully.[8]

Sam never had a mill in Chilliwack again, but because of their liking for the district he and Elizabeth continued to make their home there. Although after a year of commuting he built a house in Abbotsford near the mill yards, the family residence was always in Chilliwack until Elizabeth's death in 1916, and the local paper always referred to Sam as a Chilliwack resident. This remained the place for which he felt the strongest attachment, and when he eventually died—in a completely different part of the province—it was the Chilliwack cemetery on the mountainside which became his last resting-place.

His association with the Abbotsford mill did not last more than two or three years. Probably, with his highly individualistic temperament, Sam craved more independence than he was able to enjoy in a company owned chiefly by his brothers. He and Arthur were too unlike to get along smoothly together, even though each of them had his own area of decision-making—Arthur managing the office and Sam running the logging operations. Once again Sam acquired a mill of his own, the Shearwater mill at Clayburn.

Sam took on this mill some time after 1912, but little else is known of this brief episode in his life. An older resident of the Clayburn district recalls that the millsite was at the corner of Seldon and Clayburn Roads, not far from the main Mission-Abbotsford highway. He says it was an average-sized mill—about 60 feet in length with a lean-to—and that it functioned with the circular saw which pre-dated the band saw. It produced poles and sawn lumber. Sam seems to have run the Shearwater mill just for two or three years in the period of the first World War and given it up at about the time his wife died.[9]

Elizabeth had been suffering from cancer since late in 1915. Twice she had been operated on, and each time the family had hoped that this was a cure, but in late April of 1916 a third and very serious operation made it clear that her illness would be terminal. She left the Vancouver General Hospital at the end of May in a state of great weakness—she was barely able to sign her will on May 30—and she spent the last days of her life at her home in Chilliwack, where she died rather suddenly on June 2.[10]

Elizabeth was only forty-four at the time of her death, but she had married young, so she left three adult children. Rosanna, whose twin had died at birth, was twenty-four; Ernest was twenty-three; and Howard (a strange personality, said to be "as weird as his father") was twenty-one. Sam continued to look after their interests and find them employment throughout his life.

It was somewhere at this point that Sam felt that he had to make a complete break with his past life. He had finished with milling, as he thought, and he was seized with a great urge for a complete change of scene. Unexpectedly, he bought a ranch in Alberta. Perhaps he was partly inspired by Joe's enjoyment of the open-air life on the spacious acres of the Chilco Ranch and Will's enthusiasm for his model farm at Weston, and in any case Sam had kept a farm through most of his years in Chilliwack. The exact locale of the Alberta ranch has never been firmly established, but it is believed to have been near Hardisty, on the Battle River east of Edmonton.

Sam's years in Hardisty were few, and his life there remains a complete blank, except for the fact that while he was on the farm he met and married a widowed lady with the same name as his first wife—Elizabeth. Elizabeth Swanson was of German origin herself, a fact that aroused some prejudice among certain members of the family, as World War I was then in progress and feelings of hostility sometimes ran high. Those who remember her describe her as a quiet and pleasant woman with a lovely daughter named Camille, who was later to marry the M.L.A., Barry Mather. At the time of her mother's re-marriage Camille was about six years old.

Possibly with his changeable disposition Sam would have tired of the ranch before long, but fate decided his future for him when Arthur became too ill to manage the Abbotsford mill and died shortly after. In this emergency Sam was the only person who could take Arthur's place.

He gave up the farm in Alberta, cheerfully declaring to a reporter that "when the opportunity offered, he stepped right into the work again and wild horses would not tear him away from the smell of the sawdust and the whirr of the saws." He admitted too: "Ranching did not pay. In fact, there was a serious loss."[11] He seemed happy to be in charge, and full of ideas for new improvements. Joe was still the majority shareholder and president of the company, but Joe had no desire be tied down to Abbotsford when he was anxious to pursue his speculations in mining, logging and property investment.

Sam threw all his energy into the work. Said the reporter: "The photo of the man who has never found big boss Trethewey at work at the mill . . . has yet to be taken. The last time [I] was out at Abbotsford, he was out on the pond cutting ice from the logs to get enough lumber to feed the capacious saw of the mills. He sets the example and his men follow close on his heels. As a consequence the mill is always on the go."[12]

He took on Arthur's role not only as the manager of the mill, but also as a leader in community affairs. He was president of the baseball club, he was a director of the local branch of the B.C. Automobile Association, and he and his wife hosted the strawberry socials and other polite events in the social life of Abbotsford in the 1920s.

But this sort of dutiful social activity was not nearly enough of an outlet for Sam's high spirits and overflowing energy. Above all, he loved to dance, and the fact that he was an appalling dancer, who capered around his partner like a heavy-footed spider, made no difference to his pleasure in this entertainment. But he tried in vain to persuade his quiet wife to go out with him. He gave her money for clothes, and was then shocked to find that she had prudently put it all into bonds for the future.

Once again, Sam had married a rather prim and conservative woman, similar to his first wife (the Tretheweys always married lady-like women—except for the ebullient Reta), and it was an attraction of opposites that had its problems. Whereas his first wife had been firm enough to keep him in line, the second Elizabeth did not know how to deal with a temperament like Sam's, and the result was that he simply went ahead and had a good time without her. He made several lady friends, but his chief companion was a lady who claimed to be an illegitimate daughter of Queen Victoria. He met her when she had arrived in town in 1923 to run one of the cafés, and as they both enjoyed dancing, the two of them went all over the district together to the different dances that were advertised.

It was one of these convivial outings that landed Sam in jail. He had rounded up a group of friends to drive down to a dance across the border, and because of Prohibition, he had smuggled in an ample supply of liquor and rented a room in a hotel in Lynden to use as a bar. The constant coming and going between the dance hall and the hotel room soon aroused the suspicion of the authorities, and the federal officers came in and raided the room. They took Sam off to jail, where he seethed with fury for the whole weekend.

"Samuel's temper was at its greatest peak when he was in jail in Bellingham," says Clarke Trethewey with some relish. As Howard Trethewey put it: "Father was so goddammed mad, he could have walked across the border, jail cell and all!" Sam had to wait until Monday morning to come before the judge, who fortunately took a broadminded view of the whole episode. Ruling that the court was only interested in professional bootleggers, he handed Samuel his car keys and advised him to go and get a hair-cut, but not to stop, just to keep on going until he had crossed the border. This little incident kept Abbotsford gossip circles busy for some time.

He adored fast cars, and in fact his chief criterion for a new car was its capacity for a fast start and a high rate of speed. Any passenger in his car would inevitably endure a scary ride, as he wove in and out of the traffic like a reckless teenager. The narrow gravel roads of that era only added to the hazards of the journey. On one occasion when Sam had been taking his lady friend to a dance, driving at his usual mad rate of speed, she said to him: "Sammy, you sure hit the high spots this time." He grabbed her leg and replied: "Yes, and the low spots too!"

Elizabeth must have been greatly relieved when suddenly Sam decided he had had enough of sawmills and wanted to leave Abbotsford to go into the more exciting occupation of mining again. Possibly there was more to it than this—perhaps a policy disagreement at the mill. It is significant that when Sam sold his interest to Joe in January 1926, the company secretary, James McGowan, who had been with them for seventeen years, also resigned and left the district.[13] There was, however, no known rift between the brothers.

Once again, Sam wanted a change of pace, only this time it was not ranching but mining which attracted his errant fancy. A little mining on the side was always a recognised activity among the Trethewey brothers, and Sam was no exception. Even when he was at the mill he had held mining properties, one near Kamloops and another near Pincher Creek, Alberta, though apparently he had never developed either of these. Now he was suddenly in a hurry to start up with a working mine, so he immediately began hunting around the province for some worthwhile property to develop, and only a month after selling his interest in the mill he was the instant owner of a mine in the East Kootenays at Atholmer. Why wait?—two weeks later he was off to Atholmer again and the project was under way. [14]

As it was not his plan to be tied to the site, he employed his son Ernest and son-in-law Jacob McDaniel to take charge of developments at the mine, and he bought a family home in Vancouver.[15] The B.C. Directory now described Sam as "retired", but actually nothing could have been farther from the truth. Forever on the go, he was busy making active plans for the future. Elizabeth and Camille were to see very little of him in their Vancouver home—but this was nothing new for a Trethewey wife.

Like all his other enthusiasms, his mining interest too died away, though Ernest and Jacob stayed on at Lake Windermere, apparently to run the mine. Only two years after his purchase of the mine Sam had a new venture to occupy his thoughts. Surprisingly, it was another sawmill.

While he had been prospecting near Kamloops previously, he had got to know various figures in the lumber industry there. He had even had a pole-logging company himself, worked by Ernest and Jacob. His latest idea was that he should go in with one of his Kamloops friends, Harry Turner, and buy the Kamloops Lumber Company, which ran a sizable sawmill of long standing. His wife remained in Vancouver, but his son Howard came up to Kamloops with him.

Sam was now sixty-seven, and still full of enthusiasm for new enterprises—retirement as far from his mind as it had been with his father at the same age. His partner, Harry Turner, was fifteen years younger than Sam himself, and had a solid background in lumber sales, having worked with the Arrow Lakes Lumber Company for some years. Together they bought the mill from W.A. Foote in March of 1928, a deal "involving approximately $50,000", according to the local newspaper.[16]

Unfortunately, Sam never had a chance to develop this mill in the way he would have liked. He died unexpectedly only seventeen months after coming to Kamloops, having run the mill for only two seasons. His life was cut short by a road accident which took place just outside the town. He and a "yardman" from the mill, J.H. Turner (presumably his partner), were on the Savona Road one dark night on their way home to Kamloops, when a vehicle came up behind them, blaring the horn and attempting to pass. Turner, the driver, edged over towards the bank, but the road surface was greasy and the shoulder was soft and unstable. The ground gave way under their wheels and the truck overturned.[17]

Turner came out of it with barely a scratch, but Sam's head had been driven down on his chest by the force of the impact, and he was taken to the Royal Inland Hospital in considerable pain. In themselves his injuries were not life-threatening, and he was said to be in surprisingly good condition for a man of his age, but almost at once pneumonia set in. He had been admitted on Sunday night, but by Tuesday he was so ill that a will was drawn up on his behalf. It was read over and explained to him in the presence of Harry Turner and a nurse, who acted as witnesses. He appeared to understand it, and with a faltering hand he made his mark, a shaky cross. He died at 8.15 the next day, September 25, 1929.[18]

Sam was not buried in a Kamloops cemetery, nor in the family plot at Mountain View cemetery in Vancouver. Appropriately, his funeral service took place from the United Church in Chilliwack, his chosen home for so many years, and this was followed by the impressive graveside service of the Order of Excelsior Lodge No.7 at the Chilliwack cemetery on the mountain. Brethren of the Order assembled from as far away as Abbotsford and Mission, as well as Chilliwack.[19] It was plain that Sam was widely known and liked throughout the district, and was respected too, in spite of his foibles, for his long and influential association with the Fraser Valley.

END NOTES

1. Mrs. Margaret Weir (née Hutchinson), interview with Alan Trethewey and the author, 1991.
2. *Chilliwack Progress,* Feb.28, 1906.
3. *Chilliwack Progress,* Mar.11, 1903.
4. *Chilliwack Progress,* July 8, 1903
5. *Chilliwack Progress,* advertisement running from Mar.22, 1905, through the rest of season.
6. Everett Trethewey in conversation with Alan Trethewey, 1992.
7. *Chilliwack Progress,* Oct.6, 1909.
8. *Chilliwack Progress,* Feb.23, 1910.
9. Walter Whiteley, conversation with the author, 1992.
   Pacific Coast Lumberman, May 1920. 'Clearwater' appears to be a misprint for 'Shearwater'.
10. *Chilliwack Progress,* June 8, 1916.
    Will of Elizabeth Ellen Trethewey, GR 1052, Box 60, 8911. Provincial Archives of British Columbia.
11. *Western Lumberman,* Feb.1920.
12. *Western Lumberman,* April 1920, p.34.
13. *Abbotsford Sumas Matsqui News,* Feb.4, 1926.
14. *ASM News,* Mar.4 & Mar.18, 1926.
15. *ASM News,* Apr.8, 1926.
16. *Kamloops Sentinel,* Mar.2, 1928, p.1.
17. *Kamloops Sentinel,,* Sept.24, 1929, p.1.
18. Will of Samuel Dunn Trethewey, GR, File 17939, PABC.
19. *Chilliwack Progress,* Oct.3, 1929, p.1.

Edgar Trethewey and Margaret Church on their wedding day.

Alice Arm, the logging town where Edgar and Margaret spent part of the
1920s.

Native canoeists transporting supplies across the Lillooet river. Trethewey
Logging Co., 1930s. *Trethewey family archives*

Allis-Chalmers tractor and Carco arch used for hauling logs and breaking
up log jams, Lillooet River. Trethewey Logging Co., 1946.

Trethewey family archives

A river-going tractor. *Trethewey family archives*

The Church family ranch and corral at Big Creek where Margaret Trethewey
grew up. *Joan Campbell*

Tennis court at the Church ranch, 1917.
Joan Campbell

Margaret Trethewey on Marsinita at an equestrian event.

Maloney, Seattle

The Maple Ridge Riding Centre, founded by Margaret Trethewey.

Trethewey family archives

Vernon Preparatory School group, c.1935. (3rd row, centre) Rev. Augustine Mackie; Mrs. Mackie to his left: Hugh Mackie to his right. (Top row, 4th from right) Alan Trethewey. (2nd row, extreme right) Richard Trethewey.

Trethewey family archives

Alan (left) and Richard (right) in uniform in World War II.
Trethewey family archives

The bay on Marble Island west of the Queen Charlottes' where Alan made
his rescue attempt.
Trethewey family archives

Alan Trethewey.

Trethewey family archives

Bob Cattermole (left) and Bob Kenny (right) at Peace Dam site.

Trethewey family archives

Ivan Wells at Buttle Lake, 1957.

Trethewey family archives

Jim Douglas and Ralph Douglas of Douglas Plywood Ltd.

Trethewey family archives

The historic McNair shingle mill, Port Moody. A 19-machine mill, owned by Trethewey Industries Ltd. from 1956 to 1965. *Trethewey family archives*

Dismantling the battleship HMCS *Ontario*, 1959.

George Allen Aerial Photos

Snag clearing at Lake Almanor, 1963.   *Trethewey family archives*

Possible the largest float camp of the time (150 men), Buttle Lake, 1957.
                                        Trethewey family archives

Trethewey-Cattermole Contractors' stump-splitting device, 1964.
Trethewey family archives

Large spruce in the Queen Charlottes', 1970. Alan Trethewey beside log.
Trethewey family archives

Riv-Tow preparing to load logs from Queen Charlotte Timber to barge to Vancouver.

Trethewey family archives

The Beaver float plane. Edgar in foreground, 1962.

Trethewey family archives

The Seabee seaplane at Fire Lake, 1957.

Trethewey family archives

14

Jim: 60 Years a Lumberman

Ihit was 1939, and the tall, spare figure of an elderly man could be
seen standing on a logged hillside above Harrison Bay. He
looked down at the wide waters of the bay and across to the distant peaks of Mount Cheam, gleaming white against an ice-blue sky.
It was a familiar scene, but one whose serene beauty never failed to
stir him. For the past few years he had been running a logging camp
on the hillside above the Bay, but he had known the district long before this time—in fact, it was forty years ago that he had first begun
to log in the forests of the Harrison watershed. Before that, he had
been a lumberman too, going all the way back to his early youth in
the pine woods of Muskoka.

Jim Trethewey was now eighty years old, but still a lumberman.
He had been running a little mill and logging camp in the Lake
Errock-Harrison Bay area throughout most of his seventies. Logging
was his chosen life and, in any case, retirement was a word almost
unknown to a Trethewey. Even now he had little urge to retire, but a
heart condition had slowed him down, and his doctor had decreed
that the time had come. Jim was in the process of dismantling his operation and saying a final farewell to the life he loved.

Of all the brothers Jim had led the least spectacular life, though
it may have been the happiest and it was certainly the longest. He
had not lucked in on a great fortune like Will, nor had he made inspired investments like Joe. He had not become known for a large
mill like Arthur, nor even displayed the wild exuberance and
eccentricities seen in his brother Sam. He was a respected employer,

he was a family man with several children, and he had been happily
married to the same woman for sixty years that spring. These are not
qualifications for making the headlines, and so perhaps it is not surprising that very little seems to have been written about this successful and likable Trethewey.

But although Jim was not the flamboyant type, nor was his name
associated with any one particular district, his lumbering operations
over the years unquestionably helped to create prosperity in many
parts of the Fraser Valley, just as his brothers' had done. Chilliwack,
Harrison Mills, Haney, and Surrey, for instance, were all places
where his enterprises made a difference.

"James was a perfectionist," says one retired logger who worked
in one of Jim's logging crews in the 1930s. "He set himself and his
men a high standard in any project he decided to take on, and insisted
on a high quality of production."[1] He had been raised on the work
ethic. Like his brothers and sisters, he had been expected not only to
be self-reliant and hardworking, but to try to excel in whatever he
set out to do, and this early training remained with him.

Though Jim had paid one visit to British Columbia in the 1870s
soon after his father came out,[2] he had had no great urge to pioneer
there like his impulsive parent; in fact, he was the last one in the
whole family to make the decision, and did not leave Muskoka until
four years after the rest of them. He was content with his life in Ontario—his lumbering work in the pine forests of Muskoka, and his
family life with his wife Libby and his little daughters Olive and
Muriel. Besides this, with his prudent temperament he may very
well have thought it wiser to wait until the railway was finished and
economic prospects more certain.

Jim had lived in the Muskoka Falls community for longer than
anyone else in his family, and it must have been with some reluctance that he gave up these familiar surroundings for the unknown province beyond the Rockies. Still, his wife's family was
moving west too and the future looked promising, so the year 1887
found him and Libby and the children making the long train journey
across the continent to join their relatives.[3] When they alighted
from the train at the sparse new settlement of St. Mary's Mission,

his father and mother were waiting there to welcome them—and, what was more, to present them with a plan of action!

It must surely have been his father's idea that Jim and Libby should start running a hotel in Mission. Jim, contentedly logging the forests of Muskoka, had never contemplated this sort of life, and Libby at the age of twenty-seven certainly had no experience in ho-tel management, but James senior's mind with filled with visions of the prosperous town that Mission was destined to be, and he could clearly see a profitable role for each of his family there. As we have seen, James's enthusiasm was hard to resist, and the young couple soon found themselves the proprietors of one of the many new ho-tels which were rapidly sprouting up in Mission.

Strong Presbyterians, they were anxious that their hotel should have a better reputation than some of the more rowdy establish-ments in town, so they advertised it as a temperance hotel.[4] There was more than a hint of nostalgia in the name they chose for it—On-tario House—but they threw themselves into the new project with their usual determination and evidently made a success of it. James senior had shown his usual acumen in the choice of the site he had earmarked for the purpose, which was on the slope just above the new railway station and convenient for passengers. Jim and Libby regularly boarded the CPR men as well.

This was the only period in Jim's life when he did not call him-self a lumberman. Hotel-keeping can hardly have been a congenial occupation to him, and when his father suggested the mill operation at Elk Creek, he must have been thankful to give up the hotel busi-ness and in 1892 return to the forest industry where he truly felt at home.

From the age of thirty-three to thirty-nine he ran the small sawmill at Elk Creek in a comfortable partnership with his brother Arthur. The two of them made a good team. They got on well to-gether, trusting each other's business judgement and sharing the same balanced approach to the problems of management, and they were prepared to stay in partnership when they launched their ma-jor project in the form of the big mill at Harrison River.

The story of Jim's and Arthur's attempt to move into the big league of mill ownership together has been told in Chapter 8. Sadly for Jim, the most audacious venture of his whole career was to be wiped out for causes beyond his control. At Harrison River he had to face the two major crises of his life: first came illness and then a fire. It was a most tremendous blow for him that it ended as it did, for he was never in a position to undertake anything in the same class again. These years at Harrison River must have been the low point of his whole career.

At what stage in the development of the project Jim developed rheumatic fever is not very clear, but his illness forced him to withdraw from active management for some time and his convalescence was a long-drawn-out affair. No doubt he retained shares in the company, so it must have come as an appalling shock when the mill burned down in 1903 after running for only three and a half seasons. Jim and Arthur were not completely ruined by this debacle, but they did scale down their activities considerably for the next few years. They were to join forces one more time in the mining venture in the Queen Charlottes', but after this they were never again in a partnership together. When Jim logged for the Abbotsford mill, it was on a contract basis.

From the time of the mill fire onward Jim worked as an independent operator. His next move, after the Harrison Mills fiasco, was to buy 160 acres of land in a different part of the Fraser Valley altogether—a little settlement called Webster's Corners, in the pleasant rural community of Maple Ridge.[5]

As a lumberman, Jim viewed the district with an eye to the timber, which was still barely touched outside the central area. He had valuable timber on his own land, since only 15 acres was cleared at the time when he bought it, so he built a sawmill there and gradually logged off the property. He was able to locate his mill right beside a well-travelled road, for one of the great advantages of his quarter-section was that it had frontage on Dewdney Trunk Road, which was then the principal route through the northern part of the district. In the early days it was just a horse-logging operation, though later Jim invested in a steam donkey. His daughter Josephine used to have the job of firing the mill, which ran by steam.[6]

Like his brothers and sisters, Jim was a sociable person and one who had a strong sense of community. Every winter he and Libby would hold a party for their neighbours and other invited guests, who would come from all over the district, even as far away as Pitt Meadows. Most local gatherings relied solely on local talent to supply the entertainment—and there were many good singers and musicians in these country districts—but Jim would go to the trouble of hiring an orchestra to supply the music and make the party a real occasion. Jim was very musical himself and Libby was an excellent cook and a warm hostess, so these parties must have been just as enjoyable to them as they were to their guests.

As he gradually logged off the acreage, he began to sub-divide it, until he was left with only 37 acres. They were a close-knit family, so two of the lots went to his daughters, Mrs. Josephine Bowell and Mrs. Olive Hall and their husbands, who lived on the property for many years.[7]

As well as taking out the timber on his own land, Jim was doing contract logging for the Brunette Sawmill Company, which owned large tracts of forest in the Yennadon district on the north side of the South Alouette River, only a couple of miles from Jim's home. The company's sawmill was on the Fraser at New Westminster, so logs were sent down to the mill via the Alouette River at the time of the spring freshet. (It is hard to imagine logs being floated down the Alouette today, but the river was much deeper then.)

Even as late as the 1970s, longtime residents of Yennadon were able to point out the spot where the Trethewey log dump used to be—a deep part of the Alouette just east of Maple Ridge Park—as well as the line of the Trethewey skid road, which went straight up north into the bush from the log dump.

The old skid road had quite a story attached to it, and the Yennadon oldtimers were eager to tell it. It was a story that concerned the famous American train robber, Bill Miner. Half a mile up the skid road, hidden away in the bush, there had once been a little cabin. According to everybody's firm belief, this had been one of Miner's hideaways, which he had used while he was planning one of his raids. Many years after Bill Miner's time, some boys hiking up in the forest had rediscovered the little shack, and in it had made a most exciting find. When they peeled away the oilcloth that covered the built-in table, they found a wad of old newspapers, and after stripping these away too, they exposed a square wooden tube in which small objects could be stashed away—surely the perfect hiding-place for the loot from Miner's robberies! According to one version of the story, the boys had also had the thrill of finding a nickel-plated revolver inside this tube.[8]

Was there ever any confirmation of this legend? Unexpectedly, the story surfaced again in recent years from an independent source —Jim's son, Everett, who was by then in his ninety-seventh year. When Everett was a boy staying with his father at the logging camp, he had often met the occupant of the Yennadon cabin. He was quite under the impression that this man had been none other than the celebrated outlaw. Miner had been in the habit of asking Everett to do errands for him, like bringing vegetables and supplies to his cabin up the skid road. In return he had given Everett "shin-plasters"—the slang name for the old 25-cent bill. In spite of Miner's rather sordid record of crime, he was always able to make himself popular and agreeable in his rare spells in the ordinary community, and young Everett, like everybody else, had apparently found nothing disquieting in the personality of this man.[9]

After about ten years in Maple Ridge, Jim moved on again—this time to carry out logging contracts in Surrey. The Brunette Sawmill Company whom he had been logging for in Yennadon had some prime timber stands there, so it was probably because of Brunette that he went into this new area. First he logged around Craig (one of the stops on the B.C. Electric Railway) and later in Newton, where he put in one of the many logging railways which criss-crossed Surrey at this time. As one of the old-time loggers tells it, Jim's was not a fancy operation—just a short piece of trackage and a loco which was one of the very oldest and came from the east coast. He cut long timbers, possibly for scow bottoms.[10]

Jim and Libby never set up residence in Newton where he worked. Now in their early fifties, they had no desire to start homesteading all over again in the deep forest of Surrey. Instead they opted for the comforts of city life and a home just across the river in New Westminster, where they remained for the rest of their lives.

One rather puzzling aspect of Jim's association with Surrey concerns the controversial Green Timbers issue. This famous stand of prime timber was once one of the glories of the Surrey district, regarded with awe and admiration by every visitor who walked through its groves, but Brunette had the timber rights to it in the days before World War 1, and they planned to log it. They offered the contract to Jim Trethewey. What transpired between the two parties we do not know, but according to Jim's daughter Mildred, he turned it down because "there was something about the deal he did not like."

Looking into the background of Green Timbers history, it is easy to see that it would have required a considerable degree of indifference to public opinion to have taken a logging saw to these beautiful trees. Even as early as 1911, this square mile of splendid timber was so famous in the Lower Mainland that the Vancouver Board of Trade was already urging the government to preserve it as a park and a tourist attraction. With its tall trees soaring to a height of 200 feet— perfect timber, with beautiful long straight clean boles— this grand old piece of woodland seemed ideally suited as a place for the education and enjoyment of the public. It also had the advantage of being easily the most accessible stand of virgin forest left on the Lower Mainland. Given all this controversy, which mounted as the years went by, it would not be surprising if this was the reason for Jim not wanting to become involved.[11]

Jim's logging contracts in Surrey seem to have lasted for a period of about four or five years. Still contracting to the Brunette Sawmill Company, he spent the spring and summer of 1917 running a logging camp at Port Elizabeth on Guildford Island with his son-in-law, Jack Bowell.[12] Around this time too he worked with another son-in-law, William Hanna, logging on the north side of Harrison Bay, but for reasons unexplained this did not work out too well, and the partnership did not last long.

In the early 1920s Jim was logging up Harrison Lake with his son Everett, who had been working up here for a few years as manager of the Harrison Lake Logging Company Ltd. Everett went up to Alice Arm shortly after to work for his uncle Joe's new logging operation on the inlet, and Jim is believed to have spent some time there also. In general, it seems that he probably spent the 1920s chiefly in managing one or other of the Tiethewey logging camps or contracting for them.

But as the Abbotsford Lumber Company fell into difficult times on the onset of the Great Depression, its operations began to shrink drastically as one bad year followed another, and Jim was not able to count on the succession of work which had been so plentiful before. By now, of course, he was seventy years of age and it would not have been surprising if he had decided it was time to ease off, but either from choice or necessity he carried on almost as before. He spent the last working decade of his life logging in a small way around Harrison Bay and Lake Errock.

He built a small water-powered mill on the slope above Lake Errock. "Up the mountain behind the mill were little streams," says Kenneth McKellar, "and he had a wooden stave pipe running down to the mill. It tapered near the bottom, producing a lot of pressure, and the water came boiling out." The mill was equipped with an edger and a wood conveyor, and produced mostly short lengths for door stock. Logs were winched to the mill by steam donkey. Jim would stay in a cabin near the mill with two of the fallers during the working week, but get home to New Westminster for weekends.[13]

Retired loggers Stanley Browne and Kenneth McKellar, who worked for Jim at different times in these years, have nothing but praise for him both as an employer and as an individual. "He was a real gentleman," they say. "He was friendly, and he had a good sense of humour. His employees stayed with him for years." They remember him as a great perfectionist who demanded a high quality of work, but also as a person who inspired loyalty through his comradely attitude towards his employees. "I don't like to think of you as working *for* me; I like to think of us as all working *together*," he would tell his men, and he received their affection and respect accordingly.

After he finally retired from logging at the end of the 1930s, he did not retire from activity—he merely turned to a different sort of craft, which was essentially another aspect of his affinity to the life of the forest. He began to manufacture beautiful objects out of wood.

Every morning he would go into his workshop where he kept his lathe, and he would enjoyably spend his time at his hobby of woodwork, producing finely made wooden bowls, bracelets, buttons, canes, lampstands, and jewellery boxes, which he either sold or gave away. He donated the canes to the Shaughnessy hospital for veterans in Vancouver. With his high standards of workmanship James had considerable skills as a cabinetmaker also, and he produced several pieces of beautifully finished furniture. His daughter, Mildred, owned an intricate cabinet finished with diagonal inlays of maple and cherry, and other relatives were the fortunate recipients of some of his fine burl coffee tables.

His retirement years coincided with the period of the second World War, and it was Jim's great desire to live long enough to see this war come to an end. His wish was rather strangely fulfilled. On the morning of August 14, 1945, he heard the announcement of the final surrender of enemy forces in the Pacific: the world was finally at peace. Later that very same day he collapsed and died. [14]

At the time of his death he was eighty-five years of age, and had outlived all his brothers by nearly two decades. Jim and Libby had celebrated 65 years of a contented and understanding marriage only the previous year, and in the absence of this loving companionship life could never again have quite the same meaning for the surviving partner. Libby survived her husband by only six months, dying on March 28, 1946.

Their children were Olive, Muriel, Josephine, Mary Ann, Everett, Bertha, Mildred, and Gertrude, most of whom lived into their eighties and nineties. Muriel (Ella) died young at the age of 34.

END NOTES

1. Stanley Browne, retired logger, in conversation with Alan Trethewey and the author, 1992.
2. *Fraser Valley Record*, Mar.9, 1939.

3. Historical notes on the James E. Trethewey family, written by Donna Pound (Jim's grand-daughter) for a family reunion in 1989.
4. *B.C. Directory,* 1891.
5. Assessment rolls, Maple Ridge.
6. Kenneth McKellar, retired logger and husband of Jim's grand-daughter, in a telephone conversation with the author, 1993.
7. Assessment rolls, Maple Ridge.
8. Mary Legge, interview with the author, 1970.
   Edward Shoesmith, interview with the author, 1972.
9. Everett Trethewey, in conversation with Alan Trethewey, 1991.
10. McKellar conversation.
11. G. Fern Treleaven in *The Surrey Story,* 1970, suggests a subsequent Trethewey connection with Green Timbers twenty years later. He states that it was the Abbotsford Lumber Company that logged the last 200 acres in 1930, after placing advertisements in the papers and warning the public that it might regret its indifference in time to come (the government had refused to buy the land for a park.) I have been unable to trace these advertisements, and newspaper accounts all identify King-Farris as the logging company involved. The Trethewey family have never heard of any connection with Green Timbers in this later period.
12. *Western Lumberman,* June 1917, p.41.
13. Browne conversation.
14. Mildred Kitching, conversation with Alan Trethewey and the author, 1991.

15

The Two Sisters—
Elizabeth and Emma

Nineteenth-century women tend to be more nebulous figures in history than their male counterparts. Their entrepreneurial talents had less scope; their role in society depended very much on their husband's status and type of employment; and their views and personalities were seldom thought important enough to be recorded anywhere. This is certainly true of James and Mary Ann's daughters, Elizabeth and Emma. Their lives have faded into insignificance beside the bold, brash figures of the male Tretheweys. Though their brothers rose to prominence and left their mark on the history of British Columbia, the two sisters lived in relative obscurity and met with the usual fate of female anonymity. Stories about their lives are few, and even the bare facts are scanty.

What is very clear is that these two sisters could hardly have led more different lives. Emma's was a placid, predictable life, financially secure, domestically serene and successful; Elizabeth's life was deeply troubled, seldom free from financial anxiety and scarred by repeated disillusionment in her relationships with men.

They were both hardworking women, brought up in the same work ethic as their brothers during their childhood years in rural Muskoka. They were used to the frugalities of the pioneer life and they ungrudgingly put all their energies and enthusiasm into coping with similar conditions when the time came to marry. They demonstrated, in fact, all the characteristic Trethewey talent for organisation, especially in their maturer years.

Elizabeth, born in 1864, was the older of the two girls by seven years. Like the rest of the family she was expected to contribute to the family income as soon as she was past childhood. She was evidently clever with her needle and did sewing for some of the neighbourhood families, for the census of 1881, taken when she was just seventeen, gives her occupation as "seamstress".

She married just a few days after this census was taken. As was usually the case in these sparsely populated rural areas, her choice of partner was restricted to someone in the immediate neighbourhood (it was amazing that so many of these marriages turned out as well as they did), and Elizabeth's husband, Joseph Taylor, was almost certainly one of the Taylor family who had a large holding quite close to the Tretheweys. All we know of him is that he was born in England and he was nine years older than Elizabeth.[1]

Soon after Elizabeth's wedding, Mary Ann began planning the big move to join James in British Columbia, taking her younger children with her. Elizabeth was eager to go out west with the rest of her family, and her husband apparently was not averse to the idea at the time, so not long after they married, they became swept up in James's plans and joined the migration west.

They all spent the first year living in the Fraser Canyon, because this was where the job opportunities lay. The work of building the railroad was in full swing. Some of the Tretheweys found work cutting ties for the railroad, but Elizabeth's husband Joseph had a different expertise—he was a plasterer by trade, and he was able to make a living by doing any plastering required for the CPR stations on the new line.

Elizabeth was pregnant when she arrived in British Columbia, and she gave birth to her first child, Albert, in the spring of 1882. Two years later there was another baby to look after—James Edmund—but this did not prevent her from working with her husband as his assistant in the plastering business. Elizabeth did such things as mixing the plaster.[2]

Oddly enough, the year 1887 found her back in Ontario, where her third child, Paul, was born. We do not know whether Joseph had returned there for reasons of work, or whether he was, in fact, with her at all. However, they were both in British Columbia again by November of 1889 when Elizabeth's father made over to *her*—not to Joseph—two lots in Mission above the railway station (just where the main highway now curves round.) The object of this was for Elizabeth to build and operate a small hotel there, next door to Jim's and Libby's Ontario House.

Elizabeth ran this hotel, Albion House, for a matter of about four years, and it gave her some experience which—as her life painfully unfolded—was to be more valuable than she could ever have foreseen at the time. Joseph was still with her when the 1891 census was taken, and he was listed in the 1892 B.C. Directory too, but after this he vanishes from the picture. He deserted his wife and three little children, and returned to his old life in Ontario.[3]

What caused this rift nobody knows for certain. The only explanation ever suggested is the one which Elizabeth's nephew, Clarke Trethewey, puts forward in his notes on family history. According to Clarke, the couple eventually came to realise that they had a serious difference of viewpoint over the way they felt about pioneer life in the West. Elizabeth had adapted to her new life, she enjoyed British Columbia, and she wanted to stay with the rest of her family. Joseph, who was older, had a stronger attachment to Ontario and longed to return to the old life there. Neither would yield, so Joseph just walked out on his family and left. He later divorced Elizabeth. Curiously enough, many years later, he married the mother-in-law of his eldest son, Albert.

For a short time Elizabeth helped her mother as a nurse at Mary Ann's nursing-home in Mission,[4] but it was not long before another man came into her life. By the end of 1894, the pretty, thirty-year-old Elizabeth was married to a new husband by the name of McLeod, and in November 1895 she gave birth to her only daughter Violet.[5] But very soon things began to go wrong again: she discovered that she had married an alcoholic. It was not in her temperament to accept this sort of a life for herself and her children for very long, and quickly this marriage too ended in divorce.[6]

For the next two or three years it was a struggle to make a living.

Her grandson, Frank, believes that she was running a boarding-house in Vancouver during the late 1890s; his father, Paul, remembered standing on a street corner selling newspapers to bring in a few more dollars to the family exchequer. Then along came logger William Dolby (or Dalby).

Fair-haired, blue-eyed Elizabeth—far more vulnerable and impulsive than her tougher sister Emma—was still susceptible to masculine charm in spite of her disillusioning experiences, and still hopeful of achieving a happy married life. Rather precipitately, she once more plunged into matrimony, and towards the end of 1900 her last child Arthur was born.[7]

Her three oldest boys had now left home, and Jim and Paul were working at their uncles' sawmill at Harrison River. Elizabeth went with her husband and Violet and baby Arthur to the logging camp in the Port Moody-Coquitlam area where William Dolby worked. With her usual readiness to do her share, she became the camp cook. [8]

But once more, Elizabeth had made a dreadful mistake—the same mistake—for Dolby too turned out to be a heavy drinker who could not control his drinking, and once more she cut free from a bad marriage without lingering in the relationship in the unlikely hope of improving it. By the time of her father's death in 1906 she was living apart from Dolby on Keefer Street in Vancouver.

This was Elizabeth's last attempt to establish a traditional home life; from now on she was definitely on her own in bringing up her children and earning a living. What she did during the next few years is not known, but by 1919 she was living up at Ocean Falls, employed as the housekeeper in charge of the cleaning women at the big company hotel there.[9] She no doubt got the job through her son Jim, who worked as a log buyer for the Ocean Falls Company for several years.

She was not without support from the Trethewey family during hard times. Clarke believed that his father, Arthur, had helped her out from time to time, and he thought that Joe, who was always a generous man, would have done so too. Elizabeth's mother, Mary Ann, who lived with her on Keefer Street during the last two years of her life, left her all her investment income, such as shares in the

Providence mine, interests in the Harrison Mills company, and interests in mortgages. Besides this, nearly ten years later, when Joe died, she received the very substantial sum of $10,000. This must have enabled her to retire—she was by then sixty-three—and she spent the last few years of her life in California, probably to help her daughter Violet, who had become addicted to drugs, as Clarke Trethewey sadly records. Elizabeth died in 1932, and is buried in the Mount Pleasant cemetery in Vancouver near her parents and other relatives.

The younger sister Emma was unlike Elizabeth both in looks and temperament.[10] In contrast to Elizabeth's fair colouring, Emma had the brown eyes and darker brown hair of a different side of the family. In Emma's heavier looks one can see a hint of Mary Ann's directness and determination, more so than in Elizabeth's finer cast of features and more sensitive expression. Did James's imaginative and impulsive temperament find an echo perhaps in his daughter Elizabeth? Emma certainly seems to have inherited the very different qualities of her mother, Mary Ann: she was strict, religious, forceful and extremely capable, a woman very much in charge of her life and those around her.

Emma was not quite eleven when her mother came out with the younger children to live in British Columbia. From an early age she must have helped her mother in their little general store in Mission, and this is where she may have met her future husband, Richard Brett, when he came into town from Dewdney to do business. She may also have known him through her brothers Joe and Sam, who were farming on Nicomen Island on homesteads not very far from Richard's.

Like her sister, Emma married at the age of seventeen and, like her sister, married a man nine years older than herself. Richard Brett had settled on his land in 1885,[11] so his farm would have been reasonably well established when Emma came there four years later to be his wife. Like the other settlers, he went in for mixed farming. In 1893, when he wrote a few notes for a government agricultural report, he mentioned that he was growing crops as well as raising cattle and hogs. He was contending with the usual problems that farmers have to deal with: he said that he had lost 14 hogs to disease, and that the skunks, racoons and wild cats were constant pests (the skunks and racoons in this district still are!)

Emma lived in the Mission area longer than any others of her family, but when her brothers wanted to dispose of the Elk Creek sawmill, she and Richard took advantage of their offer and moved to the Chilliwack district, where they stayed the rest of their lives. When the Jim Trethewey family left Chilliwack for Harrison River in April 1900, the Bretts moved into Jim's and Libby's house on Prairie Central Road.[12]

Richard and Emma still continued to farm now that they lived in Chilliwack, but now they also had the sawmill as an extra source of income. They did their own logging on a small scale up the mountain behind the mill—probably horse-logging, said Emma's daughter in later years—and they kept the sawmill running for a matter of ten years or so, even replacing the old mill machinery in 1906.[13] No one else operated there after Richard, and the machinery was sold to E.C. Eckert. As for the grist mill, it was seldom used after James senior moved to Vancouver, except to oblige a few local farmers[14]

The Bretts developed their land into a prosperous dairy farm, de-scribed as "one of the choicest in the valley", and Emma led the hardworking life that any farmer's wife in pioneering days would have to assume. Besides doing her expected part in all this, she took on an extra job as well, delivering mail. The post office which was es-tablished at Elk Creek in 1908 was located in some little nook in the Brett home on Prairie Central Road, and Richard was appointed postmaster. But although her husband had the official appointment, very often it was Emma who did the hauling and faithfully made the rounds regardless of the weather. Between them, she and Richard looked after postal services until 1913 when the Elk Creek post office was shut down altogether.[15]

Of the two of them, Emma was undoubtedly the more forceful partner, while Richard was known to be of "a retiring and modest disposition". Still, this did not prevent him from living up to his obligations in the life of the community. He was a member of the Chilliwack municipal council for over five years as well as being a school trustee, and his opinions and character won general respect. A series of strokes eventually slowed him down and put an end to public life. He was obliged to give up the farm on account of his health, and in 1925 a final stroke was responsible for his death at the age of sixty-two.[16]

Emma lived on for another thirty-three years, busy and capable as ever. At weekends she would often organise family picnics or berry-picking expeditions, which were happy and enjoyable outings for her numerous grandchildren. Always on these expeditions Emma would be wearing her special apron with a rock pick in one pocket and a bag for rock samples in the other, for, like all the rest of James's offspring, she was an avid prospector at heart. She was always on the look-out for some rich vein that "looked promising", and was probably very knowledgeable about ores and mineralogy. Apparently she never took her interest any further than this, but her son Enos did own a gold mine in Ontario.[17]

Emma's grand-daughter, Elaine Mitten, tells one amusing story, which perfectly illustrates Emma's instinct for action and optimism in time of crisis. The incident occurred in 1935. Emma's son Earl was flying back from eastern Canada with a new plane and had given the family his expected time of arrival in Vancouver. They waited to receive his phone call, but the hours went by, and even allowing for bad weather or other hold-ups, the fact had to be faced that Earl was well overdue. Everyone sat there worrying, but Emma knew she must take some sort of action to remedy the situation. What could she do? She would see her fortune-teller.

She promptly put on her best clothes and went off across the river to visit Mrs. Spinks, described by Elaine as "fortune-teller, seer, tea-cup reader and card reader extraordinaire". The sitting went well. Mrs. Spinks took Emma's hands, gazed into her eyes, and said: "Do not worry, my friend. Your son is walking in rough terrain amid odd-shaped mounds and peaks. I can see railway tracks. He and his friend are safe. You will hear soon." Emma felt better: she had dealt with the situation. As it turned out, all went exactly as predicted. Earl and his friend did manage to walk out of the bush after making a forced landing in Montana, and they did actually reach a railway, just as foretold by Mrs. Spinks. He was able to telephone his mother to reassure her the very next day.[18]

Sadly, Emma did lose two sons, Roy and Enos, to aeroplane crashes. She had lost her first two children in infancy, and only one son, Earl, and a daughter, Beatrice, survived her when she died in 1958. Emma spent the last eighteen years of her life living with Beatrice in her home in Chilliwack, active almost to the last.

Emma remained a formidable character right into old age. "Grandma Brett was such a strict Methodist that drinking, card playing, dancing or betting was a sin, so she never allowed it in her house," recalls Elaine Mitten. (Emma must have been horrified by the life-style of her brother Joe!) Elaine tells how the whole family would rush around "like crazy persons" hiding any beer bottle or sign of liquor in the house before their grandmother came for a visit. In reality Elaine's family hardly drank at all, but they knew that the mere thought of it would send Emma into a state of shock. "She would give everyone a horrible lecture and make everyone uncomfortable. That was her way, she couldn't just ignore it."[19]

Right into her eighties Emma was still driving her car in her usual vigorous style. She was still occupying herself with her usual church work and organisations such as the Orange Lodge and Rebekah Lodge.[20] She died at the age of eighty-seven, the last survivor of all the remarkable children of James and Mary Ann.

END NOTES

1. Census, 1891, New Westminster District, No.14, Mission area.
2. Frank Taylor, Elizabeth's grandson, in conversation with Alan Trethewey and the author, 1992.
3. Taylor conversation.
4. B.C. Directory, 1894.
5. Census, 1901, Vancouver, Sub. Dist. 2, p.6.
6. Clarke Trethewey, historical notes.
7. Census, 1901 (see end note 5.)
8. Ibid.
9. Taylor conversation.
10. Ibid.
11. Land assignments, GR436, Carton 47, Provincial Archives of B.C.

12. *Chilliwack Progress,* Apr.25, 1900.
13. Ibid, Feb.7, 1906.
14. Beatrice Walker (née Brett), taped interview with Lilly Tyzio & Shirley Gronich, 1980. Chilliwack Archives.
15. Cecil Coutts, *Cancelled with Pride,* Cecil C. Coutts Publishing, 1993.
16. *Chilliwack Progress,* Dec.2, 1925.
17. Elaine Mitten, *Oh Dem Golden Slippers,* Chilliwack, 1994, p.75.
18. Ibid, p.47.
19. Ibid, p.194.
20. *Chilliwack Progress,* Dec.10, 1952.

16

The Depression Years:
Edgar Carries on

After the fast-paced, almost frenetic, rate of achievement during the first thirty years of the 20th century came a lull in the advance of Trethewey ambitions. Four of the five brothers were now dead, and the last survivor was into his seventies. With these larger-than-life figures no longer bestriding the scene, the next generation lacked the colourful aura and the confident gusto that had characterised the Trethewey image for so many years. They had little chance to develop any such persona either, for confronting them was the Great Depression.

The Coniagas fortune had been widely dispersed after Joe's death in 1927, for although he had died a wealthy man, he had left a large family of seven children for his money to be divided among. Besides this, the trustees of his estate had been obliged to sell many of his assets—particularly his timber limits—at the most unfavourable time, during the 1930s. Had the Vancouver Island timber been retained another couple of decades, it would have had a truly staggering value. As it was, his heirs were not left in a position of immense wealth.

Of the three sons who might have taken on the mantle of leadership, Edgar was the only one capable of handling the business responsibilities. His older brother William suffered from an emotional or mental fragility which made him unable to cope with ordinary life, though he is said to have been of a studious turn of mind, an academic who shut himself away with his books.[1] As for Joe's adopted son Joey, a wild youth, he was still a minor at the time of Joe's death. Everything had to devolve upon Edgar, alien as this may have been to his natural temperament.

Father and son could hardly have been more different in their approach to life. Edgar was quiet and mild in manner, Joe loud and flamboyant; Edgar was non-drinking, Joe enjoyed his liquor and gambling in uninhibited fashion; Edgar was happy with solitary pursuits, such as his lapidary hobby in later years, while Joe spent his life restlessly pursuing one new business interest after another.

Not that Edgar was by any means a dull and serious character. He enjoyed dancing and playing the violin, and his photograph as a young man shows a humorous twist to the mouth and a kindly look in the eyes. His son Alan writes: "Dad was a very tender, honest and hardworking man. I never heard him raise his voice in anger or speak badly of anyone. He lived by high standards."

Although Edgar was one of a family of four surviving children, he had been brought up as an only child in the home of elderly people. After his mother's tragic death the whole family had been split up, and he and his brother and two sisters sent to live in different foster homes. Edgar, who was only one month old when his mother died, did not have even any residual memory of life in a family of other children, for he was cared for by his uncle Jim Trethewey's parents-in-law, the Springs, who were more like grandparents to him than parents. [2]

Albert Spring was sixty-five and Jane sixty at the time when they undertook to raise Edgar. Rather strangely, they had chosen to live far from the rest of their family in one of the most isolated parts of Maple Ridge—at the northwest edge of Yennadon, cut off from the rest of the community by the swamps of Sturgeon Slough. The nearest school for Edgar at that time was a 4-mile walk away.

It was probably a staid and sober upbringing for a young child. Kindly as they must have been to think of rearing an infant, the Springs were very much guided by strict Presbyterian principles. We are told that many Yennadon families of that era regarded even a friendly game of cards as a sinful sort of pastime,[3] and Albert, being an elder of the local Presbyterian church, probably concurred in these views.[4] Both he and his wife were beginning to show their age as the 1890s dawned, and in April 1894 Albert passed away.

What happened to Edgar after this is not very clear. Jane Spring was "well up in years and frail", according to one account, and she decided to move out to Dewdney to be near her son Isaac.[5] It would seem likely that the nine-year-old Edgar went with her. However, by the time of the 1901 census, he and his brother and sisters were all back with their father Joe, who had now married again and was living on his farm in Richmond.

According to family tradition Edgar worked for a living from the age of thirteen or fourteen onward, just as all his cousins—the Tretheweys, Bretts and Taylors—were expected to do. Very likely he was given a job at the Trethewey logging camp on Harrison Lake while his uncles Jim and Arthur were running the sawmill at Harrison River. Edgar could hardly have foreseen then how much of his life would be spent up in the watershed of the Harrison, nor even pictured himself then as the future owner of a large logging company. Far from it—his interest as a young man seems to have been in farming.

By the age of twenty-two, in fact, Edgar had his own farm to manage. It was in Maple Ridge, and it must have had strong sentimental associations for him, for it was close to the only real home he had known as a child when he lived there with the Springs. The South Alouette River meandered gently through his land, whose level acres—one day to be cultivated fields—lay spread below the twin pinnacles of the Golden Ears mountains. It was then mostly a tangle of scrubby bush and the pink-plumed hardhack, with only a few acres cleared by the previous owners, the Dales.[6]

Edgar must have been very much enthused at the time, because in 1907 he went off to take courses at the Ontario Agricultural College in Guelph. Academically, his two years there were of little value. He soon realised that his few years of education at a small country school had been completely inadequate as a preparation for these theoretical courses, for his marks in the Christmas exams went as low as 3 out of 100 in Botany and rose to only 48 out of a 100 even in his best subject, Animal Husbandry. His standing at the end of his first year was 114th out of 116, and in his second year 81st out of 88. He failed several courses and left without qualifying for the Associate Diploma which was normally the end-product of the first two years.[7] As is the case with many other successful people, his examination results did not reflect his true ability, for he went on to become a respected figure in the lumber industry and a recognised expert among lapidary hobbyists.

Undeterred by this lack of academic success, he went back to the farm and started to bring more of it under cultivation. Although it was basically good soil, built up from fertile river silt, it needed clearing and draining, and this he did with the help of Chinese labourers working with wheelbarrow and shovel.[8] As the assessment records show, the next five years saw another 20 acres laboriously brought into cultivation by this method.

But after his father bought the Chilco Ranch in 1910, Edgar spent most of his time in the Chilcotin, as a manager of the ranch. One of the biggest projects he oversaw was the construction of the huge irrigation system which Joe needed in order to maximise his vast acreage. This irrigation ditch extended over a distance of 20 miles, from Big Creek to the Chilco Ranch, and took several years to complete.[9]

He entered into the social life of the district and he visited the homes of the neighbouring ranchers—particularly, as time went by, the Church family at Big Creek. Of the four lovely daughters of Herbert Church (all of whom acted as a magnet to the eligible bachelors of the district), it was Margaret who attracted Edgar's attention as she grew up. The understanding between them developed slowly, for she was ten years younger than he was, and even then they did not exactly rush into matrimony, for he was thirty-four and she was twenty-four when the wedding took place in 1921.

Their first home together was on Edgar's Maple Ridge farm, which they called Coniagas, after the celebrated silver mine. According to one relative, the young couple also had another name for their abode—Sinners' Roost. This was possibly in reference to the weekend dances they would sometimes hold (surely quite innocuous affairs in reality, especially as she and he were both non-drinkers!)[10]

Joe seems to have been very much in control of Edgar's life even after his marriage. Having worked for his father at the Chilco Ranch for several years while this was Joe's big interest, Edgar continued to be his father's righthand man even after Joe sold the ranch and came to Abbotsford to take charge of the sawmill. Joe had suddenly become excited by some interesting mineral prospects up the northern coast, which was his chief pre-occupation with the area, but at the same time he also planned to make a paying proposition of it in the form of a logging operation. He needed a manager to oversee the logging, so Edgar was despatched to this rather dreary spot to look after the business for his father.

Coniagas remained Edgar's and Margaret's home base from 1921 to 1927, but from 1923 onwards they were both spending a good part of the year at the new logging camp at Alice Arm. Huddled in the mountains a 100 miles north of Prince Rupert, Alice Arm was a primitive little mining town which had suddenly come into existence to service the famous Dolly Varden silver mines ten years earlier. It lay at the end of a rain-soaked inlet, overhung by high mountain ranges. At the 55° latitude it was cool and damp even in summer, and was altogether not the most prepossessing of places to live in.

Just the same, Margaret joined him at Alice Arm soon after the first baby, Richard, was born, and stayed there with Edgar for much of the time, though they both spent some winters back at the Coniagas farm.[11] However, their next two children, Alan and Bill, were both born up here in the primitive surroundings of northern British Columbia. Surprisingly, there was a hospital on this remote inlet, at the small copper-smelting town of Anyox 18 miles away, and this was where Margaret went for the births.

But their quiet life at Alice Arm ended abruptly with Joe's death. The logging operation was winding down at that point. Most of the timber had already been cut by the end of 1925, but Joe still had booms in the water, so Edgar spent 1926 in shipping these out. The mining claims were still active, and Joe was constantly travelling up there himself to keep a personal eye on developments. But in 1927 Joe became ill with cancer, and Edgar must have realised that the time was coming when he himself would have to take over the heavy responsibility of his father's complex business interests.

The year 1927 saw Edgar and Margaret still at Alice Arm, but this was their last season. In the early autumn the call came to return urgently to Abbotsford, for Joe was sinking fast. They arrived in early October. Before the end of the month Joe was dead, and Edgar had inherited all his business responsibilities.

Joe's death meant big changes in Edgar's and Margaret's lives. They immediately moved to a house in Abbotsford to live near the mill, but Edgar was too attached to his farm in Maple Ridge to want to sell, so for the next twelve years they leased it out to a series of other families. Edgar was at once appointed president of the Abbotsford Lumber, Mining and Development Company. The mineral explorations which had appealed so strongly to his father did not have the same interest for Edgar, and he decided to restrict operations to lumbering only, so a total re-organisation of the company occupied most of the year that followed. Finally, on December 29, 1928, it was reincorporated as the Abbotsford Lumber Company (the name the original mill-owners had used a quarter of a century before.)

Unfortunately for Edgar, he took over at the beginning of the most difficult years in the history of the company. The timber around Abbotsford was almost exhausted, and it was obvious that the mill could not go on in this location much longer: it was no secret to the Abbotsford community that its major industry would soon be lost to the district. It was not an immediate concern, for Joe had had the good sense to buy up several small pieces of woodland between 1925 and 1927, which at least gave Edgar some breathing-space to consider his next move. At this point he took it for granted that in the near future he would be building a new mill. Certainly he never contemplated being without a mill: it was merely a question of finding the right location. But before this decision became urgent, external circumstances took matters out of his hands, for he was faced with the grim emergency of the Depression.

The Wall Street crash of October 1929 hit the lumber industry almost immediately. By June of 1930 the Abbotsford Lumber Company was reported to be struggling, and by July it was forced to

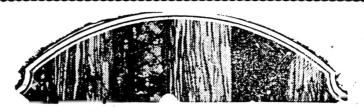

Advertisement in the Abbotsford-Sumas-Matsqui News, April 25, 1928.

make heavy lay-offs. This measure must have been adopted with the greatest reluctance by a company that had always prided itself on looking after its workers. When it came to the crunch, it was the Asian workers who were first dismissed—all of the 40 or 50 men. In those days the town would have been outraged had the mill done anything else. Edgar cannot have been very happy at having to make such a choice, in view of the good relationship which had always existed between his family and the Asian community, but public opinion undoubtedly favoured the decision.

"The Abbotsford Mill has set a worthy example," lauded the local paper. "Would the hundreds of other lumber operators in this province follow the example of the Abbotsford Lumber Company, probably unemployment and consequent privation would not face the white mill hands of B.C. in this period of industrial depression."[12]

In spite of these cut-backs 1931 and 1932 were no better. However much Edgar might have wished to support the economy of the town, he had no choice now but to shut down the mill at the end of 1932 and sell off the machinery, as well as disposing of all his logged-off land around the district. All that remained of the busy Abbots-

Carefully-Milled Lumber and Shingles

Are an important requisite of structural workmanship, and are undoubtedly well preference. Labor cost is lower, and your buildings are more durable and permanent. For 20 years the Abbotsford mill has maintained High Quality—and does today.

ABBOTSFORD LUMBER COMPANY, LIMITED

EDGAR J. TRETHEWEY, Pres.   A. VAN PUYENBROEK, Secretary.

Advertisement in the Abbotsford-Sumas-Matsqui News, May 29, 1929.

ford operation was the lumber yard in town, which carried on for another forty years.[13]

Even in 1931, Edgar had still not ruled out the idea of building a new mill. Though he was reported to be looking at several different alternatives, he was reluctant to move out of the Fraser Valley with all its family associations. Surprisingly, the location he was considering the most seriously was only a few miles away from the old mill, but in Matsqui municipality beside the river and just west of the Mission bridge. He even had tentative plans drawn up for this site,[14] but a realistic look at circumstances forced him to think better of the idea. Mills were shutting down everywhere, and until the economic climate improved, Edgar decided he would have to limit himself to logging on a retail basis only.

Debating where to acquire new timber limits, he found his thoughts returning to the familiar setting of the Harrison Lake forest district, which he knew so well and which his family had been linked with for nearly forty years. Brooks-Scanlon had owned the extensive timber limits at the head of Harrison Lake for the past twenty years and had once had ambitious plans, but apparently they had not been active there for some time. They were willing to sell, and for a figure of $35,000.00 Edgar became the owner of the entire timber holdings of Brooks-Scanlon—beautiful stands of prime timber on either side of the Lillooet River as far as the north end of Lillooet Lake. This amounted to 250 million board feet of timber. [15]

Unfortunately, the tough times of the Depression years forced Edgar's company to let go four-fifths of this purchase. The Lillooet Lake holdings went to Peter Bain of Whonnock, and some of the timber on the west side of the river was let go for taxes, but in the end Edgar was still left with a sizable 50 million board feet of standing timber. It was at about this time that he formed the new company, Trethewey Logging, as a companion company to the Abbotsford Lumber Company which operated the lumber yard.

For a couple of years he leased a shingle mill—the big Harrison Bay shingle mill at the mouth of the Harrison River—but this only led to more problems, which ended up as a court case. In August 1933 a fire had broken out and destroyed the kilns and the drying-sheds as well as 3 million shingles, though luckily the mill itself was saved. The owner, G.W. Beach—a difficult character at the best of times—sued Edgar for negligence. Luckily for Edgar, he was able to prove that he had observed all the usual fire precautions, since the markers on the water barrels were all at the bottom, showing that they had been full and ready for use, as required by their agreement. The case ended favorably for Edgar. [16]

Edgar's logging started off at the head of Harrison Lake in 1933, though he did not begin major logging until the 1934 season. He organised it as a river drive, floating logs down the Lillooet River into a catch-basin at the mouth. It was important to make the catching-boom extremely secure, because of the violent winds that tore down the lake between the mountains, so he took every precaution. He had the area enclosed with bundles of enormous timbers, 180 feet in length, and bound together with heavy cable. These were held in place with massive crib anchors, 14 feet square and 14 feet high, filled with rocks and tied with cables. Yet in a really bad storm all this would break loose as if it were matchwood, and logs would scatter all over the lake, mixed up with driftwood and debris. This would involve countless hours of work in sorting through the huge entanglement of timber and extricating each individual log.

As his crews worked their way farther up the Lillooet, Edgar ran into greater difficulties with the river drive. The Lillooet was a twisting and turning stream, treacherous with snags and roots, and islanded with a maze of sand bars where logs could run aground, so that as the distance grew, his crews were having to spend increasing amounts of time in unblocking log jams that resulted. Edgar attempted to cope with this problem in a novel way by putting a tractor in the water to shift the logs that had got stuck. "A river-going tractor is news even in this fast-moving age of machinery," declared the *Abbotsford Sumas Matsqui News* in 1939.

It must have been an impressive sight to see this cumbersome machine labouring in the fast-flowing stream, but it was a method that would only work in shallow water. In deeper water the crews used donkey engines on the bank and a cable across the river. The work of stringing the line from the donkey engines was given to the natives of the Douglas and Skookumchuk areas, because they were so extremely deft at handling the canoes in turbulent water. Their technique was to use poles to edge along the sides of the river, but to change to paddles as soon as they needed to get into mid-stream and manoeuvre about, while taking the line across. They never wore life-jackets; they could not swim; yet they never once had an accident.[17]

From the early 1930s onward Edgar was rarely at home. He lived up at the logging camp on the Lillooet, managing the operation but sharing in all the hardships of life in the woods. "He worked actively in the bush, never afraid to do the lowliest job or the toughest," says Alan. "Tent camps were the norm and mosquitoes were in absolutely the greatest abundance. Many working men wore mosquito netting over their hats and covering their faces." The only times his children remember him coming home were when he had business dealings in Vancouver—but this, of course, was the normal Trethewey way of life, in the tradition of his grandfather, his father and his uncles

Finally the Depression eased and by the end of the 1930s Edgar was in a position to make more choices about his business future. In his own mind, Edgar had always seen himself as a mill-owner. He had regarded these last five or six years of retail logging purely as a temporary expedient before resuming a sawmill operation at some new site. The Tretheweys had always run mills as far back as Edgar's memory went, and he intended to continue in the family tradition. In about 1940 he went into partnership with an associate named Bob Simpson and built a new sawmill on Mitchell Island in Vancouver. With a capacity of about 75,000 board feet a day, it was comparable in size to the Tretheweys' former mill at Abbotsford. Bob financed the mill building and Edgar threw in the timber. It ran as a joint project for about five years, but finally Edgar decided to phase out some of his business activities, and he withdrew from the partnership. Bob Simpson then kept the mill and Edgar took back the timber.[18]

After Edgar turned sixty in 1946, his thoughts began to turn to retirement and the prospect of some leisure pursuits. His business was still divided into two companies: the Abbotsford Lumber Company and the Trethewey Logging Company. His three eldest sons were only just over twenty, but Edgar must have had confidence in their ability, for he now handed over the Abbotsford Lumber retail outlet to Alan and Bill, 49 percent to Alan, 48 percent to Bill and 3 percent still left with Edgar.

What was to be done with the logging company? The oldest son, Richard, was not available, as he was making the Air Force his career; Alan and Bill were fully occupied with the lumber yard; and J.O. was too young to take it on. In the end in 1947 Edgar arranged to sell it to his younger cousin Leslie Trethewey (Arthur's son) and a partner named David Harding, with the agreement that they did not have to make a payment on the purchase price until 1949. It was a deal that was never completed, for, as it turned out, the market for logs was so poor in this period that when the two years were up, Leslie was obliged to bow out. The camp sat idle for a year.

Then in 1950 a crisis arose. A competitor applied to the government for an auction of the timber right in the Port Douglas area, and Edgar feared that if the timber went to another company, it would destroy his own position in the Lillooet Valley and probably mean the end of his own logging operation. The family rallied round to save the company. Alan eagerly agreed to step in and head Trethewey Logging with 50 percent of the shares, while Richard and J.O. were to be silent partners with 25 percent each. (J.O. later exchanged his shares for Alan's interest in the Abbotsford Lumber Company.) The plan worked: Edgar bought the timber for double the upset price, Alan moved into the Port Douglas camp, and Trethewey Logging was in business once again.[19]

Now that he had some leisure time, Edgar was able to indulge in his favourite hobby of rock collecting and lapidary work. He had always been knowledgeable in mineralogy and geology—surely no Trethewey could be otherwise, certainly not a son of Joe's—and had always enjoyed heading off into the bush on a rock-hunting expedition whenever he could spare the time. Now he was free to explore the province at leisure for any rare specimen of rock he wanted to collect, and he was at his happiest on these solitary wilderness trips, prospecting up in the hills on some rugged mountain trail. "He would arrive home with his camper straining at the axles, his family wondering at the superhuman efforts required to load the beloved rocks," remembered his daughter-in-law, Lois.

Back home from these trips, Edgar spent many happy hours in the special workshop he had built to contain his collection. Most of his evenings were spent in cutting and polishing the beautiful specimens he had obtained. Eventually he had the idea of making pictures sculpted out of the brilliantly hued rocks, and the artistic side of his nature began to find expression in these wonderful three-dimensional landscapes, rich in subtle colour harmonies and full of strange depths and reflections—their glittering waterfalls, snowy peaks and mossy crags all inspired by the natural variations and striations of the rock itself. His most ambitious work was a massive picture which measured a full 39 by 27 inches, had a thickness of 10 inches, and weighed perhaps 90 pounds. He gave this to the Matsqui-Sumas-Abbotsford Historical Society, where it has been displayed from time to time in their museum.

"Dad loved to play chess," adds his son Alan. "After he retired, he would often spend all day with his best buddy over the table, but would always be home at dinner time."

Edgar was fortunate in having many years of retirement in which to develop his leisure interests, and he was eighty-two when he died in early 1969. His quiet, gentle, unpretentious character was respected by all those who knew him, and more than one person has summed up his qualities with the words: "Edgar was a real gentleman."

END NOTES

1. Cora Trethewey, interview with a representative of the Matsqui Sumas Abbotsford Historical Society, 1982.
2. Census, 1891, Maple Ridge area.
3. Bertha Roberts (née McDonald), interview with the author, 1971.
4. *Maple Ridge Gazette*, Centennial issue, ? 1958.
5. Land records and agent's notes, GR436, 9998 BCL, Carton 50, p.0065, Provincial Archives of B.C.
6. Ibid, GR436, Box 78, 3287.
7. Examination Record, Ontario Agricultural College, Guelph, 1907 & 1908.
8. Margaret Trethewey, interview with the author, 1972.
9. Information from Bill Trethewey.
10. Mildred Kitching (née Trethewey), conversation with Alan Trethewey and the author, 1991.
11. Various references in the *Alice Arm & Anyox Herald*.
12. *Abbotsford-Sumas-Matsqui News*, July 9, 1930.
13. Ibid, Nov.2, 1932.
14. Ibid, May, 1931.
15. Information from Alan Trethewey.
16. *ASM News*, June 7 & Aug.30, 1933; Feb.13, 1935. Information from Alan Trethewey.
17. Information from Alan Trethewey.
18. Ibid.
19. Ibid.

17

Margaret, a Pioneer in B.C. Horsemanship

To most of the residents of Maple Ridge, Margaret Trethewey had a much higher profile than her husband. Anyone who rode a horse was familiar with the name of "Mrs. T", as she was fondly (and respectfully) known. Edgar did not enter into community life to any extent, and in any case his business kept him away at the logging camp for most of the time. Margaret, on the other hand, quickly surfaced as a community leader in any district in which she lived. First in Abbotsford, and then in Maple Ridge, she made a name for herself in organising sports for young people. Eventually, her name would become known throughout the province, and in other parts of Canada too, as one of the outstanding pioneers of British Columbian equestrian sports.

Her love of horses went back to her childhood days in the Chilcotin. Always there had been horses in her life, growing up on the Big Creek Ranch, and she could not remember the time before she was confidently riding her first pony. All of the children had learned to ride bareback, as her father thought this was safer for them when they fell. Soon they were "first rate riders", he wrote in his memoirs. As they grew up, they all had their own horses—at least two horses each.[1]

Where her father had got his love of horses from, no one knew. The Churches were an English family of scholars and artists, and it must have come as the greatest shock to the senior Church (a university professor) when his two teenage sons came to him and broke the news that they wanted to go out west and live the cowboy life. At that point they had never ridden a horse in their lives! Riding lessons were quickly arranged, and before long Herbert Church and his brother were on their way to the new life in Canada.

"Before leaving the Old Country one had the notion that riding the range after horses or cattle would be all fun and sport," he admitted later. But though Herbert's visions of a pleasant, easy life had been swiftly dispelled, the realities of pioneer life had not deterred him. He had applied himself determinedly to learning the ranching business, and he had gone on to create his own ranch in Alberta from land that had never been farmed before. At the same time he used every opportunity to enjoy outdoor sports (passing this enthusiasm on to his children too), and somehow found time for cricket and tennis and polo in the midst of his hardworking life. Horses remained his great love, and he had found a way of indulging this interest by creating a sideline in horse-breeding and training, and had acquired a considerable reputation for his expertise.

Margaret (or Madge, as she was known in the family) was born in 1897, while the family was still living on their ranch south of Calgary. She was only six when the family moved to the Chilcotin, and all her childhood memories were of life on the Big Creek Ranch in isolated wilderness conditions. Once again her father was creating a ranch completely from scratch. The only road into the property was an Indian trail just wide enough for a wagon to edge through. The nearest family was two miles away, the nearest doctor 90 miles away. In winter the temperature was sometimes 40° F below zero.

Until Margaret was about ten years old she must have been taught at home, for the little log schoolhouse at Big Creek did not open until January 1908. Basically it was just for the benefit of the two large local families, and when these children grew up, the school had to close for lack of numbers. Margaret, who was eighteen by that time, taught the youngest children at home for a while, though later they went to private schools in Victoria and Yale.

Margaret had known her future husband since she was thirteen years old, ever since Edgar's father had bought the Chilco Ranch at Hanceville in 1910. The two ranches being only 20 miles apart, their families must have been acquainted as neighbours right from the start. Edgar and Madge must have played tennis together, attended the big annual event of the Riske Creek horse races, and met at social gatherings at the homes of local ranchers for several years before she was old enough to think of romance.

When Edgar Trethewey stood at the altar with Margaret Church on a wintry February day in 1921,[2] it was a union of two outstanding families. Each of these families was distinctive in its own way. By now the Trethewey name was well known in lumbering and mining circles. Joe, in particular, had a high profile. "Mr. Trethewey is one of the best-known mining and ranching men in British Columbia", commented the *Ashcroft Journal* in 1922.

But Margaret's family too brought exceptional qualities to the marriage. The Churches, who had come from a privileged background of education and social standing in their English origins, were from a line of intellectuals and academics. Her father, Herbert, besides being a well-known Chilcotin rancher, was an occasional newspaper contributor and later the author of a lively book about his pioneering days. The cultural gifts of the Churches and the business acumen of the Tretheweys were to make as fortunate a combination in this marriage as the qualities of the Tretheweys and the Ogles had done nearly seventy years before.

The two families could hardly have been more different in background, education and inherited traditions. "The Tretheweys were rough, hardworking men," says one acquaintance who remembers this generation. Joe, moreover, had quite a reputation for fast living. The Churches, on the other hand, had a circle of acquaintances drawn largely from the upper-class English families who had ranches in the Chilcotin. Back in the Old Country, in the days when Edgar's ancestor, Samuel Trethewey, was at work in the lead mines coping with faulty engines and flooded soughs, Margaret's grandfather and great-uncle were preparing for their college years amid the "dreaming spires" of Oxford University. At the time when Samuel was hacking pathways in the Muskoka forest, Alfred and Arthur Church were enjoying a scholarly life as lecturers and researchers at their English colleges.

Nevertheless, in the pioneer life in Canada, both Edgar's father and Margaret's father had had to face the same sort of hardships while getting established. Margaret and the other children had grown up accustomed to milking cows and helping with farm chores and coping with wilderness conditions. Different as their antecedents may have been, in their immediate background she and Edgar shared the same practicality of outlook and the capacity for putting their best efforts into anything they set out to do.

It was just as well that Margaret had so much capability and strength of character (she was, in fact, a much tougher and stronger character than the gentle Edgar), for she had to manage everything at home and bring up five energetic children virtually singlehanded. She soon showed herself to be a born organiser and a person who made things happen.

Abbotsford seemed to her, as her children grew older, a place lacking in healthy social activities for young people, so she decided to do something about it. She started a badminton club. This was an immediate hit with the youth of Abbotsford—"It transformed life in Abbotsford for us," says Alan's wife Vivian, one of her early players. But for Margaret Trethewey it was never enough just to have a bit of half-hearted fun. You had to excel. Spurred on by her determined coaching, her players soon made a high standing in provincial tournament events, and were surprised to find themselves winning large numbers of prizes and trophies.[3] Her sons Richard, Alan and Bill became top players. Alan had outstanding ability, though his mother made him practise so hard that one onlooker became quite concerned: "I thought he was going to drop from exhaustion!" He was at one time the under-fifteen champion of British Columbia.

Besides organising the badminton club, Margaret also taught tennis—they had had a tennis court at the Big Creek Ranch—and she was, in fact, responsible for getting the clay tennis courts built at Abbotsford. (She was later to do the same thing in Maple Ridge.) As well, she started a children's garden club. The youthful gardeners were divided into different age groups and had to keep gardens that were regularly inspected. Here again, the competitive element was a strong factor, and the children were expected to work hard at their projects and exhibit the results at agricultural shows. [4]

Margaret herself won prizes for her flowers and her needlework at these shows. Her creative ability also found an outlet in wood-carving, in which—being Margaret—she developed considerable skill and achieved beautiful results. To help to put her children through private school, she decided to put her talents to profitable use and sell her output. One of the Trethewey relations found her very early one day on her way to the market in New Westminster with her smocking and her preserves. "Madge, why are you doing all this?" she asked. "Well, Edgar can't give me all the money I need for their schooling," she replied. According to this source, Margaret undertook to supply the school with huge amounts of canned corn and other produce in a type of barter arrangement towards tuition fees.

By the end of the 1930s Margaret was becoming concerned over the problem of how best to direct the lively energies of her three teen-age boys. Abbotsford was not exactly Sin City, but just the same she thought the open-air activities of life on a farm might be better for them, especially remembering her own happy years on the Big Creek Ranch, and in 1939 she and Edgar decided to move back to the Haney farm.[5] (This may have been a personal sacrifice to Margaret in some ways. She once said rather wistfully to this writer: "Abbotsford will always be home to me.")

During the war years Margaret channelled her energies into food production as her contribution to the war effort. She stocked the farm with sheep and Cornish game birds, and there must have been cows too, for her daughter Phyllis remembers taking butter and cream to the farmers' market in New Westminster every Saturday. Phyllis also took roasting chickens in, and has vivid memories of preparing a hundred birds for market every Friday night! Margaret did vast amounts of preserving and was a tireless worker, though she was always helped by her "farmerettes" from England—girls whose passage was paid for by the British Government to work on Canadian farms so that the men could go to war. "Bill was in on a lot of pranks pulled on [these girls]," says Phyllis, "some definitely not nice!"

Now that she was back in a rural area, Margaret's early love of horses came to the fore again and soon she was the owner of two mares which had once been race-horses—Regal Rose and Lady York. Riding became a part of family life, just as it had at Big Creek.

Her interest in horse-breeding, which was to have such an impact on horsemanship in British Columbia, really began as a result of the two younger children, Phyllis and J.O., wanting to compete at the local fairs. Margaret decided to start raising her own horses, but she wanted horses of a finer breed than were available locally, and so, around 1944, she took the major step of importing an Arab stallion, Nuri Sinbad, known in the family as "Sinny".[6] (This is believed to have been only the second Arab stallion to be brought into British Columbia.) She and Edgar leased out the farm in 1948, so that Margaret could then devote all her time to this exciting new enterprise.

She set up a breeding program, and she began training young riders in dressage. They came from as far away as Vancouver to be coached by Margaret—"She was a superb coach," says J.O.—and eventually she took parties to compete in the Royal Winter Fair in Toronto, where to their surprise and delight they placed extremely well even in their first season. She sent her riders to international events; she engineered the first Western Canadian Dressage Championship (held at Coniagas); she started the first Pony Club in Britsh Columbia. When Margaret was around, there was always action. "If there wasn't a horse show to prepare for, then Mrs. T. (as her younger friends called her) would suggest we take a short trip or have a party or trail ride—or put on a show—or buy a horse [often on someone else's behalf]—forever something on the go," wrote one of her best riders, Barbara McCauley Marsden.[7]

Margaret's great ambition was to open a major riding centre in Maple Ridge. This was a very big ambition for such an undeveloped rural area, but miraculously she made it happen. Just east of Coniagas there was a very suitable acreage on the old Edge homestead, and this she hopefully bought for the future riding centre. Bolstered chiefly with a great deal of faith and vision, she somehow managed to find the necessary funding, and soon the old farm acreage was transformed into the Maple Ridge Equitation Centre, which had its official opening in 1955.

One of Margaret's new ideas was to hold one- and two-day riding events at the centre. Here again, she was a pioneer, for "eventing" had not been known in British Columbia until then. It became an extremely popular innovation, eagerly looked forward to by the riding community, who assembled at the Maple Ridge centre from far and wide. Under her energetic leadership these projects could not but flourish.

All that was needed to fulfil her dream completely was an indoor riding arena. Even this eventually became a reality (though not during Margaret's ownership), when Charles N. Woodward generously financed the construction of this facility in 1964.[8] It became a tremendous attraction to riders from all over the Lower Mainland, and was visited by equestrians from all over the world.

Margaret eventually retired from the Riding Centre and sold it in the early 1960s, but lived on at her Maple Ridge home until her death in 1976.[9] She was described then as "a living legend", and even fifteen years later was the subject of a glowing tribute in the magazine *Horsin' Around,* in which she was given her rightful recognition as one of British Columbia's foremost equestrian pioneers.

This would certainly have pleased her, but what might have touched her even more in this tribute might have been the feeling of indebtedness on the part of the generation she had influenced, who spoke of her with affection and gratitude as a "leader who inspired young and old alike to achieve and to be winners in the game of life."

END NOTES

1. H.E. Church, *An Emigrant in the Canadian Northwest,* Methuen & Co. Ltd., London, 1929. The stories concerning the Church family are taken from these memoirs, as well as from Patrick A. Dunae's *Gentlemen Emigrants,* Douglas & McIntyre Ltd., Vancouver, 1981.
2. *Ashcroft Journal,* Feb.18, 1921. The wedding was on Feb.7 in Victoria.
3. *Abbotsford Sumas Matsqui News,* Mar.9 & Aug.9, 1939, and many other references in this paper.
4. Ibid, July 27, 1932. Margaret holds her first children's flower show on her lawn

5. Ibid, Aug.9, 1939.
6. *Horsin' Around*, July 1991, p.13, article by Sharon Stewart and J.O. Trethewey, entitled "A Tribute to 'Mrs. T'".
7. Ibid.
8. *Maple Ridge Gazette*, 1971 newspaper clipping.
9. Ibid, June 2, 1976,

Beverly Hills Oil Associates' drilling tower in the heart of Beverly Hills, 1979.
Note the high school alongside.   *Trethewey family archives*

Working on a paving contract, mid-1960s. Gordon Zacharius (left), Bob Kenny (right). *Trethewey family archives*

Mineral exploration in the Yukon. (Left to right): Roddy Watt, Jim Carabetta, Bob Kenny, Alan Trethewey, Robin Trethewey. *Trethewey family archives*

Gold Run exploration in the Yukon. Working the Ross sluice box.
Trethewey family archives

The journey to the Sky Ranch. *Trethewey family archives*

Alan Trethewey at the Sky Ranch. *Trethewey family archives*

On an African safari. Rhino charge, photographed by Alan at uncomfortably close quarters, 1964. *Trethewey family archives*

Alan's yacht, the *Mir*, 1972. *Lois J. Kennedy, Newport Beach, California*

Richard and Elizabeth Trethewey, 1980s. *Richard Trethewey*

Clarke Trethewey, family historian.
Trethewey family archives

Phyllis and Bruce Watt. *Trethewey family archives*

The official ceremony to honour the Trethewey family's gift of Trethewey House to the Municipality of Abbotsford, 1981. Alan at the microphone; Mayor Dave Kandal, front right.   *Trethewey family archives*

Margaret Trethewey and her sons and daughter. (Left to right) J.O., Bill, Phyllis, Alan, Margaret, Richard.   *Trethewey family archives*

Missing from group photo: Tye (top), Christopher and Tessa (centre), Barbara and Toby (bottom).

H. Simpson

Alan and Vivian, their five sons and their families at the Vicarro Ranch, 1989. Top row (left to right): Will, Derek, Brig, Nini, Regan, Bruce. Second row (left to right): Kyla, Phyllis Godfrey, Sam, Casey, Alan, Vivian, Andrea, Rosie, Tara, Katie, Ian. Family dog Chico.

18

Alan Transforms Trethewey Logging

In 1950, Trethewey Logging seemed to be on the point of extinction. Yet only three years later, this same company was showing a profit of a rumoured million and was about to take off into the most ambitious series of enterprises that the Tretheweys had known since the days of old Joe Trethewey. How could all this have happened so quickly and what was the reason for this extraordinary turn-around?

Things were looking black for the logging company by 1950. Edgar was sixty-four and virtually retired. His experiment of leasing the company to his cousin Leslie Trethewey had not worked out financially, and besides, this, Edgar was facing imminent competition from a rival logging company that wanted to get into the Port Douglas area.

After struggling to keep the company afloat during the Depression years, he was deeply reluctant to let it go without some final effort for survival. The sense of family tradition weighed heavily upon him too. For over half a century there had been Tretheweys logging on Harrison Lake, and he himself had owned these particular timber limits for something like twenty years. It seemed unthinkable to give up now.

Suprisingly, the son who stepped in to save Trethewey Logging was his second to oldest son Alan—Alan, who had thankfully opted out of the logging business and life in the woods only a few short years before! Since then, his perspective on life had changed. He badly wanted a chance to give his ambitions more scope, and all at once the prospect of running the logging company seemed like a golden opportunity to make the most of.

When Edgar turned over the company to him, merely in the hope of maintaining the status quo, he could have had no conception of the venturesome plans that were turning over in his son's mind. Nor could he have remotely foreseen that within the space of five years this young man would not only have created huge profits for the ailing company but transformed it into a major name on the British Columbian business scene.

Anyone meeting Alan Trethewey for the first time should not be deceived by the quiet, low-key manner and the mild, unassuming approach. Although this is his preferred style of transacting business, it also happens to mask great strength of purpose, a willingness to take risks, a capacity for tough decision-making and hard bargaining, as well as physical courage and quick thinking in the face of danger.

Appropriately enough—for a future lumberman—he was born and spent the first three years of his life in the remote logging and mining settlement of Alice Arm. After his father took over the management of the Abbotsford mill, the town of Abbotsford became his home for the next twelve years. Then the family moved back to their farm in Maple Ridge, and he spent the last few years of his teens on the Coniagas ranch. Like his brothers, he spent several years at a British-style private school, the Vernon Preparatory School, "a wonderful school," says Bill Trethewey, and one whose discipline (and canings!) they never regretted. Alan finished his education at the Maple Ridge High School.[1]

When Alan graduated from high school in 1942, he could hardly wait to enlist. To him and his friends it was the most exciting opportunity of their lives and the possibility of being killed or wounded never even crossed their minds. Like the rest of these eager 18-year-olds, Alan saw himself as a fighter pilot, so it was an extreme disappointment to find that pilots were not required at that time. Instead, he was picked to be a Wireless Air Gunner.

This was anti-climax enough, but by a ludicrous series of developments Alan proceeded to bring a much worse fate upon himself. Since he had become very friendly with someone who was training as a straight Air Gunner, Alan decided he would ask to transfer to the same course so that they could stay together. He asked for a hearing and told the board a tale about wishing to change because he hated wireless. To his dismay, when their decision came, he learned that they had deferred him to *ground crew* for the next six months. Alan was devastated. In vain he told them that he really did not mind wireless after all. For the whole of 1943 he was tied to a routine of general duties loading R.C.A.F. tug boats with supplies for stations on the coast of British Columbia.

In retrospect he considers that this deferral of air-crew training was probably one of the lucky breaks in his life, as the chances of survival for an air gunner in 1943 and 1944 were slim indeed.

Marble Island, where—now a corporal— he spent most of 1943, was a place that would be forever etched on his memory. It was the site of the most westerly radar station in Canada, and a place of extreme isolation, a most desolate piece of rock 12 miles west of the Queen Charlotte Islands. Because of its exposed position, the landing of supplies was difficult even at the best of times and only took place every few months. In the course of one of these landings a tragic accident occurred, in which Alan played a heroic part in attempting a rescue.

It happened on New Year's Day, 1944. No one had been able to get off the island for months because of the high seas, but in spite of the weather the authorities had decided to try to land some men and supplies. The dinghy that was bringing them in had just left the mother ship, when there was a cry of "Boat upset!" Alan rushed to the clifftop to see one man clinging to the boat and two others desperately trying to swim to shore. One of them was doomed, for he was trapped against a high sheer cliff, but the other had fought his way to a rocky cove directly below where Alan was standing. Alan threw down a life-preserver on a rope just as the man disappeared beneath the surface, and for a moment there was hope, because his arm appeared above the surface right in the middle of the life preserver. Unfortunately he wasn't touching the side of it, and before he realised it was there, he sank under again. So close and yet so far! Again he came to the surface, but now he was unconscious. Quickly Alan scrambled down to the foot of the rocks with absolutely no intention of going into the water, but just to see if he could manage to reach him from the shore. When he saw the man only six feet away from him, he knew he could not stand by and do nothing. "I didn't think twice. I jumped in and grabbed him with one hand and grabbed the life-preserver with the other."

For some time Alan managed to hang on this way, but eventually he was forced to use both hands to cling to the life-preserver, and he had to grip the unconscious man between his legs to support him. Submerged more than half the time by the gigantic breakers pounding over him, Alan hung on grimly, while the rest of the party on shore formed a human chain down the cliff and attempted to haul the two of them in. But in those freezing waters it was a struggle that Alan could not keep up indefinitely. Battered by the waves and numbed by the icy cold, he was finally obliged to relinquish his hold, and was dragged to shore himself, exhausted and suffering from hypothermia.[2]

For this act of bravery Alan was mentioned in despatches and was awarded the Oak Leaf Cluster.

During 1944 he finally received the aircrew training that he wanted, and graduated as a Pilot Officer with a Bomb-Aimer wing badge, but too late to see any action. By this time the war was in its final stages and he never had the opportunity to go overseas.

Edgar expected all his sons to learn the logging business. In spite of, or perhaps because of, his years at Guelph, he had little faith in theoretical learning, and he believed in training his sons early on in the value of hard, practical work. As teenagers they had to spend their summers working at the logging camp, and as a matter of course, on his discharge in mid-1945, Alan went to work there to be groomed for management.

Up at Port Douglas he learned every aspect of the logging business. He drove every type of vehicle that they used there and he learned to operate every piece of equipment. Like his father, he gained an invaluable personal experience and practical knowledge of all the jobs which his employees would be required to do.

But just before Christmas 1945, Alan quit, after enduring a horrendous month of bitterly cold weather. Temperatures had been so low that the caterpillar tractor would only start up in the morning if he lit a fire underneath it to get the engine warm enough to turn over. He had had enough of the logging company—as he thought then—and so he entered the other division of his father's business, the building supply company.

But after two or three years of working at the lumber yard (and eventually taking over management), Alan was starting to feel a little bored. Something in his ambitious nature began to stir. Certainly he could make a comfortable living by going on as he was, but he now recognised the old Trethewey urge to look for something more challenging. And so in 1950 when Edgar needed someone to take over Trethewey Logging, Alan forgot all about the rigours of his previous experiences, and told his father he was definitely interested. His brother Richard, who was enjoying an adventurous career as an Air Force test pilot, came in as a silent partner with a 25 percent share.

Alan's wife, Vivian, whom he had had known since the days of the badminton club and married in 1948, was just as thrilled with the idea as her husband. Like Alan, she was a hard worker and ready to put all her energy into revitalising the logging company: she insisted that she would be the camp cook, book-keeper and first-aid attendant, all in one. She was well prepared for any of the rough conditions she might be faced with at the Port Douglas camp, as the old farmhouse they were living in had had no electricity or running water for the first year.

It was a historic site up there at the head of the lake—one of the most historic sites in the province. Port Douglas was just about as old as the colony of British Columbia itself. In the early days of the gold rush it had been the starting-point for the most travelled route in the whole of British Columbia—the Harrison-Lillooet route via river and lakes to the upper goldfields.

But after the Fraser Canyon road was built, the whole Port Douglas episode faded from memory like a dream. By the mid-20th century it was hard to believe that thousands of miners had ever been this way with their pack-horses or mule trains. The shanties of Port Douglas had fallen into ruins and eventually burned down; the Douglas trail had greened over and its bridges rotted away. True, the government had rebuilt the road during the Fire Mountain mining rush of the 1890s, but half a century later it had once again fallen into disrepair. Alan would be the one to rebuild this historic road.

His first action, before even going up to the camp, was to seek out one of the very best and most reputable yarding and loading contractors in the business, as he was convinced that this would set the tone of the whole operation. He found the person he wanted in Albert Wells, a much respected operator, and gave him the contract. Albert's son, Ivan, who became a personal friend of Alan's, went up to Port Douglas to carry out the work, and with him came Ivan's brother-in-law, Peter Androniak, and other loggers of his team. In all, Alan had about 25 employees when he first started.

In spite of the efficiency of his work-force and in spite of the fact that the price of logs nearly doubled that season, Alan was down $82.50 in his first year of operation!

But the second year saw a distinct upturn in the fortunes of the company, and from then on he never looked back. One of his first objectives was to start converting from a river drive to a truck-logging operation, as far as this was feasible, for the stiff gradients on the old road ruled it out in many sections. Where it could be done, it cut down tremendously on labour, as it saved so much on handling. With the river drive they were continually having to contend with the problem of untangling log jams or shifting logs that had got beached on sand-bars, and it was quite usual for logs to be handled several times over before they arrived at the catchment area at the mouth of the Lillooet.

Despite the best planning, accidents do happen. It was one of these log jams that led to the Tretheweys' most serious misadventure on the river. Alan, together with Ivan Wells and Peter Androniak, had gone out on the river in a flat-bottomed skiff powered by an outboard motor, to try to connect a cable from the cat-yarder on shore to the log jam in the middle of the river. They ran into some problems with the cable, and Alan and Ivan were just attempting to pull it free when suddenly the boat made a downward lurch and disappeared beneath their feet, never to re-appear. Everyone was now in the water, struggling for his life—70 feet from shore and no one wearing a life-jacket. The current was running fast and the three men were swept rapidly downstream; the man on shore couldn't keep up to the pace of the river as he tore after them along the bank.

Alan, being a good swimmer, had managed to strike out to within 30 feet of the shore when he paused to catch his breath. Suddenly the undertow caught him in its grip and he found that he couldn't keep his head above water. "My God, I am going to drown," he thought. Something inside him told him not to panic. He took a deep breath and let himself sink down, thinking one last time of Vivian and his two boys, when to his amazement he felt river bottom beneath his feet. Now he knew he had a fighting chance. He kicked himself up to the surface, went down again, pushed up again, and struggled on in this way until he arrived at a bend in the river. The water was shallow here, but the racing current still had him in its grip and carried him helplessly along, rolling him over and over, and pounding the breath from his body. Then suddenly—miraculously —he was out of it. By an incredible piece of good fortune he had come to rest in safe water. A large cottonwood tree had floated down the river and become lodged against the bank with its roots in the water and its top on shore, and this had created a shallow back eddy. It was the only place of safety in all that stretch of the river. Alan had come to a stop with his head just out of the water, but the current still surging past him on either side. For half an hour he was too shaken to move. Finally he summoned up his strength to shuffle inch by inch to the cottonwood root that had caused the eddy and slide slowly along the trunk of the tree to dry land.

Ivan Wells survived the accident by clutching an empty 5-gallon gas tank which came bobbing past, and paddling himself to a small log jam, though nearly drowning beneath some logs as he clawed his way to the surface. Peter Androniak was swept away by the current; he was not a strong swimmer and he was never seen again.

After surmounting the financial problems of the first couple of years, the company prospered. Alan opened an office in Vancouver, he built a new home, and Vivian quit her job as book-keeper and camp cook.

But his big break came in the summer of 1953 The B.C. Electric Company was about to construct a major new powerline from Bridge River, running down the Lillooet River and Harrison Lake to the Waleach-Surrey right-of-way south of Rosedale, and they were inviting tenders for clearing the right-of-way. Alan realised that here was an opportunity not to be missed, but he needed someone to share the costs. He discussed the idea with Robert Cattermole, who was also logging near the head of Harrison Lake, and they agreed to put in a joint bid for the clearing of line and the building of an access road.

Alan and Bob were successful in their bid, and so began a long and totally amicable association. Forming Tenas Operators for the clearing work and Lillooet Operators for the road work, they contracted to deal with the section from Port Douglas to Lillooet Lake along the east side of the Lillooet River. Since one of the great advantages of the contract for Alan was that he was going to end up with a far better road for his truck-logging, it was agreed that Trethewey Logging, independently, would share the cost of the first 15 miles with B.C. Electric.

Alan had a sense of being linked with history as he reflected that they would be following in the footsteps of the Royal Engineers who had surveyed the original wagon road nearly a century before. Some parts of the B.C. Electric road would follow the exact line of the Engineers', though most of it would be using vastly improved gradients. The contract could hardly have been better for Trethewey Logging, for not only would they make a handsome profit on the deal, but they would be left with exactly the road they needed to get their truck-logging into full operation.

This was the turning-point in Alan's career. The financial success of this contract dramatically changed his life and made it possible for him to start up new ventures in a range which had not come the way of anyone in his immediate family since his grandfather, old Joe Trethewey, was alive.

END NOTES

1. Most of the information in this chapter is taken from autobiographical notes by Alan Trethewey, compiled in 1992.
2. *The Royal Canadian Air Force 1939-1945 Book,* pp.123, 124 photocopied, no date, no further detail.

19

"Go ahead or go home!"

From now on, it was "all systems go". For the first time in his life Alan had some significant capital to invest, and for the first time his entrepreneurial talents had full scope. Now began the most exciting and creative period in the whole history of Trethewey enterprise since the family entered British Columbia three-quarters of a century earlier. Even the legendary Joe had not owned such a plethora of companies, nor branched out into so much diversification as his grandson coolly proceeded to do during the 1950s, 1960s and 1970s.

With his new partner, Bob Cattermole, he launched into a profusion of major enterprises. Few projects were too large or too complex for Alan and Bob to tackle. With monster machinery that would have made past generations of Tretheweys stand in awe, they set about changing the face of British Columbia and parts beyond. They went into muskeg, swamp and forest, building miles of road, clearing vast acres of timber from reservoirs, stringing powerlines across mountain peaks, boring deep into the earth in search of minerals. And, as a continuous background to it all, remained the lumber industry. On a much larger scale than ever before, they set up logging camps all over the province. They bought or built a series of sawmills. By the late 1960s it was British Columbia's largest independent logging operation.

"Go ahead or go home!" became the catchy new slogan of the

Trethewey-Cattermole partnership in these years, as one project followed another at a dizzying rate of progress. Alan was willing to take chances in a way that his father would never have dreamed of—though, to his credit, Edgar never attempted to interfere or offer advice. His daughter-in-law, Vivian, says: "It was not a family that discussed things very much, though I am sure they were proud of their sons' success. I think that Edgar may have been a little nervous of some of the expenditure on new machinery, but he kept it to himself." Machinery was indeed a major aspect of Trethewey-Cattermole operations, and a heavy investment. Like the old Tretheweys of long ago, Alan never hesitated to try out the latest inventions in modern machinery and frequently pioneered new techniques himself to suit the job in hand.

So many projects were in full flourish by the end of the 1950s, including his brother Bill's window factory in Abbotsford, that Trethewey enterprise attracted the attention of the *Financial Post*. A lengthy write-up described the tremendous range and variety of their projects. What impressed the writer of this article was the versatility of the Tretheweys, and their adaptability in innovating new ideas. They "won't put up risk capital," he noted, "[but they] deftly put the lie to the suggestion that Canadians lack business enterprise."[1]

Alan's first big opportunity after his initial success with the Port Douglas road was at Buttle Lake on Vancouver Island. He and Bob Cattermole were now firmly allied as Cattermole-Trethewey Contractors, (though they each maintained their own separate companies as well), and it was as Cattermole-Trethewey Contractors that they jointly took on a huge land clearing contract for the B.C. Power Commission, which was about to inundate acres of forest at Buttle Lake in Tweedsmuir Park in readiness for the Upper Campbell dam. It was nothing less than landscaping on a gigantic scale. The water level would have to be raised by 30 feet; 2,000 acres of virgin timber would have to be cleared; and finally 600 acres of designated beaches would have to be restored by stumping and grading. At that time (1957) it was the largest clearing and clean-up operation in the history of British Columbia.[2]

The Trethewey talent for innovation was already apparent even in this early project. It was at Buttle Lake that Cattermole-Trethewey Contractors first saw the possibilities in the flotation method of disposing of brush during the clean-up process. With this system, once logging was completed and the lake filled, any debris that remained would be floated to the shore for burning. Alan and Bob considered this method so effective that they decided to use it on a much larger scale at a later project at Yuba Lake in California, where they deliberately employed it for moving logs as well as brush and debris. They were able to do the Yuba job for half the original cost ($2,500,000 instead of $5,000,000) by using this system.

Their projects had already begun to penetrate into the United States by the early 1960s—Washington, Oregon and California— so Cattermole-Trethewey Pacific Inc. was formed in 1962 to conduct the American operations. One of the most difficult contracts they ever undertook was at the Lake Alamanor reservoir dam site in California. This was an old reservoir which had been flooded in the days before World War I, leaving thousands of standing trees in the water. The requirement now was to clear 9,000 acres, but of this acreage *one-third* consisted of these old inundated snags, which had to be cut between 8 and 15 feet under the surface! "This unsightly morass," wrote one contemporary reporter, "had a dampening effect on most aspirants . . . Cattermole-Trethewey's Land Clearing Division won the contract and literally sailed through it."[3] Moving around the snags on rafts, their crews harvested the timber by means of a very simple device evolved by Bill Owens, the head of construction, and Art Gobin, in charge of clearing. Originally they had experimented with elaborate machinery such as a high-powered hydraulic underwater sheer, operating from a barge, and also a 12-foot hydraulic under-water saw which mowed through the stems like hay, but in the end they had come back to a very basic method. All that was used was a heavy-duty power-saw with a 15-foot extension on the blade, and this was handled by a single operator working on a raft consisting of six empty gas drums. The simplest and cheapest method turned out to be the best.

Cattermole-Trethewey's use of unconventional machinery made

the headlines in trade publications again in 1964, but this time with a major invention—a mechanism for splitting stumps. It was custom-built for another job in California. This time they were at work in the Sierra Nevada Range, clearing for a hydro-electric complex east of Auburn. They were dealing with dense timber, where the usual process of dynamiting the larger stumps would have been very costly in time and powder, and so the idea of splitting the stumps mechanically was born. Their device consisted of a "stinger"—a wedge-shaped point 7 feet in length and 14 inches deep —mounted on the rear of a Caterpillar DG9 with a rake on the front. The operator would approach the stump in reverse, thrust through it to split it, then swivel smartly round to scoop up the splintered roots or pieces with the rake—a process that took only minutes, as opposed to nearly an hour using dynamite. "We had the stinger built to our specifications specially for this job," commented one of the job superintendents, Tony Fischer, "but it looks like we're going to use it from here in on."[4] This proved to be true: they never went back to the use of powder. The stump-splitter rapidly caught on in the logging and contracting business generally and became universally adopted, ending up as the accepted method in use to this day.

But all this was only one side of Trethewey operations during the '50s and '60s. At the same time Alan was expanding the lumbering business at a phenomenal rate. While still keeping up the Port Douglas operations, he began logging in an area quite outside his previous range of experience—the Cariboo. This was done in conjunction with his good friend, Ivan Wells, whose idea it was, though sadly the partnership of Trethewey-Wells was broken up prematurely by Ivan's early death at the age of thirty-nine.

Dire prophecies always accompanied any transition from Coastal logging to Interior logging, as the techniques in each were so different. The extreme climate of the Cariboo and the thinner stands of timber were factors that could work against great profitability, and experts in the lumber industry would speak gloomily of the "long history of economic disasters" that had befallen anyone foolish enough to tempt fate in this way.

But because of their adaptable outlook Alan and Ivan apparently managed to overcome these problems. "Trethewey is young, shrewd, far-sighted, imaginative and an exceptionally able administrator with the courage of his convictions," wrote one journalist. "Wells is also young and sharp . . . He has been well schooled in both Cariboo and Coast techniques. He has developed the delicate art of fostering better labour-management relations to an incredible degree."[5] It was a well-matched partnership.

Bob Cattermole, though not mentioned in this article, was also involved in the Cariboo experiment, but in a separate area. Cattermole-Trethewey logged on the east side of the Fraser, and Trethewey-Wells on the west side in the vicinity of the Gang Ranch.

Bringing logs down from the Cariboo had its problems. For the first few years it was a river drive, and it was a drive on a massive scale, encompassing a distance of some 300 miles down the churning waters of the Fraser to the mills at the coast. In spring it was always quite a spectacle to see the vast accumulations of logs (90 percent of the year's production) being swept downstream in the powerful flow of the annual freshets. But one year nature outdid itself. It was the year when Alan achieved what might have been thought impossible: he managed to create a log jam that blocked the Fraser River from shore to shore.

"We didn't try to do this," remarks Alan, perhaps unnecessarily. "It just happened all on its own." The ice had formed early that winter (1963), and it had begun to block a quiet stretch of the river near the Gang Ranch. Large quantities of bundled tree-length logs began to drift up against this icy barrier, and as the winter went on, they gradually piled up into a gigantic mass of timber amounting to about 12 million board feet. When the ice began to melt in the spring, all this shifted downstream until it arrived at a point where the river narrowed considerably. There it jammed, and nothing would dislodge it, not even their attempts to blast out the key bundles of logs.

Obviously something of cosmic proportions would have to happen soon—the spring freshet was reaching its peak. "The break came in late May, and she all went out at once," recalls Alan. "I was walking on the jam the day before it let go, and it was quite a sensation, as the whole thing was moving up and down. In fact, it made one very uneasy being on it, as you could tell it was going to break at any moment."[6] When the log jam finally gave, all hell broke loose. Cables snapped, bundles were torn apart, logs broke in half, as the great mass of timber hurtled on its way in the fury of the current. It was an awesome sight at the Hell's Gate rapids to see huge truckload bundles of logs tossed on end and sucked down into the whirlpools like flotsam, as they shot through the Fraser Canyon.

Contingency plans had been made well ahead of time to deal with the inevitable emergency. At the catching-grounds, powerful floodlights lit up the water at night so that work could go on around the clock. Nearly every beachcomber in British Columbia had been rounded up in advance to lend a hand, so most of what passed beyond the catchment area was salvaged, and as a result, very few logs were lost to the ocean. Because of this whole extraordinary chain of events, Alan has the dubious honour of being the only person ever known to have jammed the Fraser River.

It was soon after this episode that they decided to give up the river drive and erect their own planer mill at Chasm near Clinton. It was a large mill, capable of turning out 30 to 40 million fbm, and built on the most modern lines entirely of steel. Typically, it featured one significant innovation, in that all the machinery was installed at an elevated level above a solid concrete floor, thus eliminating the usual pit where accumulations of water would freeze in winter.[7] The rough lumber that supplied the planer mill was produced by 35 small bush mills which the company installed and which were operated by various contractors.

This mill was one of a series owned by Trethewey companies in the 1950s and 1960s. The best known of these was the historic McNair shingle mill at Port Moody, whose origins went back to the early years of the century. With 19 machines and 80 employees, it was one of the largest shingle mills in the province. Alan kept it from 1956 till 1963 when it ceased to be financially viable, though he recovered his losses by selling the property for a housing development.

Immediately on disposing of McNair, he bought the controlling shares in a very large mill indeed—the Douglas Plywood plant on Annacis Island, owned 25% by the Douglas group and other key associates. In terms of employees, this was the largest mill he was ever involved in, with a workforce of 400. The fact that this investment was made in the same year as the construction of the mill at Chasm indicates the tremendous rate of company expansion in the 1960s. Besides these, Nalos Lumber Ltd. at False Creek also came into the Trethewey orbit in 1965: this was a good-sized mill producing high-grade cedar lumber and turning out 60 million board feet a year.

Their logging operations were far-flung now, ranging from Pitt Lake in the Fraser Valley to Juneau, Alaska, and including North Bend, the Cariboo, Narrows Inlet, Wakeman Sound, Warner Bay, Nikite River, Powell River, and even Peel Inlet and Rennell Sound in the Queen Charlotte Islands. Curiously enough, one of these latter camps was only a few miles from where Alan had nearly drowned during his rescue attempt in his Air Force days. "And to think that I said I would never go near the place again!" he reflects now with some irony.

They also moved into the log export business, hiring Jack Sexton, the manager of McMillan and Bloedel log supply, to run the division. He not only sold their own logs, but also bought and sold many million feet more. Later, in 1978, the management of this division was taken over by one of Alan's sons, Regan Trethewey.

A great deal of the timber was in isolated valleys and hillsides and could only be reached effectively by air. All the Trethewey brothers had their pilot's licences and flew extensively, but they depended on good bush pilots for their regular commercial work. Alan at one time owned the majority shares in Cascade Air Services, which operated out of Chilliwack. His partner in this was Ron Wells, for whom he had a very high regard, considering him the best bush pilot in British Columbia. But Cascade did not prove a moneymaker, so in the end Alan disposed of his interest. He and Bob Cattermole eventually owned their own aircraft—ending up with a handy little fleet of float and wheel planes, not to mention two helicopters.

Their ventures in flight led to a number of close calls, both on business and pleasure. "Having the plane always created a certain amount of excitement," recounts Alan. "One time, in the Seabee, I had a faulty fuel gauge and I ran out of gas just after flying through a snowstorm about nine miles from camp. I had a choice between landing in the Lillooet River or on a small lake which was 95 percent covered with ice. It took me just five seconds to decide—it was the lake! We touched down on the ice at 80 miles an hour and went skooting ahead, not slowing down a bit, till at last within 100 feet of the far end we broke through the thin ice. I had just time to spin around and turn the aircraft to avoid going into the trees that grew into the water. We eventually had to take the wings off the plane and tow it to Harrison Lake, as the lake was so small that we did not have room for a take-off."[8] This was but one of many similar episodes in a life full of lucky breaks.

Expansion was still the name of the game, even after fifteen years of business activity. Starting in the mid-1960s Alan and Bob plunged into a whole new series of operations, which took in road-building, sewer construction, strip mining, pipelining, and even high-tension powerline work. At one point in Cattermole-Trethe-wey operations their pay-roll swelled to a peak of 1500 employees on one project alone—and this was exclusive of other Trethewey-owned companies.

The most famous of all the projects they engaged in in these years was the giant Peace River power development in the north-central part of the province. At the time, this was the largest single hydro project anywhere in the world, larger even than the Aswan dam. One of the first three contracts for land clearing at the dam site in 1965 went to Cattermole-Trethewey Contractors, with the happy upshot that they were afterwards given contracts for the clearing of several sections of the right-of-way between the dam and Vancou-ver—ending up as the largest single clearing contractor on the whole project. From then on, over the next fifteen years, they were en-trusted with a whole series of contracts in each new phase of this grand scheme for hydro-electric power and, in fact, during the 1970s became B.C. Hydro's leading powerline contractor.

In total they cleared over 6,000 acres on this project, working in extraordinarily adverse conditions for much of the time. The terrain was rugged. In one area the men had to climb up half a mile of steep, boulder-strewn hillside before even starting their day's work, while some of the section between Boston Bar and Agassiz was so difficult that the crews couldn't use machinery, but had to employ hand methods. They endured conditions of extreme cold too, as they contended with the brutal climate of the north. Temperatures of 40° F below zero awaited them at the dam site, where the work had to be completed within a time limit of six weeks, while in the Pine Pass section they persevered under the constant threat of heavy snowfalls that sometimes dumped as much as 15 feet of snow at a time.

One of the Trethewey hallmarks on any project was the customised equipment which they used to speed the work, and this job was no exception. A special cutting-blade was manufactured which would work on all but the largest trees. It was an improved version of an existing type of blade and it consisted of razor-edged knives fitted to the blades of D8 and D9 tractors. When this went into action, its efficiency was impressive. As one observer described it, it skimmed effortlessly through the trunks of 2-foot-diameter trees "like machetes cutting sugar cane."[9] Even more important than this was an ingenious device known as a "U" blade, for which they had to thank the inventive mind of their General Manager of Construction, Bill Owens. Mounted on a bulldozer, this was a wide U-shaped blade like a scoop, which was intended for the job of pushing the waste timber and brush into piles ready for burning. Because of its impressive width and size it was capable of dealing with much larger quantities than had been possible previously, and it greatly speeded up the work of clearing. With such machinery at their disposal, it was not surprising that Cattermole-Trethewey soon had a reputation for being "geared to clearing projects requiring plenty of muscle."[10]

But Alan's and Bob's involvement with the Peace River project was not limited to land clearing. As a result of their original contract they decided to bid on a further development of the work—the powerline installation. Had they any previous experience of such work? No, but innovation was what the Trethewey-Cattermole partnership thrived on, and they were more than ready to launch Catre Hi-Line expressly for this new field of enterprise. Obviously they were not going to be able to handle such complicated work without bringing in someone who had highly specialised experience of hydro-electric projects, but they were fortunate enough find just such a person in Jim Carabetta, who had been the engineer in charge of B.C. Electric high voltage transmission construction and who now came in with them for a 20 percent interest in the company.In the event, Catre Hi-Line was the only Canadian firm to be awarded one of the contracts. All previous competitors had been large American firms.

Alan and Bob were responsible for 50 miles of the line from Boston Bar to Vancouver, including a lengthy 6,000-foot span of the Fraser River and a cross-country route that traversed a series of jagged mountain ranges before reaching the level pastures of the Fraser Valley. They also strung 182 miles of line between the Peace River dam site and Prince George, working once again in icy temperatures and deep snow drifts during the winter months.

This prestigious job established Catre Hi-Line firmly in the field of powerline work, and they went on to a series of other major contracts throughout the 1970s. As always, they kept their methods up-to-date. For stringing the line they were quick to adopt a combination of helicopters and radio communications, and this proved the key to efficiency in the inaccessible terrain which was usually the norm in powerline work. The helicopters used for this type of work were enormously powerful, capable of lifts of up to 22,000 lb. The pilot was in constant touch with the field crew by radio contact, and throughout all the critical procedures of the work radio mobiles kept every member of the team in full communication—the helicopter pilot, the stringing foreman, and the crews operating the puller and tensioner. "Radio is the greatest thing that ever happened to this industry," enthused Vic Dirk, the construction superintendent on one of the projects.[11] Undoubtedly in these isolated areas it speeded the job, and saved both money and lives. The projects of the 1970s culminated in one more outstanding contract of provincial importance, when Catre worked on the final stage of the transmission line between the W.A.C. Bennett dam and Prince George in 1978. This included installing most of the foundations, as well as erecting 740 high-voltage towers and stringing the conductors.

Road-building developed into another major thrust during these years of expansion. Their projects ranged from Inuvik in the Arctic

Circle to the other side of the Rockies in Alberta. The Inuvik project was a particularly daunting one. "When you build roads in the Arctic, you start right from 'square-one'," acknowledged Olav Naas, the project manager. "You leave all your experience behind."[12] Catre had contracted to build 33 miles of the Mackenzie Highway going south from Inuvik, and it was their first encounter with conditions in the far north. Again, it was a challenge to devise ways of competing with the forces of nature: working in the fragile tundra, moving machinery over the permafrost, and battling the impact stress on steel, which—quoting Naas again—"raise[d] hell with the equipment", for the January chill factor could stand at a horrendous 109° F below zero. "Building roads in the Arctic," he summed up, "demands a change in attitude, a change of techniques and a learning process." Their flexible approach enabled them to master new techniques and adapt themselves to difficult conditions, and over the two years of the contract they acquired invaluable experience of working in the north.

But these problems were nothing compared with the ordeal of one of the Alberta highway contracts, which followed not long after.

The Alberta highway contract represented the most disastrous episode in Alan's whole career and the only bad memory in the history of the Cattermole-Trethewey partnership. The contract sounded straightforward enough: it was merely to build 22 miles of gravel highway in the northern part of the province in a time-frame of an estimated 3 months. As it turned out, it took Alan and Bob not 3 *months*, but more than 3 *years* to finish, and it resulted in a loss of *$3½ million.*

What occurred, as Alan tells it, was that the information about soil conditions which was supplied in the government maps and tender documents proved to be entirely inaccurate and misleading. Once their crews were on the job, they discovered with dismay that the soil in the borrow pits was different from the description supplied, and to make matters worse they began to run into muskeg and saturated conditions not allowed for in the original design. The road simply could not be constructed as designed and calculated. The only way in which they managed to complete it at all was by having a major design change, with consequent financial loss.

Outraged at the unfairness of their position, Cattermole-Trethewey sued the Government of Alberta for misrepresentation and breach of contract, and in this they had the support of the Canadian Construction Association in their defence, as this would be a test case for all contractors and would have devastating results if they lost. Unfortunately this is just what did happen. The original judgment was in their favour and they were awarded a sum of $2,500,000 (rather less than their claim, but still satisfactory), but then the case went to appeal, and to their dismay the judgement was reversed. Through an exclusionary clause, the government had successfully maintained that they could not guarantee the accuracy of information supplied to bidders. "In other words, all the information that a bidder uses to base his bids is totally erroneous," says Alan bitterly. "All in all, a terrible injustice. It caused me an awful lot of sleepless nights, and must have aged me by twenty years."[13]

It is significant that, after this case, changes were made to contract law across Canada.

In 1971 Alan suddenly sold his lumber and timber operations, and this tension-filled sale proved to be yet another of the memorable dramas played out in his career. The sale offer came right out of the blue, for the idea of selling had never even crossed the partners' minds. Alan was sitting in his office one day when without any previous warning a stranger walked in and enquired whether he would consider an offer of this kind. Although the thought had not occurred to Alan, he could certainly see some advantage in it, for he knew that if they stayed in business, they would soon be faced with very large investments in new plant and equipment, both on the Coast and in the Interior, in order to keep their timber quotas. "When a figure of $15 million was mentioned," says Alan, "this was enough to make us sit up and take notice. After all, we had been working for just over 20 years and we had started with very little. Definitely we were interested."[14]

For some months they explored the possibility with the interested party, which was a large American company, Boise Cascade. Suddenly Boise Cascade pulled out, but at this point two other companies entered the picture and began to compete for the deal, one being B.C. Forest Products, and the other, Weldwood of Canada Ltd. This element of competition was just what was needed to provide a stimulus. In the end it was B.C.F.P. that emerged as the successful buyer.

Days and nights of tense negotiations marked the final stages of this settlement. Both sides were suffering from fatigue and lack of sleep, and the atmosphere had become extremely strained, with Alan refusing to give an inch, when one more thorny question came up: was he willing to throw in the Beaver float-plane? Alan still said no. At this point his secretary-treasurer Bob Kenny broke in, in desperation: "For Christ's sake, Alan, give them the goddamned Beaver." Alan was so stunned by this plea from his own trusted negotiator that he capitulated at once; it was characteristic that he placed implicit confidence in the judgement of his top associates and had the generosity of spirit to acknowledge this. Later, the fate of a $60,000 D9 cat was settled by the flip of a coin: Alan lost![15] B.C.F.P. ended up buying 19 companies in this deal, some solely Trethewey-owned, others jointly by Alan and Bob; however, Bob did not sell any of his own companies.

At the last minute, however, one shattering crisis occurred. The lawyers for B.C. Forest Products found what they considered to be a loophole in the agreement and disputed the price. Five million dollars was at stake, for the total price would have been reduced by this amount. "You can imagine the thoughts going through my mind over the week it took for a decision to be reached. Five million was a lot of money—my life blood!"[16] The dispute went to their joint arbiters for settlement, though Alan was distinctly perturbed that it should even have had to go to arbitration. Thankfully it was settled in his favour, and Alan had no complaints over the final outcome and the favourable sale figure. Trethewey Logging had come a long way since Edgar Trethewey's struggle for its bare survival during the difficult Depression years.

Outside his major business interests in lumber and construction, Alan let his fancy range freely over a wide variety of speculative ventures—mining, oil wells, ranching, movies (briefly), and even battleships!

The battleship idea was probably the first of his more exotic types of inspiration. When he read in the paper in 1959 that the government was about to auction off the flagship of the Canadian Navy, *HMCS Ontario*, for scrapping, he had been quite unable to resist the urge to buy. "This really caught my fancy," he admits. But why did he wish to buy this ship? enquired a *Province* reporter soon after the sale. Alan deadpanned: "Because I have always wanted to own a battleship."[17] Of course!

Had he known more about the scrap metal business, he might have been less enthusiastic. It soon turned out that it was controlled by a group of individuals who were not about to allow outsiders into what was virtually a private club. He could not get a price anywhere near what he thought the scrap was worth. After a long hassle, he was allowed to sell it in Japan, and was thankful to come out of the deal with a comparatively minor loss.

Movie-making was another small aberration which did not turn out exactly as hoped. It promised well, for 1969 was the television era, and it looked as if there would be a large demand for many different types of movie. What particularly appealed to him—perhaps as a reflection of his own vigorous lifestyle—was the idea of action movies, but the National Film Board of Canada would only support a country musical. This was hardly what he had in mind, but at least it would be a start. They began shooting, but it became so difficult to meet the further conditions of the Film Board that he finally decided to cut his losses and opt out. His partner, Jack McCallum, did eventually manage to complete the film—"without the Film Board's assistance!" adds Alan—and it appeared under the title *Travelling Light*.

But it was mineral exploration which really afforded the greatest thrill to Alan and his brothers as an interesting sideline. Mining had been in the Trethewey blood for five generations now, and each member of the family had grown up on tales of mining adventures and talk of mineralogy. It was right in the family tradition—almost a natural development—that at some point his generation would go out looking for the mine that would bring untold wealth, as it had to Will Trethewey.

The brothers had a wonderful and exciting time flying around the province in pursuit of these elusive minerals. Their will-o'-the-wisp search for uranium was perhaps the most bizarre of all their endeavours, being conducted in a most hush-hush fashion for fear of competition, and also being undertaken with very little knowledge of how to go about it—the fact was that hardly anybody did know how! It was a totally new field of expertise at that time, but in the late 1950s the uranium boom was on, and it looked as if it might be very rewarding. They equipped themselves with a Piper Super Cub airplane and a strong scintillometer, and spent many happy hours hovering over the rumpled surface of British Columbia in the hope of picking up some dramatic signal. At times they actually did get very high readings, but they learned by experience that other minerals like thorium could also register strongly, and the excitement slowly fizzled out.

Once, however, they were completely convinced that they had made a spectacular discovery. As it was comparatively near civilisation, just south of Penticton, they took great pains to conceal their activities. They took their ground sample very secretly, and they stole off in the middle of the night to some remote spot to test it out. It fluoresced! They were sure that this was it. Sadly, after all this cloak-and-dagger activity, their hopes were dashed again. The uranium content was negligible.

It was in these years that Alan and his brothers Bill and J.O., and two friends, Larry Lyttle and V. Keith, formed a little consortium called Big Bend Explorations. One of their best remembered projects was a copper prospect near Revelstoke, on a rugged mountainside known as Downie Peak. Bill was the man on the spot and he had more than his share of adventures in the course of the two or three seasons he spent there in the late 1950s.

Some of his adventures involved the local wildlife, particularly some of the more persistent and inquisitive bears that inhabited the mountain with him. However, it was the problems arising from flying in and out of the area that chiefly linger in his mind today. One particular incident happened to involve both Bill and Alan, who had come out for the weekend to have a look. Bill had been using a hired helicopter that season to take the compressor and other machinery up to the tunnelling site. This was at the 5,500-foot level, but there was also a second site at the 7,500-foot level. The hillside was nearly vertical, so in order to provide some type of heli-pad at the lower level he had constructed a platform of logs right up against the cliff and resting on two topped trees on the outward side. It was a windy spot, being near the glacier, and pilots would have to choose their moment for take-off very carefully in a lull between these strong air currents.

On this occasion Alan was being flown from the lower site to join Bill, who was already at the upper site near the glacier. Just as they lifted off, a violent rush of wind suddenly took them by surprise. The copter lurched sideways, then dropped several hundred feet before recovering. The pilot wiped his brow, muttering "My God, that was close," but carried on to reach the upper site. He seemed shaken, but neither of them realised just how shaken until much later, when they learned that he had immediately flown back to Revelstoke and handed in his resignation. In the meantime, Alan and Bill were left stranded at the glacier in the freezing cold with only one sleeping-bag between the two of them for warmth and not overly cheered by the gloomy thought that the pilot must have crashed. They began to calculate the not very encouraging odds against climbing down from this sheer mountain top. Fortunately, on the afternoon of the next day, before they had made up their minds to take this chance, the helicopter at last arrived. It had had to wait for a new pilot to be flown in all the way from Vancouver.[18]

The glacier site was an unlucky place for Bill, for another time the helicopter he was in suddenly stalled and dropped into the lake about 30 feet short of the landing spot. That 30 feet seemed like an endless distance to swim in the paralysing cold of the glacial lake. He barely made it to shore. It was almost too much for the pilot, and Bill had to pull him in over the last few feet. After all these adventures, they found little of any value on Downie Peak and they abandoned the claim after expending $100,000. "We were not discouraged," adds Alan, "and we carried on elsewhere in the ensuing years."

Eventually Alan began to think that he would like to be in a larger syndicate with some specialised expertise and in 1969 he became a major investor in such a group. It was by this route that he entered into the most successful mining venture of his career —the Equity Silver Mine near Houston in British Columbia. In its day Equity Silver was the richest silver mine in the whole of North America, at its peak of production pouring forth an astounding average of 6 to 7 million ounces of silver a year. Besides this, it yielded substantial amounts of copper and gold.

A huge outlay was required to bring this mine to true profitability. To maximise its tremendous potential, they had to be able to recover a far higher percentage of the silver than was being done when they first acquired the mine in 1972. It was to take seven years and a cost of a million dollars before they succeeded. They hired the Hazen Institute in Denver to research into methods of extraction for Equity Mining (as they named the company), and in the long run the expenditure paid off handsomely, for Hazen's eventually found a way of recovering an amazing 90 percent or more of the silver content.

Even then the way was not clear, for they needed major financing to get into full operation. Placer Mining showed interest, then appeared to back off. At this point Alan himself put forth an alternative proposal, but finally a deal was made with Placer, who formed a company called Equity Mines Ltd. Placer put in $120 million and gave Equity Mining 40 percent of the equity. They also bought out the original owners' (Kennecotts) 30 percent of carried interest for giving Equity the property.

When production finally started in 1981, it was astronomically successful. The company went public, and at its peak the market value of the shares reached as much as $450 million. During the producing years, the price of silver soared, and at one point was fetching four times as much as when the syndicate first bought in. After several successful years Alan sold his shares, but now regrets that he did not stay in longer. "Hindsight is a wonderful thing," he muses.[19]

Silver was easily the most rewarding mineral commodity he ever speculated in, but briefly he was an oilman too. Alan liked nothing better than a change of pace, so when a neighbour of his in Palm Desert (where he and Vivian had a winter home) asked him if he was interested in an oil well in Beverly Hills, he jumped at the opportunity. It literally *was* right in the heart of Beverly Hills, alongside a high school and a hospital and only two blocks away from a luxury hotel often patronised by presidents of the United States. At the moment his friend's company was pumping only 10 barrels a day, but the potential was enormous, for beneath this spot in the city lay a proven pool of at least 10 *million* barrels of oil. Using Alan's initial financing funds, the two partners went ahead with the development, and after two years waiting to get permits they began construction of an $8 million "cellar"—a 30-foot deep cellar where the wells were spaced at 5-foot centres. No objections were ever raised by the high school next door, which became the fortunate recipient of a 5 percent royalty, making it one of the richest educational institutions around.

Initially the project looked like an investor's dream. The first well produced 400 barrels a day, and three years later, with fifteen wells drilled, production had reached 3,000 barrels a day. On paper this sounded good, but the operational costs turned out to be much higher than expected, while conversely the price of oil was lower than anticipated. In spite of the success of the drilling, the operation could not survive. Alan himself recovered his investment, plus a certain profit, but unfortunately the Beverly Hills Oil Associates general partnership and the general partner went into bankruptcy proceedings.

Besides being a lumberman, heavy construction contractor, highway contractor, mill-owner, movie-maker, oilman and airplane pilot, Alan was to cram yet one more career into his action-packed life: in the 1970s he became a ranch-owner. The idea of ranching had a lot of appeal, for it was something that was right in the family tradition. He had grown up with an attachment to the open spaces of the Cariboo-Chilcotin country, where his two grandfathers, Joe Trethewey and Herbert Church, had had big ranching spreads, and this was where he bought two beautiful acreages of his own.

The first of these was the Canyon View Ranch on a piece of high bench-land near Williams Lake overlooking the Fraser River. As well, he later bought the Sky Ranch in the lofty mountain country near the headwaters of Big Creek. This had a family connection, for it had previously been owned by Alan's uncle, Dick Church, and it was only about 30 miles west of the Big Creek Ranch where Alan's mother had grown up. A third operation, with 250 head of cattle, was at the Vicarro Ranch on Sumas Mountain at Abbotsford, the property where Alan lives today and which had been in the family for many years—ever since his father had logged it for the Abbotsford mill 70 years before. Alan's brother-in-law, Bruce Watt, who had been ranching in the Cariboo for over 20 years, agreed to be his manager in charge of all cattle operations.

As usual with Alan's ideas, the cattle enterprise turned out to be a large-scale affair, for as well as owning these ranches, which ran a cow-calf operation, he also bought and sold thousands of cattle through feed lots in British Columbia, Alberta and Saskatchewan. At the peak of his ranching activities he had as many as 12,000 head on the hoof in various places. Bruce Watt acted as his cattle buyer, travelling round British Columbia and Alberta by any form of transport that would take him there—motor vehicle, airplane or helicopter— to complete these deals.

The family enjoyed many good times participating in the open-air life and activities of the ranch, but eventually this phase came to an end and the two ranches in the Interior were sold. Alan kept the Vicarro Ranch, and this is where he and Vivian live today after selling their Point Grey home in Vancouver in the mid-1980s. Their ranch-style log home, with its massive timbers of yellow cedar, stands amid woodland on the sheer edge of a high hillside, with views sweeping out over the Fraser Valley, apparently isolated from civilisation, yet only minutes away from the freeway to Vancouver.

Looking back on his career, Alan stresses the importance of one particular factor which was the key to all the Tretheweys' successful operations—the wonderful loyalty and commitment of the employees who worked for Trethewey-owned companies. "The reason for our great success," he emphasises, "was not that the principals worked so hard, but that we were blessed with having not only a group of highly qualified key personnel, but also a large, capable body of other intelligent, hard-working and dedicated individuals."

END NOTES

1. *The Financial Post,* Sept.12, 1959, p.27.
2. *B.C. Lumberman,* August, 1957, p.10.
3. *Vancouver Times,* Business Review, April 1965, p.11.
4. *Forest Industries,* May 1964, p.78.
5. *B.C. Lumberman,* Nov.1959, p.10.
6. Alan Trethewey, autobiograhical notes, 1992.
7. *Hiballer,* May, 1963, p.25.
8. Alan Trethewey, autobiographical notes, 1992.
9. *Vancouver Times, Business Review,* April 1965, p.14.
10. Ibid.
11. *Pyeline Canada,* April 1971, p.1.
12. *Heavy Construction News,* Sept.18, 1972, reprint by Catre Industries.
13. Autobiographical notes by Alan Trethewey, 1992.
14. Ibid.
15. Ibid.
    Sue Baptie, *First Growth, the Story of B.C. Forest Products Ltd.,* 1975, p.258.
16. Autobiographical notes by Alan Trethewey, 1992.
17. Ibid.
18. Alan and Bill Trethewey's autobiographical notes, 1992. Their two accounts of this incident vary slightly, but the gist of it is the same in each.
19. Alan Trethewey, unpublished memoirs, 1992.

20

Epilogue

Action and adventure—these have always been the key-
words for at least five generations of Tretheweys, and
Alan's brothers and sister have been no exception to this
tradition. They have carried on the spirit of free enterprise and they
have lived lives filled with activity and outdoor adventure, often
working in remote wilderness areas to manage their operations.

Every one of the four brothers—Richard, Alan, Bill and J.O.—
has learned to fly a plane and has flown back and forth over the
mountain terrain of British Columbia many times as a necessary
part of their timber and construction operations. The oldest three
brothers each went into the Air Force during World War II, and
Richard, in fact, made the Air Force his career for a period of thirteen
years after the war was over.

When he joined up in 1941, Richard applied himself to his Air
Force training with some dedication. He remembers studying for his
courses with a diligence which would have met even his mother's
high standards: "I even refused invitations to go duck-hunting with
friends. In retrospect this is hard to believe." He graduated top of his
class in Elementary Flying School and eventually went on to become
a pilot officer. After the war he accepted a short service commission,
which was later converted to a permanent service commission, and
embarked on a career as a test pilot.

In this role he did a certain amount of research work in alternative engine systems in existing aircraft, but chiefly his responsibility was to test planes that were being returned to service after a period in storage. Not surprisingly, he had a few unpleasant emergencies to deal with in the course of his career, most notably the three occasions when he was faced with the sudden failure of both engines at the same time. But flying was the life he enjoyed, and he found his last three years in the service much less congenial, spent at a desk in the Directorate of Organisation and Establishments at headquarters. "Nothing momentous on this type of job. It was easy to accept more challenging prospects. The excitement of flying was gone."

The prospect that induced him to return to civilian life in 1958 was to go in with his brothers in a major expansion of their Abbotsford window-manufacturing plant. Bill had started this in 1952 as an offshoot of his and J.O.'s lumber yard business. He had heard of a new sashless window invented by an American, Ernest Pierson, and although it had not done particularly well in the States, Bill was convinced it had good potential. He and J.O. had begun to manufacture it at the lumber yard in Abbotsford with such success that after a few years, with sales soaring, the prospects looked very good for expansion. The $350,000 plant which they put up on the Mission-Abbotsford Highway was financed by the four Trethewey brothers jointly through their two companies, Abbotsford Lumber and Trethewey Logging, but Bill, whose idea it had been, had the chief management of it. Richard became the Toronto sales manager. Celwood Industries, as their new company was named, expanded rapidly over the next few years, adding a whole new range of products to their inventory —particularly kitchen cabinets in a very wide variety. They even put up a kitchen cabinet plant in Calgary as well. But Celwood was not a long-lived operation. The very variety of their cabinets turned out to be a factor which worked against the greatest profitability and eventually they became over-extended, all of which happened just at the time of a recession in the building industry. The result was that Celwood closed down.

Bill and J.O. continued to run the building supply store in Abbotsford until liquidating it in 1971, and they also became involved with B.C. Silo and Tank, which was a company producing concrete staves for silos. Their participation in some of Alan's mining explorations was an interesting—and often exciting—sideline of activity, and certainly added colour to these years.

The youngest brother, J.O. is named for his grandfather, the flamboyant Joseph Ogle Trethewey. According to one story in the family, his parents made a promise to the dying Joseph that they would name their next boy after him, which they duly did when he was born five years later. J.O. himself, however, when consulted about this piece of family lore, said he had never heard the story before! Be this as it may, he took on his own identity with the abbreviation "J.O.", and was never called by his full name.

Like the older boys, he went to the Vernon Preparatory School, finishing his education at the Maple Ridge High School. Too young ever to fight in the war, he helped with his mother's patriotic effort in the way of food production on the Coniagas ranch, and—like Phyllis—he particularly remembers the preparation of vast numbers of chickens for the market in New Westminster each week. He was a good rider and competed in major horse shows during his teens, but it involved a great deal of hard work and hours of training in order to come up to the standard which the whole family set itself. Although he had enjoyed the pleasure of riding and the satisfaction of doing well, he did not regret giving it up at the end of his teenage years.

Like his brothers, he was despatched to the logging camp at Port Douglas for a year to learn every aspect of working in the woods. He drove gravel trucks, he was a "cat skinner" (driving caterpillar tractors), he did road maintenance, besides taking a turn as a faller, cat swamper, powder monkey and other jobs. But although this was all useful knowledge and experience, he did not find the life particularly congenial and had no ambition to involve himself in the management of logging operations like Alan. He traded his quarter-interest in Trethewey Logging for a half-interest in the Abbotsford Lumber Company, and from then on he and Bill worked as partners in the building supply business, as well as Celwood Industries and B.C. Tank and Silo.

City life may have been J.O.'s preference and his normal lifestyle, but he too was quite often on the move about the province, travelling to look at mining claims or promote business. Currently, however, his principal business interests are focused on real estate, insurance and financial planning. He and his wife, Marlene, have also built up an Amway company, in which they have reached the seldom achieved Diamond level. He makes his home in Abbotsford, the town which has so much history for this branch of the Tretheweys.

"I think I had an inborn love of horses," writes Phyllis, the only daughter in this family of five. Horses were to be a big part of her life from childhood onward. She was eleven when they left city life in Abbotsford for the rural lifestyle of the Coniagas ranch, and she enjoyed the full benefit of her mother's growing interest in dressage and riding shows. Riding and competing in local fairs became the focus of Phyllis's teenage years. Like her brothers she did her share of farm chores, but her mother always gave all of them ample time for any sport. "She gave an enormous amount of time and energy to teach us and many other children badminton. Horses and sports made my teen years wonderful," says Phyllis.

Phyllis married at the age of nineteen, and she and her husband, Bruce Watt, immediately set about becoming ranchers. They went to live on the Church ranch at Big Creek, and they learned the business of cattle-raising from her uncle, Dick Church, who had the expertise of half a century's living in the rugged conditions of the Chilcotin plateau. Two years later they bought the neighbouring ranch, where they happily settled down for the next twenty years or so, "to raise cattle and five children," as Phyllis puts it.

The district was still almost as remote and undeveloped as it had been when Margaret was growing up there herself in the days before World War I. The nearest school (with a total count of only eight students) was the one at Big Creek, which was ten miles away at the end of a narrow dirt road, which—depending on the season—could be either muddy and flooded over, or else slippery with snow and ice. Phyllis remembers having to use a horse and sleigh to travel to a Christmas party at the Big Creek schoolhouse after one particularly heavy snowfall. "Ranching provided both wonderful and harrowing experiences," she sums up.

Phyllis now lives in Vernon, where she continues to enjoy outdoor activities—golf, skiing and gardening. Golf is the major enthusiasm of her retirement years, and not only does she enjoy playing the game itself but she has also been a course-rater for the past five years.

The current generation of Tretheweys are still as go-ahead as their pioneering forebears. All of Alan's sons have worked within his companies for varying periods of time, and each one now has his own company. Brig has inherited the Trethewey aptitude for invention, and has patented several automotive-type inventions. Bruce is in the mini-warehouse business in Canada and the import business in South Africa. He is a helicopter pilot, as is his brother Will, who makes and distributes machines, and sells chemicals around the world for the application of polyurethane products. Regan is following in his father's footsteps in the timber industry, while Derek is involved in large real estate deals in Canada and overseas. Evidently the saga of the Tretheweys is still unfinished.

The Trethewey tradition throughout this century has been to give back to the community. Abbotsford, in particular, has been the beneficiary of more than one philanthropic gesture on the part of the Trethewey family. Edgar in the late 1930s donated the land which is now the lovely Centennial Park by Mill Lake, with its pathways, shelters for barbecues, and wharves for swimming and fishing. A generation later, in 1979, Alan and his brothers started off the Matsqui-Abbotsford Foundation with an opening donation of $250,000 to be invested for the benefit of community projects. The following year the family stepped in to save historic Trethewey House for the community, buying it when it came on the market and presenting it as a gift to the municipality. This fine heritage home, built by their grandfather, Joe, is now used as a living history site and a museum centre. The district of Maple Ridge too has a memorial to the presence of the Tretheweys in the form of the outstanding rock collection which was once Edgar Trethewey's pride and joy. This superb collection of polished rock specimens which he had assembled over the years was donated by the family several years after his death, and is now on view on a rotating basis in the Maple Ridge branch of the Fraser Valley Library, where it makes a rich display of glowing colour.

Five generations of the Trethewey family have made their homes in British Columbia, and many of them still live in the country towns of the Central Fraser Valley. Their roots go deep, and the Tretheweys clearly feel a strong affinity for the beautiful green valley which attracted James a hundred and twenty years ago. This in itself is not unique—other founding families too can claim several generations in the Valley—yet certain elements in the Trethewey story combine to give this particular family a singularity and distinction of its own.

Few families indeed remain in the Valley who arrived before the CPR, as the Tretheweys did—the vast majority entered British Columbia only after the railway was built. Even fewer of these early families have so consistently displayed such outstanding enterprise in each and every generation, that special spark of energy always re-emerging. Fewer yet have exerted such a major influence on the economy of the Valley or moulded the history of their communities to such a degree. Add to this the fact that since the end of World War II their operations have multiplied on an almost unbelievable scale throughout the province and even outside Canada, and their position does truly become unique in the Valley.

James would certainly have congratulated himself on having his vision so handsomely fulfilled, and on the commitment he made when he stood at the Great Divide and looked down into the province of his choice more than a century ago.

Appendix

Recollections and Close Encounters

as told by Alan Trethewey

My earliest memories date to my family's years in Abbotsford, where they came to live in 1927 when my father took over the management of the mill.

I was not an easy child for a parent to bring up—the worst child in the family, I rather think. My adventurous nature, which was to be of advantage to me in my mature career, displayed itself early on in ways which were not always socially acceptable and which caused some concern to my parents.

I inherited in full the Trethewey fondness for practical jokes. One of my outstanding efforts in this direction was the time when I killed a garden snake and draped it gracefully around the steering-wheel of my mother's Hudson. Unfortunately her sense of humour did not extend to this little joke—no doubt it came as the last straw—for I got the worst spanking I ever received. It was one I *never* forgot.

Around this time my parents decided that we boys were in need of some consistent discipline at a well-regimented boys' school, so when Richard and I were each about ten and nine respectively, we were sent to a private school in Vernon for three years of stiff character-building. Bill and J.O. later attended this school too.

The Vernon Preparatory School was run by a very fine family named Mackie. The Reverend Augustine Mackie and his brother Hugh Mackie ran it on the spartan lines of a typical English boarding-school of that era. Every morning while at this school we were all lined up and had to roll over in a bathtub full of ice-cold water. In the wintertime, if there was no ice on the swimming-pool, we would have to dive in one side and crawl out the other—boy, were we fast!

According to historian Margaret Ormsby, the two main types of student at this school were the sons of the English ranchers in the Interior and the "dread Canadian type" from the Coast. I am sure I came into the latter category and I fully lived up to its reputation by getting into all sorts of minor trouble. If a boy accumulated enough bad marks by the end of the week, he was sent to the Reverend Mackie's study for a few strokes of the cane on the rear end: I paid many visits there. None of us ever regretted this discipline.

It was by no means an unhappy time for my brothers or myself at the Mackies' school. We liked athletics, so we enjoyed the wide variety of sports that were available—badminton, boxing, cricket, football and hockey—and also the open-air activities that were a big feature of the school. I emerged from the Vernon Preparatory School a thoroughly reformed character!

Our mother now filled our time with all sorts of constructive activities. Each one of us had to learn a musical instrument: mine was the clarinet, and later the piano. But the recreation which I enjoyed the most was badminton, and I played in all the badminton tournaments which my mother organised for the young players of Abbotsford, gaining quite a few trophies. The girls' badminton group had plenty of equally enthusiastic players. Among them was a girl named Vivian Golos, and this was how I first came to meet my future wife.

As my brothers and sister and I grew into our teens, my parents decided that we needed some responsibilities to keep us out of mischief. At our Maple Ridge farm, which we returned to in 1939, Richard and I learned to drive a tractor, and ploughed and disked many acres of hardhack in our after-school hours. We also tended a herd of several hundred sheep: I consider that my one real expertise in farming is in the handling of foot rot.

By the time Richard and I reached our mid-teens we began to spend our summers up at my father's logging camp. We were put to work on the boom, which was considered the safest job. Our living-quarters consisted of a tiny wooden shack on a log float at the catching-grounds, alongside two other shacks.

We stayed there on our own and did all our own cooking—if it could be called cooking, for our preferred menu was usually a can of Headlands Meat Balls, rounded off with a Jello dessert. Tiring of these products one day, we decided to be really ambitious and cook ourselves some French fries, relying on the instructions of the lady in the cabin next door. She said that the secret was to get the fat up to boiling point. We kept stoking the fire and getting the fat hotter and hotter, until we could hardly see across the room for smoke. Further advice was needed: I went off to consult our neighbour again. On my return, to my horror there was Richard standing in the doorway of the cabin with a flaming frying-pan in his hand! Yelling to him to put it down, I helpfully grabbed an empty box, dipped it in the lake and flung the contents on to the pan. The result was sensational: a sheet of flame erupted several feet in the air and filled the whole doorway. Richard jumped backwards into the cabin; I jumped too, but backwards into the lake. Fortunately the fire did not take hold, and by great good luck no one came to any harm.

As a teenage boy it was my great ambition to own a shot gun, and when I was fifteen, at last the day came when my father allowed me to go out and buy one. My total savings amounted to only $10, but luckily this was all that was needed to acquire one of the second-hand guns advertised in the local paper. I immediately rushed out to buy one of these and came triumphantly home with my bargain. I will never forget riding back home on my bicycle carrying this gun—hammerless at that. This treasured weapon of mine had only one flaw: whenever it was fired, it would fall into two pieces—not the greatest attribute when you happened to be standing in the middle of a ditch or slough.

My first hunt was memorable for only one thing: its remarkable lack of success. There were literally thousands of ducks in the low-lying, wet scrubland around the Coniagas ranch, so Richard and I had no doubt at all that we would bring back dozens of ducks at the end of the day. What we did not realise was that it was useless just to fire haphazardly into a large flock on the wing. It is hard to believe that you must pick out a single bird and aim directly at that one, if you ever expect to be successful. We returned home very crestfallen, for after using up fifty shots we had not succeeded in bringing in a single bird.

Eventually we began to make a habit of sneaking into a private hunting-club nearby in Pitt Polder, as the ducks were even more abundant there than on our own property. The only problem was to keep clear of the gamekeeper, a big powerful man, who would immediately chase after us when he heard shots. My brother Bill got caught on one occasion. He and his friends Brian Bell-Irving and Peter Cherniavsky had all driven in in Peter's car for a brief shoot— it had to be brief because of the warden. Sure enough, they soon saw him coming after them. Somehow they all three managed to reach the road and pile into the car, but in the general panic Peter forgot to release the hand-brake. Failing to get up any speed, he was soon overtaken and caught. This game-warden was an intimidating figure, a huge bare-chested man, towering to about six and a half feet in height, and of heavy build to match, and he was quite impressive as he made a note of the licence number of the truck. Once back home, Peter was sufficiently worried about his criminal activities to telephone a celebrated Vancouver lawyer, Reginald Tupper, about this heinous offence. The great man advised a policy of waiting, and to the intense relief of these petty poachers nothing further came of the whole affair.

But we were soon to have more momentous concerns than these to occupy our thoughts, for all this was in the early days of World War II. All three of us Trethewey boys who were of age to enlist were desperately keen to lead the exciting life of a fighter pilot, but although we all entered the Air Force, not one of us succeeded in this ambition—fortunately, as far as our future chances of survival were concerned. Richard flew Catalinas over the Indian Ocean without much incident; I became a Bomb-Aimer but did not go overseas; while Bill, who only came in near the end of the war, ended up in the Army and never went overseas either.

Richard liked flying so much that he stayed on in the Air Force after the war was over. In the end Bill, J.O. and I all learned to fly too, in order to carry out our timber and mining operations, and we had a few close calls in the course of some of our projects. Risk-taking was all part of the day's work and I think we thrived on this type of stimulus. In fact, we did not even consider it risky at the time—merely exciting.

We often flew about the province on our hunting or fishing trips. I particularly remember one of these trips in the spring of 1953, when Larry Lyttle, Bruce Watt and I decided to go on a grizzly bear hunt into the Taseko Lake area (where my grandfather had once tried to develop the Whitewater mines.) After a couple of days wandering over the beautiful mountains we had not seen game of any kind. On the third day we came across two black bears, which we shot and skinned out with the heads attached for trophies. After a few more days we decided to head for home; we had run out of grub also. Since we had acquired extra weight that the plane could not handle in one trip, we had to make two separate flights back to our starting-point near Big Creek. Bruce was to wait in an old miner's cabin; Larry and I took off.

As we headed north, we could see a storm front approaching. Before we could reach our destination we were cut off by this front of bad weather, and we had to turn back and find some unmapped lake to land on and let the storm pass over. With our fuel running low, it seemed like a very long time before we came to a small lake—and lo and behold! some moose grazing around in the snow. We taxied up to a moose and I picked out a cow, figuring it would be tender, and felled her with one shot at a range of 200 feet. We got a nice fire going, cut some small pieces of meat and put them to cook over the coals. Larry tried eating his and he couldn't eat it at all. I said: "You just haven't cooked it enough." I kept cooking my pieces, which got smaller and smaller, until I thought they were definitely ready. I could not even tear off a piece of it—it was so tough! All we could do was to chew little pieces and swallow them whole. The effects of this gourmet meal lasted with us for the next two weeks.

After this awful fare we cleared away the snow and lay down for the night on a piece of canvas with the bearskins as a quilt. You would never guess how hard it is to keep a slippery bear hide on you with the fur being down. We ended up sitting around the camp fire most of the night. Luckily we got out the next morning when the weather cleared, and made it to our destination with about five minutes of fuel left.

This sort of adventure was no deterrent to my brothers and myself. We were avid hunters of birds and big game. Regularly each fall we left on our hunting trips, setting out with dogs and gear, sometimes going to Alberta for the pheasant, duck and geese shooting, sometimes to the interior of British Columbia to hunt deer and moose. But what I had always dreamed of was to see the great animals of the African continent and experience the thrill of the safari.

In 1964 I had the opportunity of achieving this ambition. In Tanzania there was a game reserve (the Salou game reserve), which had a huge proliferation of wildlife. This was due to the fact that the area had been closed to everyone for a period of thirty years because of the infestation of tsetse fly, and the animals had multiplied unchecked. The government had now decided to capitalise on this and make some money from admitting hunting parties, so my friend Ray Bonn and I signed up for a three-week safari with a well-known white guide, Tony Archer.

The safari was to be just a part of a two-month round-the-world trip, so several of our friends decided to organise a stag party for us as a going-away celebration. Present at this event, besides Ray and myself, were Harry Bell-Irving, John Nicolls, Stuart Wallace, Peter Cherniavsky, Art Holden, Bill Owens, Gordon Zacharias, Jack Sexton and Bill Trethewey. But unknown to Ray and me, these friends had thought up an elaborate surprise for us which would make this an occasion never to be forgotten.

The dinner was arranged on very formal lines at one of Vancouver's best hotels. The dining-table was set in the suite with white linen, fine crystal and elegant silver—everything top drawer. The wine chosen was of the finest vintage from France with the proper amount of bouquet and character for this special occasion. Everything proceeded according to the expected etiquette until the moment came for the main course to be brought in. The steward advanced to the table with great fanfare, bearing an enormous covered silver platter about three feet in length, about the right size for a large salmon. Everyone waited expectantly. With a flourish he raised the lid and a dead silence followed, as all looked on with awe at the course presented. Most of us could not figure out what in the world was before our eyes. We were all completely mystified, then incredulous. Finally, in stunned surprise, someone spoke: "It's a whale's penis!" And be darned if it wasn't just that.

The author of this practical joke was Harry Bell-Irving, who had had the inspiration when he and Peter were watching a whale being cut up on the dock of a whaling-station on Vancouver Island that same morning. Harry's friend John Nicolls in Vancouver was delegated to make arrangements with the hotel for this addition to the menu, but he wisely omitted some crucial details. When Harry arrived at the hotel and opened up his box, the staff went into a state of complete shock and consternation. The catering manager was so upset that he could hardly speak. It was only with great difficulty that he was persuaded to demean his standards of haute cuisine and allow the item to enter his kitchen. As it was, the waiter who was to serve it promptly fainted at the sight and had to be sent home. By all of us guests the idea was highly applauded and the evening was a great success. (Fortunately no one was actually required to partake of this unusual dish. It was quickly whisked away from the table, and a normal entree followed.)

After this unique send-off, Ray and I were off on our safari, which turned out to be a most thrilling and spectacular three weeks. These were the days when trophy-hunting was the usual part of an African adventure, and I shot a wide variety of specimens—elephant (with 60 lb tusks), bushbuck, Cape buffalo, leopard, duiker, impala and others.

The most exciting thing that happened to me on the trip took place on a day when Ray was hunting elsewhere. Our party was on foot, searching for signs of kudu. We had just arrived at a dry watercourse when we noticed an old skinny rhinocerous making its way along the sandy river bed, undoubtedly intending to take a dip in a small pool farther up. Here was a great camera opportunity. I got out my movie camera which I carried with me at all times, and began filming, keeping pace with the rhino as he moved along. After walking a ways he spotted us; he stopped once or twice and glared, then suddenly changed direction and began heading straight towards us. When he was 50 feet away, I realised we were being charged, and I decided it was time to quit the movie business. I looked around and found that only Tony, our guide, was still with me, as the three Africans were long gone. I was about to take cover, when I saw that Tony was calmly standing his ground, elephant gun in hand. I stood beside him, watching, as this monster came pounding towards us, moving unbelievably fast for his size. He was 15 feet from us before Tony shot him right between the eyes, dropping him dead right at our feet. When we examined him, we noticed two raw-looking gashes in his side, probably from a recent attack by a lion, so this may have explained why he was not in a very good humour that day.

After this thrilling safari I never again shot a bird or an animal. Africa had been the ultimate experience, and anything else would have seemed like an anti-climax.

Because of my two near-drowning episodes when I was in my twenties (related in Chapter 18), I suppose it would not have been surprising if I had been left with a permanent phobia about the water, but this was not at all the case. I continued to enjoy swimming and boating for recreation, and liked to experiment with any type of water sport. This led to a few scary moments in my life.

One of these incidents happened quite suddenly in the middle of a carefree morning on a little beach on the island of Maui. I noticed that the young Hawaiian boys were having a wonderful time in the huge waves far out from the shore, body-surfing and riding the waves in to the beach. I could not resist trying this out, so grabbing my small rubber raft, I paddled it out to the spot where the 12-foot breakers were rolling in and positioned myself ready to catch the next big wave. I turned around to wait for it—only to find that the wave was already there, directly above me, and about to crash down on me with all its force. Down I went into the depths, and next thing I knew I was rolling over and over in the water, not knowing which way was up and which was down. All I could do was to hold my breath and hang on. When I was nearly out of breath, I suddenly popped to the surface. I was still several hundred feet from the shore, my little raft long gone and no one to help me out of the mess I was in. There was nothing to do but strike for shore and try not to panic. Somehow I made it O.K., for which I was truly thankful.

Another time I ran into trouble when we were on holiday on Grand Cayman Island. I was on a spear-fishing expedition in company with my 14-year-old son Brig, Bruce Watt, a friend of mine named Chuck Colthart and his sons aged 16 and 18. We had been swimming in a beautiful lagoon on the inner side of a coral reef that ran parallel to the shore. Seeing a gap in the reef, we entered it to explore a little way, when suddenly the current caught us its grip and swept us through the gap out into the open sea.

Each person had to make his own decision as to the best course of action. The coral reef was a maze of jagged rocks, but it seemed to me that our best hope was to try to swim through it back to the lagoon. Brig with great presence of mind had dived down and anchored himself with his spear to one of the rocks to think the situation over. I called to him to come over and we began to wind our way across the reef, taking particular care to keep clear of the sea urchins which covered the floor of the reef—their sharp black prickles could deliver a nasty sting. Our worst problem was the heavy swell, which threatened to batter us against the coral. In the end we thought of a system: whenever we saw a swell coming, we would dive down to the bottom and lie there, hanging on to some large rock, until the wave had washed over us. In this way, very slowly and laboriously, we finally reached the shelter of the lagoon.

In the meantime my friend Colthart was having a terrible time, as he was totally exhausted. His two sons, both strong swimmers, came to his rescue, each grabbing one of his arms under the shoulder and pulling him through the current. They took a different route back, re-entering the gap and working their way along the edge, where the current was slower, until they reached the lagoon.

I had narrow escapes when I was flying too. There was the time when I ran out of gas, due to a faulty gas-gauge, and had to make an emergency landing on a small, ice-covered lake. I only just had room to swing the plane around to avoid crashing into the trees at the end of the lake. The lake was so short that subsequent take-off was impossible and the plane had to be dismantled in order to be removed.

Another time Bill and I were being flown back to Mission after concluding a log transaction at Port Douglas. As we approached the Mission bridge, we thought of the high-tension powerline strung across the river and hoped the pilot had remembered it. He had not! Bill and I gasped as we headed into the line. Suddenly the pilot saw the cables, poured on the power and jumped the deadly line—another close call.

I seem to have acted as a magnet for dangerous experiences, for even as recently as 1989, I had yet another close call, which could have ended up in a very unpleasant manner. It happened in California, where Vivian and I were spending a few months in our winter home at Bermuda Dunes. We had been dining out and had stopped on the way home to pick up some groceries. Vivian, who was driving, parked the Mercedes and went into the store. As she left, she handed me the keys and told me to lock the car. "No way," I said—not wanting to appear chicken—and put the keys back in the ignition. I settled back in the passenger seat and fell into a comfortable doze. After a while some noise disturbed me, so I stirred and muttered sleepily: "Vivian, is that you?" There was no reply. "Vivian, is everything all right?" I persisted. Still no reply. Turning towards the driver's side, to my utter astonishment I saw a young Mexican seated at the wheel, driving the car. Another Mexican was in the back seat and the car was speeding along a four-lane highway in the direction of the desert, where they were no doubt planning to rob me. The fact that I had woken up too soon caused a change of plan, for they began to pull off the road into a dark parking lot. I turned round to have a look at the man in the back, and as I did so, he squirted me between the eyes with a stream of fluid from a can he was holding. I was half blinded by the spray, but so mad that I didn't think twice: I hurled myself across the arm-rest of the front seat to attack the driver. The speed of the car was now down to about 10 miles an hour, so the driver jumped out, and in mid-spring I flew out after him through the open door. I landed on the roadway, rolled over a few times, but got to my feet. I was dishevelled and minus a pair of shoes—which had fallen off as I hit the ground—but otherwise not much injured. The robbers were nowhere in sight.

"Vivian will wonder where the hell I am!" was my first thought. Luckily the car was still drivable. It had carried on in slow motion, jumped a curb and finally come to a halt against a decorative cement-block wall with only minor damage to the bumper. I cautiously edged back on to the busy highway, my eyes still sore and blurry, and drove back to Vivian, who was waiting outside the grocery, quite mystified by my sudden disappearance. The robbers were never found. I must have seemed like an easy victim—a placid-looking, silver-haired gentleman trustingly asleep in his car with the keys still in the ignition.

I wonder what further adventures life holds in store!

Bibliography

Newspapers

Principal newspaper sources

    Abbotsford Post.
    Abbotsford Sumas Matsqui News.
    Alice Arm and Anyox Herald.
    Ashcroft Journal.
    British Columbian.
    Chilliwack Progress.
    Fraser Valley Record.
    Mainland Guardian.
    Vancouver Daily World.

Periodicals

    Horsin' Around.
    Pacific Coast Lumberman.
    Western Lumberman.

Unpublished documents

    Gibbard, John E.: *The Early History of the Fraser Valley 1808-1885*, thesis (M.A.), U.B.C., 1937.
    Green, Everard: *Pedigree of the Trethewey Family*, 1912.
    Lawson, Joseph: *Letters to his wife and diary, August 1883*, PABC.
    Trethewey, Alan: *Autobiographical notes*, 1992.
    Trethewey, Clarke: *The lives of James and Mary Ann Trethewey and their sons and daughters*, 1989.

Official Publications

B.C. Gazette.
B.C. Sessional Papers.
Land Registry Office records.
Vital Statistics records.

Books

Church, Herbert E., *An Emigrant in the Canadian Northwest,* Methuen & Co. Ltd., London, 1929.
Long, Gary, *This River, the Muskoka,* The Boston Mills Press, Erin, Ont., 1989.
Mitten, Elaine, *Oh Dem Golden Slippers,* E. Mitten, Chilliwack, 1994.
Peak District Mines & Historical Society, *Lead Mining in the Peak District,* Peak Park Joint Planning Board, Bakewell, Derbs., 3rd ed. 1983.
Rogers, John (maps) & Person, S. (Sketches), *Guide Book and Atlas of Muskoka and Parry Sound Districts,* H.R. Page & Co., Toronto, 1879, 2nd offset ed. 1972.

Interviews

Stanley Browne with Alan Trethewey and Daphne Sleigh, 1992.
Cornelius Kelleher with Imbert Orchard, 1963 (PABC)
Mildred Kitching with Alan Trethewey and Daphne Sleigh, 1991.
Frank and John Taylor with Alan Trethewey and Daphne Sleigh, 1992.
Cora Trethewey with the Matsqui-Sumas-Abbotsford Historical Society, 1982.
Clarke Trethewey with Alan Trethewey, 1989.
Everett Trethewey with Alan Trethewey, 1991.
Margaret Weir with Alan Trethewey and Daphne Sleigh, 1991.
Margaret Weir with the Matsqui-Sumas-Abbotsford Historical Society, 1982.

Index

About the Author

Daphne Sleigh was born in England, in Ewell, Surrey. She attended Oxford University, where she took an Honours degree in Modern Languages. She emigrated to Canada in 1957, living in North Vancouver for a few years before moving out to the Fraser Valley in 1963. Since then she has lived in rural areas of Haney, Whonnock and Deroche.

Her interest in British Columbian history stems from her participation in the writing and production of Maple Ridge, a History of Settlement, published by the University Women's Club of Maple Ridge in 1972. She then went on to become the first curator of the Maple Ridge Museum from 1974 to 1981. After leaving the Maple Ridge district, she returned to historical research and writing, and authored two other books on local history—*Discovering Deroche* in 1983, and *The People of the Harrison* in 1990. Her book, *Discovering Deroche*, gained her the 1984 Lieutenant-Governor's Award of the B.C. Historical Federation.

Daphne and her husband, Francis, who have raised a family of three, enjoy a rural lifestyle in one of the most scenic parts of the beautiful Fraser Valley.